The Gospel of Mark
Eternity and Readiness

THE GOSPEL OF MARK
ETERNITY AND READINESS

A JOURNAL BY A LAYMAN

GEORGE ANDREW

AuthorHouse™
1663 Liberty Drive
Bloomington, IN 47403
www.authorhouse.com
Phone: 1-800-839-8640

Published by AuthorHouse 10/09/2014

ISBN: 978-1-4969-3727-8 (sc)
ISBN: 978-1-4969-3726-1 (hc)
ISBN: 978-1-4969-3725-4 (e)

Library of Congress Control Number: 2014915475

Contents

ACKNOWLEDGMENTS

I want to acknowledge a few close people to this work. First, Ruth, my wife, soulmate, confidante, and playmate. We share three decades of multidimensional life. It is her effect on me in the last few years that motivated me to begin this project. She often called it stream of consciousness. I would add, stream of *spiritual* consciousness. Second, Lamont was immensely supportive in all the stages of this effort. His ideas, support, and clarifications were greater than he knows. Third, Jane Willig did a superb job with my first draft and many more services for the book as well. Next, Ruth and I (she a member of Kol Ami synagogue) went to services where I was able to brood and consider the work I was doing in the midst of the ritual of Shabbat. Ideas that found their way into this work floated up and into my awareness many times. The time there was a solace for a week of challenges. In addition, many of the prayers in their prayer book were inspirational for the latter half of the book. Thanks, too, to the anonymous editors, a part of AuthorHouse, who did a neat job of clearing the enormous underbrush at the blog level which was the first derivative of this book. And finally, this book is all my responsibility with Divine assistance all the way.

Let me close with a prayer from St Francis of Assisi for us to end this creation:

Keep a clear eye towards life's end. Do not forget your purpose and destiny as God's creature. What you are in His sight you are and nothing more. Do not let worldly cares and anxieties or pressures of office blot out the divine life within you or in your great task of leading humanity to wholeness. If you open yourself to God and his plan printed deeply in your hearts, God will open Himself to you.

Grace and peace from God our Father and Mother, and the Lord Jesus Christ.

Amen.

The Sun rose, and the world was filled with sight enough and sound to deceive all but the deaf and the blind and the wise.

—The Ronin, William Dale Jennings

Love and do what you will.

—Saint Augustine

Love is what is left when thought has fled—not religion, not faith, but love. Love is what drives us. If there is a God, and like you, I do not believe that for a moment … but if there is, love is what brings us closer to Him. Not hate. Not vengeance. Neither orders nor rituals. Nothing from above, or below. Just us, humanity—what we French fought and lost our Revolution for. We sacrificed our ideals on the altar of the guillotine, and we learned never to do that again. Now here we are.

—Shock Warning, Michael Walsh

One person with faith is equal to a force of ninety-nine who are merely indifferent.

—Ancient Proverb

Foreword

Before she died, my grandmother gave me two books: one I still have—a Bible concordance from 1950—and the other a Bible commentary on the New Testament. The concordance got packed away with the advent of the Internet. I have no idea what happened to the commentary.

I only remember it was boring.

The book you are now reading is so vastly different from any other New Testament commentary I have used over my career that there is virtually no way to compare them. This book is clearly not boring.

I am honored to write a few words encouraging readers to explore this book fully and in a relaxed fashion. This is not a book for the beach, where noise and wind might distract. Rather, it is best read chapter by chapter when you can breathe in the author's insights as he strolls through the book of Mark.

My first time reading through each chapter came when George shared his writings in a weekly blog. This was the perfect way for me to read his thoughts—when I was relaxed and ready to take on his views and perceptions of the life of Jesus as told through the words of the oldest gospel. Reading one chapter at a time allowed me to digest George's approach to the Jesus experience through the eyes and mind of a modern layman.

This is not a scholarly book in the sense of a study of the language of the day. Nor is it a breakdown of the culture of the time, although the author does bring his vast knowledge of history to his comments. It is more a wonderful view of Jesus' life as shared though the perceptions of George Andrew.

I've probably preached around a thousand sermons over the years. Most of them were helped along by commentaries and books on Bible translations. While I borrowed unashamedly from the wisdom and studies of others, this book is a man's personal journey. It's a walk with Jesus, if you will, in which George has tapped into his intuitive side to share his view of God and the spiritual experience. He has chosen to work his magic from the contributions of J. B. Phillips, and I think he made an excellent selection. Phillips is very readable, and his choice of words adds greatly to Mark's gospel.

I have known George for many years, and although we have had theological and philosophical discussions many times, I was still surprised when he chose to write a commentary on the book of Mark. To be truthful, I was even more surprised as I read each chapter when they arrived in my mailbox weekly. His discernment is keen, and I truly do marvel at his ability to place his own worldview into the various verses of Mark.

Over lunch, I was surprised, actually more than surprised, to learn he did not use any other commentaries as he worked his way through the gospel, chapter by chapter. This takes great courage. I know from firsthand experience the risk involved when one puts one's own thoughts and judgments out there for others to read and digest. George did not waver in this book, and for that I commend him.

In his opening writings, George states that he "felt both called and impelled to write this book." Such feelings are the stuff of artists and authors who truly sense they are meant to put paint to canvas or ink to paper. It is what makes this book worth your time—the sharing of the deepest part of a person as he explores the life of Jesus. It is what makes this reading both mystical and personal. George does not shy away from sharing himself whenever the teachings or experiences of Jesus led him into that very secret place.

He also writes a simple fact, namely, "If you get God, you get Jesus." This is such a fascinating statement, and, in my view, not easy to understand. It is, however, a theme throughout many chapters, not in those words but rather in the concepts of God in daily living for the person who seeks and is aware. In a way, George deals with the crossing points of life—those places where Jesus's teachings and life intersect; where we all live each day.

I heard an old story several decades ago that tells of a meeting between the great Swiss theologian Karl Barth and the evangelist Billy Graham. They were supposedly asked to write a prayer together, a sort of united word for the people of God. After much discussion and thought from their differing theological positions, they unveiled the following: "Ground of all Being, Bless us real Good." This was the result of the union of two deeply spiritual men, both of whom had their own great truths to offer.

This book is very similar in that it brings an evangelical thrust with a powerful theological study from a layman's point of view. It is an attempt to share the gospel of Mark and the story of Jesus from the intuitive side of George Andrew.

One final thought: this is a book to be read slowly, chapter by chapter, or better yet, paragraph by paragraph. I would fix a cup of tea, take out your hard copy or e-reader, and relax with the words. Close your eyes and ponder the thoughts presented. If you're like some folks, it may help if you take some notes and write some questions. I am sure George would be pleased to respond with his own insights and thoughts.

I commend this book to you and your heart as you search for a deeper connection with the Divine.

Lamont Satterly
Search Foundation

Beginnings

The end-of-period bell rang on time at 9:54 a.m. Gathering up myself and my books, I dashed to the next class, which was sophomore math with Mr. Harvey Buren. We called him Harvby. I rolled into my assigned seat six chairs back by the window in the far row. Scattered as I was then, I just sat down and stood up after the roll was called for the prayers and Pledge of Allegiance to the flag. I stared out the window at spring and mouthed the whole set of words. I said them, but I did not attend to them. Harvby called out, "Hey, Andrew, are you a heathen?" I then got an eraser thrown at me, which struck my khaki uniform. I was enrolled in a military Christian Brothers high school in the Midwest. The year, 1964, was not the happiest period of my life.

This event did not stand out to me at all at the time, shame-inducing though it was. It did, however, add another color to the palette of my life. As did the first real effort I put into writing and going to a religious conference, where I heard about other religions beyond Roman Catholicism. This was in the time of Vatican II and efforts to open Catholicism to the twentieth century—both failed. VC2, as I call it, failed because its premise was wrong. Windows were opened, which just blew the papers off the desk. Catholicism really ended during the

Enlightenment and after the French Revolution because of its inability to thoroughly address these episodic events.

Rather than write a book about these two assertions, I decided to leave Catholicism for other roads less traveled. It is not surprising, because religiously my parents—one a Catholic, the other a Hungarian Unitarian—somehow affected me equally, as did the church I grew up in and left. I will not return; this book is not at all an attempt to make amends, as you will read. I am not a Catholic, and I will not be at all welcome in their Roman church. This book is also not an attempt at any sort of contrition, since it is not at all perfect. I have, however, experienced something that is called a *conversion.*

As you read this book that I call a journal, it will become clearer that I am a Christian. What kind I really do not know. I did move from pretty lazy secularism to a near-absolute faith in God. I think my reader will get that. Perhaps others have traveled this or similar roads with different outcomes. If you read my bibliography, there you will find certain effects untold, some good for you, some bad for you, and some ugly to you. Indifference is always an option, but I doubt that response if you are reading this book.

Of college I will add but three matters of interest to this book: First, those four years were inscrutable and difficult. It was almost like lost time, maybe a blackout. I did not fail miserably, nor did I make any lasting connections to fall back on later in life, not even a friend. However, I did learn many life-changing things. Some of those experiences are folded into the pages of this book. Second, like many of my cohort, I worked my way through college in the summers. What I did was a bit different from most of the college students at the school I attended. I got my hands very sore and dirty. I think it is called *manual labor*, and it trained me to never misunderstand those who make their living by the sweat of their hands. There is never a job beneath me after those summers. Third, I got involved with a Christian cult. While there, many of my current ideas had their genesis. It also saved my life. Fortunately, it grounded me just enough and bolstered me to go on to greater things later in my life. It also opened the doors of my perception without drugs, although there was that. I did not try drugs with them, but on my own, and I learned that there is more to living than meets the eye. I discovered that I had space behind my eyes, though I did not speak of it that way then. My consciousness was stricken by a depth that I now call mystical. Only after years of straightening myself out enough to be functional enough to have serious relationships and not veneer-covered monologues, am I able to say I grasp the true importance of that word.

I got married and divorced and married.

What is important about this rhythm is what I learned in the midst of each event. The first marriage brought the knowledge that I cannot change anyone. Try as I did, there was no possible way to make her anyone other than who she was. The adage "you can bring a horse to water" is apt, though incomplete. Of course, the horse has to be thirsty. More truly, the leader has to know where to find the water and then make sure that it is potable for the beast. You get the point. Along with this small fact came the knowledge that my egocentric views about the world and myself were not necessarily correct. In other words, just because I saw it that way did not make it so. I carried around a sense of entitlement; it was just excess baggage. I made improvements by the time I married the second time, just not structural changes.

What structural changes?

The changes show up in this book. Chapter by chapter, the gospel of Mark allows a life of thought, action, and essence to unfold. One of my friends said that writing this book took a lot of research. Very true. It has taken me some forty years of research across a variety of articles, workshops, books, lectures, and thinking to pull together enough sense to "dive into" this gospel. I felt both called and impelled to do this now. Part of the impetus was my wife's dual medical episodes, which span the life of this book and still echo in our lives.

In the book I say that if you get God, you get Jesus. Although I have shared this book with different Christians and non-Christians alike, I cannot say that either class of friends agrees with me on this point. Most kind of stared at me, trying to get my meaning. Since I do not explain this assertion well in the text to come, here is what I mean: God, Mystery, Divine Providence, Ground of Being, and other interchangeable names point to the reality that we can all experience in life daily, consciously, or unconsciously, if we are ready. If we are witnesses to what is simply going on in and around us—and this takes some preparations regarding our spirits and, more certainly, our souls—we notice it obviously and evidently in the world, in our lives, and in the lives of others.

Let me leave these two words—soul and spirit—in the most common-sense usage. We eventually notice that we are united with the mystery of life in discernible ways. What made Jesus beyond unique, but the Son of Man and the Son of God, manhood and godhood at once, was that He had an enormous experience of unprompted "cosmic consciousness" in which He became clear that He and God were one. Additionally, Jesus was there with Moses, Abraham, Israel, and Adam. This is the

Christ Event. It was a leap of consciousness. He had to "get" God and then communicate the event. Jesus's experience of the Ground of Being utilized the "languages" of second Isaiah, Elijah, Ezekiel, and perhaps others as Jewish touchstones to communicate God's news. Of course, Jesus was not the political messiah Everyman Hebrew was waiting for—or even Everyman Roman, Philistine, Persian, et al. In His communications in Mark, He did not try to portray Himself as the One. Nevertheless, the powers that be did not like this picture and killed Him savagely.

Fortunately, there are many mansions in God's kingdom. We too can know of this union with God, and know that Jesus, the first among equals, never wanted to be the head of a movement, though He did initiate Christianity, which we have sadly mixed up by overemphasizing Him, Jesus. This overemphasis separates Jesus's manhood and godhood. We have also missed the message that "the kingdom of God is at hand." This has resulted in the *guiltification* and reification of fear in Judaism and Christian accepted wisdom, behavior, and doctrine. Here is the rub. Jesus is said to have brought life abundant. Instead we are all privately and publically afraid of death, thus we miss that in death there is life. We have nothing to be worried about. After all, we were dead before we were born. Jesus pointed to His and our nature as sons of God. What more can there be? Jesus died and ascended. He took earth up (manhood), and in that Jesus gave eternal life to earth and to all on it (godhood).

Finally, I firmly believe, as St. Augustine said, that God is the ever-expanding circumference with a definite point where it stands, sits, or if you will, dances. Perhaps this is "pantheistic." Yet, it more closely relates to the given union with God. It is not to be sought; the union is secure if we witness it.

The first few chapters of this book set the stage in order to ease the reader into the gospel experience. Though you can begin there, these early chapters set the scene and tone. If you wish, you can skip around to chapters that attract you and call out to you. However, when the chapters of Mark's gospel begin, the journal about Mark's Jesus begins. There is grandeur in the process of reading it in the order it was written by Mark. I had fun with a few of the chapters, and please note that I am not making fun of the gospel, ever. I have sought to make the entire gospel more "vernacular." Still, there is a certain starkness to the writing. The left hand of God rested on Mark's shoulder in some spots. I think there is a crescendo from the first to the last gospel line with some quiet quasi-plateau sections that act like bridges to the next words and moods. And by no means did I cover every line; I tried to address what addressed me.

After the gospel ends, the book had to cover a few areas not addressed in the journal chapters. This purposely I left until the end. In closing, I call and challenge the reader to interact with the gospel in an existential way. By this I mean in a way that is down to earth. Metaphysics can come later. Although essence precedes existence, we see essence as it unfolds in life. In all major religious traditions, there comes a time when the individual has to admit two things. The individual must give up his or her separate experiencing ego and admit that individuals cannot define ultimate reality because it cannot be known. This radical admission sets the stage for another more powerful leap of faith, a vision of God that is neither wordy nor reductionistic—a fatherly man on a heavenly throne surrounded by seven levels of angels and with a Son at His right hand.

This vision is monarchical and one which we Christians misidentified in many ways. The restoration of God is Jesus's kingdom of God from which we are not separated by meta-language. It is something we can appreciate here and now, this inexpressible "something" that I name God. Without explicitly naming it, Jesus pointed to it with the words at the beginning of Mark's gospel, "The time has come at last—the kingdom of God has arrived. You must change your hearts and minds and believe the good news." And here, I send you to read the book.

George Andrew

27 August 2014

Opening Thoughts, Ruminations and Reflections

Greetings, salutations, and felicitations.

If you can, please pick up a copy of the New Testament transcribed by J. B. Phillips. It is an old version. Well, not in that it is wrong or decrepit, but it may be out of print. It is the one I am going to use to talk about the first gospel, the gospel of Mark. The motivation for this is complex and multilayered (more on this later in the work). The convention I will follow is simple: prior to each section that I "journal," Mark's gospel is cited after the title. Please read the section before or concurrently with each chapter where cited.

For now, go find a copy. It may be found in a used bookstore, Amazon, eBay, wherever, so much the better, as the hunt is a part of the process of proceeding with the book. A short note on the way to approach the chapters of this book: first, read the Mark section that is referenced; second, try to walk into the scene Mark wrote; only then read what I journal.

I chose to comment on Mark's gospel because it is the first one and it is the simplest compared to the other three, Matthew, Luke, and John. The others use Mark and either extend or embellish their thoughts and stories. Mark, if it is his name, wrote his gospel around 70 AD, we believe. Paul's book of Acts was written about 30 years after the death of Jesus. The others fell into line with John later, or so we think, getting their gospels on paper at around 100 AD. Time is important only because the oral history in these gospels wanes, and by the time it gets to 100 AD, matters are much accreted, meaning many layers on top of layers.

Oral history, as its name states, is passed down by word of mouth. It is passed on from lip to ear, from ear to lip. Remember the child's game "daisy chain"? Imagine a daisy chain, and around the center are petals spread from the center to the edge and back to the center, round and round unceasingly. In the center there is an attachment, which is where the petals are held.

When a person heard a story, he made it his, hers, or the community's. Then it was shared via a "hear" in an ear, and it was made a little different in each telling, not perfectly identical to the previous telling. At that time only the scribes were literate. Who could imagine that scribes would record this story of Jesus, as shortly after his death there were only a few counted among his followers? Perhaps there were a few scribes because someone organized the stories and gathered them and told them and retold them. Eventually there was a complete gospel of Mark, I guess, and then complete gospels of Luke, Matthew, and John. All were consolidated, more or less, at a time when they needed no more changes or just a few adumbrations, which finally culminated in a big colloquy (synod). During the synod, the Catholic Church fathers weeded out the nonstandard versions and standardize the agreed-on versions. After the talks they ended up with the four new testaments we have today. But through the ages the monks added a few changes in their transcriptions in their blessed efforts via roasted Arabica (coffee), which brings us to today.

We come to today with numerous attempts to make gospels reliable and ready to be read in everyday language. Philips is a part of this process to make the gospels easier to read that occurred in the 1970s.

I know this is a bit trite and that scholars will disagree with me. Accepted. No harm, no foul. I do believe that there are absolutes, and what I am saying may seem relative in a time of great relativity. I will leave the jot and tittle to those who jot and tittle. This is a journal, not a scholastic work. Throughout this book, I want to see what a word, a chapter, or metaphysical thought points to. What indicates to us in life, in my life, in our lives? Many will see this writing as a sacrilege, a disaster. Some may think I've been too glib about this New Testament gospel of Mark that was divinely inspired—the Word of God. It is not only the Word, it is unchangeable and established. I wish to add that in the past tradition had a vote, not a veto. This writing is perhaps a midrash. What's to come is a meditation or, well, an intellectualization or at best a struggle with the angel like Jacob's. Writing, reflecting, or theologizing about the religion in the Gospels is too often antiseptic and passionless. And the writing was scholastically dry and too dense. Jacob's struggle with the angel of the Lord, in today's words, the Mystery of Life, was an exertion, not a Sunday walk in the park. Because of that event, Jacob became a different human. I am a different human because of my encounter with Mark's gospel.

Naming is not knowing; knowing is experiencing. Consider my thoughts as an art form with a method of going from the superficial and ending with the experience of the Ground of Being's affect. I am most focused on the interior of the gospel of Mark as well as the pointers, and use of word and interesting events and unusual items therein. I will bring my best thoughts and experiences to this effort as I go through the gospel. I do not feel that any of the gospels are a road map to anywhere. They are the deep musings of a person, Mark, who is serious about his life and thoughts about Jesus.

My next chapter addresses who Jesus was, is, and will be.

THE 2,014-YEAR-OLD QUESTION

I find it hard to start somewhere on the topic of Jesus. Whether you or I start from the time of Jesus, enter the discussion in the midpoint, or start today and go backward, the issues seem immense and unscalable. As the title implies, it is a question. Could there be an answer? Who was he? What was he? Why was he? Even, how was he?

Let me reassure you that I am not starting from pure doubt. Some of you are true believers, nonbelievers, skeptics, doubters and agnostics, finally, "whatevers." Did I miss any of you? I am starting as a twenty-first-century man who knows science and follows it. I am an existentialist who is drawn to the truth. To ponder this life, Jesus's, is not to prove a point, persuade you or me, or feel superior, it is merely to talk openly about my reflections and where they will take me—perhaps us. It is an acute journey. I hope not to intellectualize, that is the worst. If that is a bias, I accept it. I do not want to fool or trifle with you.

Back to where to start…

If I start from the "beginning" about Jesus, I will get lost. I am not a first-century Jew, Hebrew, Roman, Greek, Samaritan, Essene, or rabbi. There are a few clear points to reasonably note. Jesus was baptized by

John. He was a teacher –one who points the way, a rabbi –one who is qualified to rule on questions of Jewish law, carpenter, perhaps a fisherman, a mendicant, a crucified leader. These are all available to us in Mark's gospel. I have heard that there is a work detailing the "real sayings" of Jesus. Okay, helpful to some, no doubt. I will and want to avoid this. I think that this is like counting the angels on the head of a pin. It is a matter of "expert" opinion. To what end? For the gospel to live, I have to grapple with it. I think to pretend is unhelpful—though the experts will state this is their expert conviction. Either it was an oral story first, something that moved those there to save it in their ear and pass it down to others or, as many claim, it is totally the word of God, which leaves me blind. Again, some feel that that is a meet and right place to be, blind in belief. Is this faith?

A few facts we have: there were twelve apostles, a band of disciples, followers, witnesses, and people of both sexes. These apostles were mostly fishermen. All the rest were good, stout-hearted men and women—oops, there were no women apostles. What does that suggest? There was Mary the mother, and Mary Magdalene, there were brothers and family. Yes, hard to believe.

Jesus dropped into—was born into—a time. The times were tough. Israel was occupied by the Romans and many of the Hebrews either wanted them out, wanted to coexist, or were collaborators. There was Messianic hope; the Zealots and Essenes hoped for revolution or separation respectively. Into this walked Jesus. People hoped for an anointed one—hoped, hoped, and hoped more for anyone to get them out of their daily grind and their daily limits.

Jesus was Human

I want to begin with thoughts around Jesus's humanness. Did Jesus think about who He was, what his purpose was, why He was here, what his destiny was, or how to get things done? Did He not have to think on these items? If He was human, these were natural questions.

Jesus was human. Otherwise, we are stuck at a dead end. He was so human, in fact, that He was tempted. He ate, slept, talked, walked on land, and felt emotions. He cried, bled, and experienced all that we feel, see, hear, sense, and think. This has to be so. And He did all of this with an added plus—a plus in particulars. Jesus really lived His life as an act of intention. None of this is metaphysical in the first instance.

Jesus was God. In that plus, not a metaphysical addition, but a particular manifestation of the divine, an incarnation in the midst of time by that "which is called the Mystery or the Ground of Being, God." How so? In the statement that the kingdom of God is at hand. Not to come or to be waited on, but at hand now. And it is available in life as a gift that we can embrace in our knowing, doing, and being due to the model of Jesus. Just wait and see how.

I take it as a simple and profound thought. God so loved(s) the world that God humbled Itself by coming to the world, to us, as a man in the flesh. God lowered Itself into incarnation, into a void, if you will, (though there is no such void, these are merely our projections) and forgot It was God, so that in the process of life itself, God could discover what It had created. This is not what you would call orthodox Christian thought. It is God's love of man, in Jesus's time, today, and tomorrow.

Jesus died a tragic death, grievous and painful. Not in the sense of unchosen. It was a meaningful death, an event that was disquieting. The community around him was devastated, and they scattered. Those who hoped for a mighty king, a ruler and savior, were naturally angry. Those who sensed more of what was happening were merely lost as to what was next. They made an individual and a group decision. In the midst of their lives, a "miracle" came. They sought deeper meaning, a deeper well—more grace. The cross was a beginning, not an end, and they were witness to Jesus's resurrection. Jesus did not fulfill the general dream, a resurrection of the anointed one for Israel, the Messiah; instead He became a confrontation to the prevailing matters and dreams with a life and death and resurrection fitting no patterns or abstraction. What a slap at life's modes, a total crack in the cosmic egg, so to speak!

Much more could be said about Jesus's life, and the gospel of Mark will get us therein. Find that Philips version wherever you can. The next stop is the first chapter of Mark for deeper passage into Jesus's life.

From the Bottom Up

I forgot during my previous comments to consider Jesus's experience of incarnation. Just writing this pushes me to the edge of my awareness, because to write about someone else's internal experience is guesswork and wracked with limitations. It is hard enough guessing about a living person; it is madness to consider Jesus's. Well, mad I am.

Our fear of incarnation is a fear of the void. Fear is a strong emotion. Are any weak? Fear plants us on the ground as we face an event, person, place, thing, or another emotion. I fear death. I fear the loss of a spouse. I fear suffering. This space is for your fears. I fear ____________________.

These fears ebb and wane and are stultifying. They turn you to stone or you flee.

Incarnation has a neat part: the carnation, a flower of petite beauty. In-beauty, in-born, in-blooming, in-living, in-fleshed—all of these perhaps describe the plus of Jesus's and God's relationship. It is a noun, but really it is a verb. Incarnation implies an action on or of being that puts into flesh and blood. Herein, Jesus God became terrestrial. God emptied Itself into a void earth that was Its creation.

The void has a negative tone. And, it seems to be a negative space—or an absence of space—limitless emptiness. Void is a powerful four-letter word. Void has a peculiar word, for in it is *id*. It too is a noun, but with an action implied. We know id from the Freudian definition as one of three parts of the "I." The other two are *ego* and *superego.* I am not a psychologist, still I know the id is the most basic part. I prefer to image the void as an anticipation, a waiting for fullness, as a type of awe. Earth was waiting, hoping against hope for the sunrise, for the morning star, to capture a glimpse of Bethlehem's star.

Jesus had a life experience; the closest we can get to it is via the gospels. What people saw of his daily life is recorded there. And there is much that is added. For example, other than Jesus, no one heard the voice of God at his baptism. Yet the gospel proclaims it as a public event. It makes no sense to argue about this. If you hear voices, well, even if divinely infused, the writer is giving us the voices that they heard. And from there it is *reductio ad absurdum*, meaning where we try to follow the philosopher Zeno to the end of his rope. I know that channeling was a big deal in past days. Let me put that in the class of "I'll get back to you about it." The gospels were not channeling Jesus. Yet there it is, the dialogue is as if they or the writer heard it. My best guess is that it was an act of faith by the community. Could Jesus have shared the experience? I doubt it.

Finally, His experience of vocation was more profound than ours, because it was first and it was deeper. As a trailblazer in the area of "The Hero," He proclaimed His experience daily and plainly to the apostles, the disciples, and the multitudes who followed Him.

This is a brief preamble to the work that sets out where we will go, and the considerations about Jesus's life-path, culminating in his death and rising. Throughout this writing, I use the present tense. The reason for this is the prevalence of the Gospel today.

Now We Begin: Chapter One, Verse One

The gospel begins with five lines from the prophecy of Isaiah. It is, however, preceded by "The Gospel of Jesus Christ, the Son of God …" It feels like ownership to me. Jesus owns this and the coming lines, however many. Gospel has traditionally been defined as the "good news" equal to fact, truth, reality, actuality, what's so, what's what. Literally, it is God's news or spell, a sense of awe or "magic."

What is God's word? Well, in the beginning the word was with God and was God. We are in the realm of Genesis echoing the creation myth. Jesus was a message from Go from the opening lines. God was manifested through Jesus. The manifestation is in Israel, grounded in the Tanak, totally part of Jewish culture.

What is this Son of God? This is hard to answer. Not being a theologian, what little I can guess about its origins is weak. Yet to me, the implication is there. It is close, closer than you can imagine. God's Son, Son of God, Godson. A son shares the flesh, blood, genes, culture, heritage, psyche, image, of his father. Like it or not, the relationship is close and different. The flow is two ways.

Adam was God's creation. Jesus is his son—very different, suggesting some type of choice. Yes, there was a choice about Adam. A son implies a biology, versus a creation, *sui generis.* Perhaps, a detail, but the son suggests a parallel versus a reaching down. Minute, I guess.

Jesus Christ, the Son of God, also pushes an act of faith by the writer, Mark. After all, He knows, sees, and believes that Jesus is the Son of God and is the Christ. Not Mr. Jesus Christ.

End of story—well, not really. We could stop the discussion here and now. It would suffice as an appetizer. Better to call it a prologue.

Start of the Gospel with a Special Event (Mark 1:1–5)

Paul Tillich states in one of his sermons that we all seek the mystery, depth, and greatness of our existence. So, it should come as no shock that the gospel writer Mark wanted to ground Jesus in the prophetic context of Isaiah. He attaches five lines to the opening section to make good and sure that all the readers know that Jesus was a serious event, right up there with other Jewish "saints." Of course, there are no such men in Jewish religion. Well, how about really important people, people who were very influential, wise, and good in their prophecy. *Powerful* is a small word for the work of Isaiah. He was a prophet around the time when Israel was a captive, as it was when Jesus was born. During Jesus's time it was occupied by the Romans and their Hebrew facilitators, like Herod. Isaiah is thus an appropriate one to use in the introduction as a parallel. Jesus was from the north and Isaiah was either from the south or he operated there solely. If you read the book of Isaiah you will see many parallels between Jesus and Isaiah and their times. However, this may be more coincidental than factual, or prophets are struck by the same archetype. The echoes are there.

Second, John the Baptist, to whom the Isaiah message is really directed, is no slouch either. Yes, I feel the lines are related to him more than to

Jesus. It says Jesus is the fulfillment right there in the lines of Isaiah. Well now, if *you* were a fulfillment, what would that look like? What image comes to mind here? A son of, a daughter of, a child of—definitely of someone's wish or hope or desire or want. This is bigger than hoping to win, place, or show in a competition. If there is a fulfillment, this is strong medicine. Still, John is out there too, a fulfillment. Why isn't John the big one to do the job? It is as if John is the prologue that goes missing after a single bit. Mark seems not to remember him after this. He does not become an apostle. Strange, in that he did facilitate the process in a very big way.

Well, what little I know about Judaism is that baptism is not a common event. It is practiced by only the most Orthodox Jews and Hasidim. And, at that time, at the beginning of the Common Era, well, I am ignorant. I think it was a very unorthodox action to baptize in the river Jordan in that time. In the gospel there is an allusion that John baptized in the desert; that must have been in the northern part of the Jordan, then. Everyone came to him, as stated there in the first paragraph. City dwellers went to the desert. Pagans went to see him too. (Look up what pagan really means.) It appears to be a very large conclave to be baptized as a sign, "the mark of a complete change of heart and forgiveness of sins." *This* is not a small matter! It was a public event and a public confession of sins. Holy moly! Imagine, if you will, what a contemporary event might look like. Go ahead. Surely this is the end of times to witness this, or is it merely the beginning of time? This was some major mojo. John proclaimed baptism as the mark. We have marks in other places too. Cain's mark comes to mind. Others? A mark is seen, and a mark is an idea of inner change. This is called a *sacrament*. It is a special event, in all senses of that term.

We begin with a baptism of many people by John. What is the complete change of heart so many came to be baptized into? I have changed my shoes, hair, mind, and heart, but only occasionally. The heart is a major thing to change, and it is hard to do. It is hard work. Hard like it takes time, effort, thought, practice, and discipline. And, it is an act of love. It is action with, because, and for something, somebody, and some way. Change like this goes deep. It is a 99 percent reformation of you throughout the dimensions of your life, in your heart, and inward to your innermost self. The last one percent is the hardest. Oh, and once in a while, maybe never, it happens on the road home. Bam. I have had it happen only once in this manner, while making a bed as a young boy. Usually it is like threading a needle in the dark, blindfolded with a howling wind in your face on a rolling ship by yourself in storm facing a time limit.

Why?

Why change your heart, I mean? After all, change comes in two ways: via a traumatic event or insight.

And it is a choice. Faced with many choices, we choose to completely change our hearts. Oh, and many don't even notice the choice; they are too immersed in their stuff. The option to choose is hidden to them. Or they are too weak to observe it. Perhaps out of pain we choose to not choose (trauma). Out of some deep separation and alienation after you can go no further away from yourself and all that is negative and your creaturely illusions, then you completely change your heart. This may be called hitting bottom. Here is the other change (insight) where you leave behind a negative and illusory life, and turn towards a life of fullness and abundance. You see plainly what is not full and abundant, and you choose to change your heart. You change yourself inside out and become baptized in forgiveness. You go forth because you have been tapped.

Nah, just walk back to the river, watch it flow, and wait for the anointed one to do it for you (or to you). Whoever the anointed one is what every man waits for. This is a choice to remain sensual man.

A short digression for those wishing it were otherwise.

There is the One, Jesus, in this case. Then there are the deeply touched ones, the apostles; then the disciples, who see and have a lesser faith; and then there are the multitudes who hear; and then there is a vast rest. It is always that way. The leader of the core cadre, then the party, then the proletariat, and then the lumpen masses. Go ahead, try it yourself. Is it otherwise? It is this way in the hive, the school, the street, in corporations, etc. Here is the point. It is all good the way it is. To rail against this givenness is mere entertainment.

The complete change of heart is to know this, to take care of business in the midst of this, to do what needs to be done, and not to blame.

Oh, and then I can spot and remove the stud from my nose on behalf of your existence. This is the change of heart.

From the Desert (Mark 1)

In the beginning, we read of a baptism along the river Jordan. John comes from the desert, Mark says. What is the desert as an image, reality, and its meaning?

If we note that there are a few major symbolic images, like a mountain, the sea, the forest, the river, the setting sun, the night sky, and the desert, these evoke immediate associations, memories, stories, feelings, and signs. The desert is one that predates most. We come from a desert past, all of us. You know the Rift Valley, the cradle of humanity. The human genome originates in the deserts and savannas of Africa. It has to have affected us with a deep imprint, a vibrant imprint spanning millennia.

Some immediate thoughts come to mind when I imagine the desert: vastness, quiet, sand, sun, dunes, heat, cold, granular, water's absence, clear sky, dryness, snakes, and a few hardy insects. Is there more you can think of? Well, wind storms are also there. There seems to be no one there but you. You are alone. Maybe there is God. This place is the opposite of a garden, yet this place has a touch of the "vision quest" in it. It is a place where nomads live and where monks went in the tenth century to live in huts and pray. The Essenes were associated with it too, as was John the Baptist. The desert is a great place, I suspect, to sort yourself out and become grounded, to en-soul, so to speak.

From there John came to baptize. As a man who had lived in the desert, I guess for some time, he was considered a "holy man." A desert spawns a certain mind among its inhabitants, and if they can reflect on themselves and the soul, well, maybe holiness falls into place. A fully realized man can baptize into forgiveness and change hearts. (Speaking of changing hearts, the heart has been thought of as the seat of the soul. To change a heart is easier to grasp than to change your soul.) Is this what caused Jesus to be baptized? Was He trying to complete or initiate His mission by this outward mark of holiness? This was Jesus's first public appearance, you notice.

Mark remarks that John was dressed as one from the desert with camel hair, leather belt to tie it, eating honey and wild locusts. This is in contrast to any city dweller or other type of Hebrew from Jerusalem or Judea. Though everyman was simply festooned in those days, John was very rustic. John was from the rural districts and a peasant opposite the city. Another image: he was a handyman in the sense of helper. The detail regarding John here is amazing. Nowhere else in Mark's gospel is there this level of description; his dress and food were meant as a symbol. John had the image of a prophet, but no prophet was a Baptist. They anointed with oil, a kind of baptism. The only other similar specifics that we read about are when they clothe Jesus during his passion and death. Both appear for a reason—both are meant to convey an impact, to make the men seem alive and more real, so meaning-true. They conveyed or echoed the symbols of honey and locusts of the Israelites' experience in the desert, thus becoming closer to God. Since this was a time of bedlam, John the Baptist imaged authentically the call back to the desert or God—to return to what is important, real, and faithful. John was squarely in the prophetic camp, but with a difference: the call to visibly change your life—mark it with water, a symbol of life and awareness flowing from the forgiveness of sins. But again, where the prophet anointed with oil, John anointed with water, common material for every man. But in the desert, water is more important than oil. No water, no life! Oil, well?

The "forgiveness of sins" phrase is very powerful. Who can forgive? Why is it needed? How come? And then what is sin? How does one come to have one's sins forgiven? Some more major mojo!

A few points for sure.

Forgiveness starts with living. It is not about running away from anything. It is facing head on what is at hand right now. Forgiveness is not the end of the process; it is the initial step from the realization that you are responsible for your life. "I did it." All of it, not excluding that part over there and not missing what is under the rug, the crumbs of your life, the shards of gravel from your passages down life's roads, the thick layers of protection—all of these for sure! There is no other way or step to take to get from a life of disarray and disorganization to a life of forgiveness in the midst of the internal and social bedlam.

Sin should be a four-letter word. Sins? What is this? Oh boy. My bad. The best I have here is that it is separation from ourselves, others, and the Ground of Being, from our past, present, and future. We are beyond alienation or enmity. Somehow we are totally insular, isolated, cut off, and outside. Notice I did not mention actions because this state produces actions that are sins—full of sin.

To become aware and witness yourself in sin can lead either to forgiveness or more separation. We have no control over the results of facing our lives as sinners except the desire and impulsion for forgiveness as a means out of the state of sin. It happens or it doesn't happen. Here is where baptism is so vital to the process.

And then, Jesus showed up in those days.

An Overlooked Phrase (Mark 1)

The first three paragraphs of Mark's gospel have been *much* described and discussed. They begin with the line, "The Gospel of Jesus Christ," followed by the stanzas from Isaiah, next John the Baptist's activities, then the description of John and his mission, or burden, to baptize with water and of Jesus to baptize with the Holy Spirit. The Holy Spirit baptizing, what might this be?

Baptism is a rite of passage or an initiation that is both individual and a step toward bringing the individual into a community. There was no such thing in the Jewish religion of the time; there was circumcision, which other gospels refer to, and there was earlier a cultic washing, not an immersion, as we read in this gospel. Here it appears that Jesus's baptism is an initiation into His calling, to His holy life. Where before it seems He was dead, after the baptism He is alive, called to existence. This section raises an interesting point regarding John: who baptized him? The Holy Spirit? Yes. In the desert, John was initiated enough that he could lay his hands on Jesus and anoint Him not with royal oil, but rather with common, everyday water. This first washing away brought Jesus to the life of grace in a very everyday manner, perfect for the common man of the time to witness. The Holy Spirit is a symbol of the soul purified, or another way of saying it, a change of heart.

There is one small detail to bring up once more.

Again, what is a complete change of heart? Well, since it is mentioned in one breath with forgiveness of sins, there would seem to be a connection. The adjective *complete* is telling. Is there any such thing as an incomplete change of heart, or a-let-me-think-about-it change of heart? Partial anyone? A "previously owned" change of heart? Well, you get the message; there is no *maybe* in this phrase. Termed *metanoia*, a change of heart is more powerful than a change of mind, it seems to me. As heart is a center of life, pumping and feeding the body with its actions, a change here is noticeable and internal. It has an enduring impact. A change of heart may be an attack that affects the whole body. This is not quite what I mean by a change of heart. It does suggest a big event, however.

It is also a major chakra center in eastern mystical experience and thought. This space is just below the throat and the head chakras, which are even more elaborate than the heart spot. A change of heart then, as a central and unbidden organ, becomes a frequency for the whole body and is tied to the mind in supreme effort. And it is the second-to-last thing to go at our death. The heart is also imaged as the seat of all emotion.

The heart's change and sin's forgiveness are yoked in this manner. The change is slow, medium, fast, quick, or sudden, and each possibility can arrive at the same place—a new state of heart. A change of heart can be a thoroughly effective experience. (It does imply a change of mind as well. See below.) The forgiveness of sin is what the heart is processing. Sin, as I said earlier, is separation. This is an event or experience in the present past. Forgiveness is the sense of living now, untethered by the event or experience of separation. Forgiveness implies a togetherness, union, or a bridge among our many pieces of life. So a change of heart is the forgiveness of sin as an experience marked by baptism. Again, the forgiveness of sin is in terms of our self, others, and the Ground of Being.

A mental change seems rational. A logical process to handle new information can change your mind. It seems to me we are in our minds a lot. It is not very easy to change our minds, either. Our minds really get in the way of our hearts, and vice versa. It appears, though, that our minds are more rigid than our hearts. To change our minds is like "the show-me state" or Thomas in the New Testament regarding Jesus after resurrection. We are skeptical and too gullible at once. Driven by our beliefs, we see what we want to see and hear what we want to hear, and seeing is believing. We disregard the rest.

Again, not just any change of heart; it is the complete change. Also, it is implied in the sentence that it is the complete forgiveness of sins, a thorough change and a total forgiveness. This implies that it takes us to and removes the original state of sin as said in Genesis.

If the Garden is original unity within and without, everything together—the geographic Pangaea in a state of wholeness and with an absence of consciousness—then this mark or step of baptism is the unity of opposites in ourselves and those baptized, where there is not a return to the Garden, but rather a union in consciousness of dynamic, diverse parts including self, others, and God. It is a union in diversity.

Still at the Beginning (Mark 1:1–19)

I am still stopped by the opening lines of Mark's gospel, unsure whether I am done.

"The Gospel of Jesus Christ, the Son of God, begins with the fulfillment of this prophecy of Isaiah …" Then follow the five stanzas of Isaiah.

The feeling I get as I read the opening line is that the lines are lines of faith or, more precisely, a proclamation of faith by the faith community. This line is written after the facts of the matter. Jesus lived, died, and generated a community of faithful who attest to life with these words. Stripped down to the matter at hand, Jesus fulfilled the prophecy of Isaiah. We call his action or life the symbol, Son of God. Many people can fulfill a prophecy. A few can move mountains, and One can create them.

Who has not sensed *deja vu* in reading the first line? I do not mean to be superficial, but it starts with this little twitch, like I have been here before. Then it extends to the concise and glorious, like St. Malachy's prophecy of papal lineage or, to the truly ridiculous, Nostradamus's predictions. Finally, we have to step back in awe. The last piece of the New Testament, the Revelation to John, is a sublime *magnum opus*. All of these, to a greater or lesser extent, open our hearts to the Transcendent. Then we look back, think back, maybe write it down to memorialize the event in a bit of 20/20 hindsight, like Mark's opening line.

What matters here to me is the need to fulfill or justify Jesus or God to the reader who is or is not faithful.

The audience two thousand years ago is mixed between the community of the faithful and yet-to-be. The faithful are set. Who needs the convincing? You do! The reader and the people of the time need to sense the enormity of the event, as if "Ol' Ike can do it." But they chose Jesus and not another. He was to be the imprimatur, Jesus to the Jews, Hebrews, et al. And if that ain't enough, well, it was prophesied there in Isaiah, and that is big to the yet-to-be-convinced. There, you see, this was all set up long ago and here you are seeing and reading of it now!

God moves in mysterious ways, Its wonders to perform; they are awe inspiring. However, some say the prophecy regarded John more than Jesus. Yet it matters not. John was clearing the way for Jesus to move onto the scene. And he was! The prophets set the path to Jesus and John completed that road. Jesus and John were a team, I am sure.

John began the work of transformation with water. Jesus completes the transformation with the Holy Spirit. Water is a good symbol of life. Of course, you can drown in it too, in an exact spoonful. The Holy Spirit facilitates the transcendence to the whole scene. All at once we have the Trinity in action—God speaking, Jesus wet in the water, and the Holy Spirit floating over the scene, giving voice for the "three man group." "You are my dearly beloved Son, in whom I am well pleased." If I were the writer, I would have added an exclamation point! This is a very powerful scene here. God, Son, and Spirit manifest so soon in the drama. It is all too much already in the first chapter. What more can there be? Much more drama later; for now, the baptism is the opening act. And John has been doing this for some time, not a month or two is my sense. He is heralding a person who will come. He will be stronger and more powerful in that he cannot purely untie this one's shoes, and this one will bring the Spirit. Jesus has arrived.

As the baptism proceeds in the span of a few minutes, "all at once" in the present moment at hand, you might say Jesus saw the heavens open, and we read that He hears a voice in the words from heaven, "You are my dearly beloved Son, in whom I am well pleased." My, what a 1,000 percent affirmation, and so early in the story. To this point Jesus has done nothing. It seems again like the earlier prophecy, meaning awe-filling. And empowered by God acting in real time, God envelopes Jesus in total acceptance. (A great father.) Is this the outward sign of the incarnation? Realize that Jesus has done nothing … diddly. And the Spirit, as a dove manifest above, is God speaking to us, and Jesus is baptized by the Holy Spirit. It is a cosmic scene. The paths are being made straight starting now.

What is the Holy Spirit? Good question.

I Jumped the Trinity

I guess I was too excited to notice, but I introduced a concept with no explanation. I talked about the Trinity and assumed everyone has some knowledge thereof. There is common knowledge, scholastic and existential, and kinesthetic, as in having an experience.

The event of the Trinity early in the story of Jesus caused me to ramble about it rather than build an existential basis for the discussion. The Trinity is the hardest concept to ground because we are talking about three parts—Father, Son, and Holy Spirit—that are individually weighty topics. When combined into a triune whole the topic takes on a high level of poetry. There has been a lot written about God, a lot about Jesus the Christ, and correspondingly, a lot less about the Holy Spirit. I ended my last post with the question *what is the Holy Spirit?*

Can we start with the thought question *what is the Holy Spirit not?*

We know, though vaguely, that there can be sins against the Holy Spirit. These are big sins, so the New Testament says. The words are "beware of the sins against the Holy Spirit," or something to that effect. How can you sin against a spirit, Holy or otherwise? Well, sin as separation may suggest a barrier from, before, or around this "spirit." Suspicion offers me that these may be willful acts more than thoughts, consciousness, or a state of being. Yet, a state precedes behavior. For example, indifference about the fruits of love suggests despair over loving and living. The best fruit is faith, and more than anything else this is what mixes the Trinity into a salad salted with hope. If God is faith, Jesus is love, then hope is the Spirit. This is internally what men have called purity of heart, this integrity synonymous with it is called righteousness.

The "ghost," if I may, is not a ghost like Casper the friendly ghost you read about or know from the comic books. It is not a stand-alone entity that hunters are chasing or an apparition in a story, nor an entity that John-Roger is trying to bring to you or words a person is trying to convey that you need to hear. These are another type of spirit, and they are not necessarily holy except that they may engender or prompt some holiness in the observer coincidentally.

You may be able to fill in some blanks about what the Holy Spirit is not. Please tell me.

What is the Trinity, then?

I have to rely somewhat on a work I stumbled across while listening to a tape by Thomas Moore of care-of-the-soul fame. The book is called *Three Faces of God*, by David L. Miller. The book is very good and out of print, so if you seek it you will have to find it used. Try to find it, as it covers this with great insight. I will try to briefly communicate its ideas and words around Trinity. However, his work is based on material that comes from many sources, and some of it may seem off-putting to some of you.

The Trinity is in the gospels. There are many antecedents to it in life, other religions, and in literature. Each tries to wrap around life experience a trinitarian pattern or form, perhaps from ontology, sensing/imaging the structure of being. Phew. The Trinity, then, is both an evocation and a concretion of activity in our self-God, Son, and Spirit. This suggestion comes from Augustine and others of his time, and recently Carl Jung. The best that I can say here is the offering by Augustine, "One person, three substances," is the prevailing faith or dogma. This certainly suggests a tri-partite psyche. More phew! Also, according to the book, there is likeness and unlikeness in relationship to man. Second, in the scriptures, if we are created in God's image and God has made Itself known in life, and we are in life, thus we are like God. And if God extended Itself to humanity or humanness in Jesus, and to us, the relationship is like father and son. The relationship is love and is the third part—that is the Spirit. And it is more. It is unlike anything we can imagine, see, sense, touch, taste, you get it. It is a mystery. It also raises the question, what is love?

Placed then in the context of life, it is like and unlike anything we have or will ever have. A great line in the book is, "God likes odd numbers." The best we can do is contemplate, love, and remember life. To go down, in, and around, is to be a discoverer or explorer in our self. The suggestion, finally, is that it is a mystery of unity, belonging-ness, identity, and difference. If you work it out, you are amazing. *The Three Faces of God* tries, and we can read and absorb it well, I am sure.

Now back to our previously interrupted program in Mark 1:1–9.

Here we see Jesus getting and knowing the initiation He is going through in the baptism experience. At that time He must have felt ready for the mission He crafted for Himself. The baptism is the moment of His depth experience of the holy. From the water, not even dry yet, I guess, He is "[S]ent (by the Spirit) at once into the desert for forty days and while there Satan tempted him."

As if the Trinity was not enough of an experience, next comes Satan.

Before We Leave the River

Reflecting on the last thoughts, a singular thought rose above the rest. The Trinity has to be discussed more prior to going into the desert.

The Spirit appears above the baptized Jesus as a dove. The phrase, "You are my dearly beloved Son, in whom I am well pleased!" lingers as an echo in a canyon. This is a phrase of great satisfaction, pleasure, joy, and love. Of course, again, this is metaphor and transcendent poetry. Yes, I know. "God spoke to us here," some think and say. It is written. I concur and gently add that this was the best Mark could write in the moment about the event of Jesus's inspiration arising from the baptism. It was God's delight to have inspired Him into a calling. Mark got it!

The interaction of the three in one was a relationship of tremendous love. The Spirit is an image of it and more, a dynamic that draws the three together and states that the greatest of these, faith, hope, and love are the foremost.

Later, a more full definition of what love is and is not will emerge.

To the Desert and Back Again (Mark 1:9–14)

The narrative is young. Mark's gospel has barely begun, and so far we see drama beyond measure. I don't recall my baptism, and I doubt you do either. Here we see Jesus at the age of thirty. I suspect that when I was thirty I was past what I thought were simple things and into cars, women, and jobs. Since this is Jesus, He staked out his vocation in the baptism event. He is anointed by his Father and enjoined by the Holy Spirit to hit the desert sands for forty days—not unlike the Jews led by Moses. That event was a transformative experience to the Jews, during which they sorted out who they were, where they were, to what they owed allegiance, and so much more. The desert experience was a community building event for the Jews. This experience was like that for Jesus, I think, and much, much, more. Mark had to ground Jesus in the Jewish experience even if Jesus was a Jew. This made Him a continuation of the tradition, and beyond and outside of it. So powerful was the message of Jesus, so discontinuous, that there had to be an anchor.

Moses led the Jews through the desert experience, led by a Spirit, a burning pillar. Jesus it is said, is led, nay *sent* at once, or "driven"(KJV) by the Holy Spirit, to venture into a period of reflection, a quest for more, a deeper well, a deeper inner experience. This is a time to journey inside. The Jews also got deep in the desert. Imagine it, if you can. Again, the King James Version says it well: not desert, "wilderness." Have you ever been in the wilderness?

Jesus's experience is solitary. The Jews did it as a large group on its way to becoming a community. Both covered a lot of geography. Forty days in the desert is not a simple thing, neither is forty years. Your life changes there, or you die, or Satan swallows you up piece by piece, step by step.

Jesus is there with a few other forces, it is written: The Holy Spirit, the angels, wild animals, Satan, and of course, the Father—six actors in Jesus's internal drama. A fuller account is communicated in other gospels. Here Mark says it in two sentences.

Okay, in the desert there are many wild animals. So what! Ah, but this is it. First, think, if you can, about a kind of a high experience. Typically, it is what is now called a *rush.* No drugs will work here. A great something—it leaves you a bit up there, inflated, like a balloon full of helium. Not very well grounded, you are all high spirit, "high as a kite." It can be soulful. Yet, it is too light; no weight, a gossamer wing. The gospel says that the Holy Spirit sends Jesus to the desert. The wild animals and angels are there. The "wild animals" suggest instinctual and untamed characteristics, perhaps the Greek muses, furies, and nymphs, while the angels assist to help keep matters from getting out of hand. Can I say Jesus had a great internal struggle to make sense of "You are my beloved son?" If you heard or felt this type of grace, these words, you'd run to the desert or somewhere to sort out the meaning of the event too. There is yet another piece or part to see.

The desert is grounding in another way. If water is the fluid dynamic of the unconscious, the desert is the grinding of or the pulling down of the soul. This is a contrast. Water flows through the sand and is cleansed of the impurities. A charcoal filter, it seems to me.

All this had to happen right away after the baptism. And the desert was the perfect setting to deal with the pride that can come if you are chosen by the Transcendent. And if you really want to be the Chosen One and you ask, can it be me? And is this really happening? Who else here can handle this? Dear God. And who can pull this off besides me and put it all together? And so it probably went, out in the desert heat, I am sure. Jesus had the Holy Spirit to guide Him, not protect Him from Satan but to hold his hand as He wended His way through the grains of thought, emotion, and a type of passion. Here there had to be the Almighty to see to it that the battle occurred.

What does this mean? Phew! I hardly know. What I can guess is that Satan has to be faced right away, now, and not delayed. A confrontation like this is better done while you are hot. Secondly, the inflation has to be contained. Can we agree that Jesus must have felt a huge pride about this? There had to be a temptation to be prideful or else the emergence of the Devil would not have occurred. The elation must have been the size of the Garden of Eden, and it could not stay this way. Put aside all the thinking about whether Satan and God are heads and tails, and whether one is good and the other evil. There are thousands of books about this, read as many as you wish. My thought here is that Jesus had to face his internal demons and get them in line. He had to get them to fly in formation and control them as best divinely and humanly possible.

Jesus had to face what all of us have to face. In the baptism, to some extent, He made his choice to have a mission. There was the quality of the Man of God, which He assumed. Next, Jesus had supreme virtue, the incarnation. Finally, He had a vocation, a calling that He took on. God laid Its hands on Jesus and made Jesus His Son. Jesus had what we call a "terrestrial goal." Perhaps then a bit inchoate, not a fool's errand by any means, He was informed by what I just laid out. The goal was the delivery of the kingdom of God in such a way that everyman gets it, at least those who choose to be entirely new men and women.

As I have said before, so much has happened so far and I have covered so little of Mark that I am amazed. I am barely away from the station, barely covered a few text lines, and it feels I have logged a lot of thoughts. There is a lot more to cover.

Jesus stayed in the desert for forty days, I assume fasting and contemplating the events to come, truly in the mode of a human being anticipating upcoming people, places, and things. But maybe not. He had to have been praying. About what? Maybe his vocation, calling, mission, purpose, journey, future actions, and current thoughts. He had his wits about him, the wild animals were there, instincts and angels/muses all catalyzed the process. He was sheltered and dissolved his inflation. Forty days is a long time for Jesus to quest.

Yet, from there Mark states that it's after John's arrest that Jesus shows up in Galilee. What took you so long? Where in God's name were you? Why did John's arrest prompt Your arrival? I ask.

And from then it is clear: Jesus was proclaiming the Gospel of God! I think this is the first and only time Mark puts it this way. The "Gospel of *God*" (my emphasis). And of course, this is the way it had to be, for in the desert, Jesus and God communed, so to speak, and Jesus got it. Or He grasped what that baptism was all about, it was about the news of God's love for the world and its lowering into life God's drop of truth—all of life is good, all of life is received, all of life is open and we—you—are accepted.

Now this is not written in Mark. This is my thought from years ago and my own journey to seizing and being seized by it.

Jesus said it this way: "The time has come at last, the kingdom of God has arrived. You must change your hearts and minds and believe the news." Yah mahn! So what is the good news? Tell me!

First, I see it this way: the time is now. It is here this second. So we are enveloped by the kingdom of God, and this is what it means to be surrounded. What is it? Hm, it is what you are looking at just now. Not this page, but the life you have all around you. Examine it. Well, it is not too great just now. How can this be anything but crap? Perhaps it is not just outside, it is also what is inside you. As creations of God, we forget the awe, fear and trembling, and wonder that we are. The kingdom of God is at hand outside and inside.

Second, the line following carries this off well, "You must change your heart and minds and believe the good news." Let's decode this some. Heart, mind, and beliefs cover what we are made of. Anything else? We have to change it all. And I think that requires a total transformation and not a bit less. This is very much like being pregnant. Either you are or you are not. For us men, either we are circumcised or we are not. There is no halfway in either case. What specifically has to be transformed? It says to change our hearts, minds, and beliefs. From what to what? If we X (you fill in the blank), well, you need to consider A, not P or Q. Perhaps it is as simple or complex as forming a living and loving heart. For the mind, it may be a mind that seeks synthesis between thesis and antithesis. And as for your beliefs, begin assessing them one by one. Become a fully reflective self.

This all only scratches the surface. There are books. There are movies. There is poetry, art, interaction, and self-reflection. A great deal is available from the present and the past. Begin now—today. Really look inside and sincerely peer outside. *This* is the *good news*. Everywhere.

A Short Question

Again, after some period of thought, I realized there is a question hiding in the closet.

Jesus, from who-knows-where, comes into Galilee "proclaiming the Gospel of God." Brusquely stating that the time has come, it is here and now, "change." It is a bit like the play, *I Love You, You're Perfect, Now Change!*

Why?

What was wrong that had to be "fixed" with us, the community, the society, the culture, and so forth. Speaking to "you," you have to change. Mark is putting it bluntly, from Jesus's mouth to your ears.

Also, it seems to me that this line about change, a total transformation, is better put out at the end of the play, movie, book, story, or whatever. It is definitely an affront this early. Like any play that has acts and drama and meter, a pace, a low point where the major protagonist and antagonist get it on and get nasty, thesis and antithesis arrive at a synthesis. Not right off the top, boom, the message. No waiting for the right moment or time. This drama has the point up front.

Still, *why*?

Mark puts it up front and center. After John is off to jail, Jesus bounds in from somewhere and says, I got it out in the wilderness and this is *it*—change to the core, now. *Your* waiting is over. Stop fooling around and …

Why?

For the next sixteen chapters we see the answer, a bit. We are not well. Well is not the right word. Maybe we are off center, off the mark, missing the bull's eye with our total being. You feel it, see it, taste it, know it, act it, and hear it over and over and over and over.

Yes, we are struck in God's image. And, we have free will, free to be ourselves. Who are you, by the way? Who is asking? *Why*?

Still Here A-Wondering

Yes, I am still here wondering and wandering in the maze or labyrinth seeking answer(s) to the questions of *why* change and *what* to change.

Some have said that all writing is autobiographical. If Mark even remotely adheres to that, then the question that I am trying to make out—*why*—is a pan-human question. You have asked yourself the same question before. By writing this gospel, Mark tries to bring to the market place this question in the form of Jesus, the Son of Man. Jesus was the answer to that *why*, coming from the market place. Jesus, at that second, not earlier or later, proclaims in the opening line, "The time has come at last." You secretly waited, hoped, wanted it to come. It has come at last. The great song by Etta James by that title—what longing there is in that song! Why did Jesus wait so long, so to speak? You waited, and at last the kingdom of God has arrived. And what is that? Hold on.

Why do I have to change? You go first and I will follow. I am not so bad, you go. You have all those issues. Past, present—right now you are and will be fouled up. I'll watch and learn. Go on. I am just the way I am. I've tried and tried and failed and failed, and who cares anyhow? This change business is really hype. The results are not what they are cracked up to be—two thousand years and you see what a mess we are in? And we are to change that? All that? Now?

And so it goes.

Or doesn't.

It stops and unwinds. Life is a bitch and then you die, many say.

I had the chance to go to a B&B in Princeton over a Labor Day weekend. It was pleasant being with my wife. As I walked down the path there, a leaf fell. It was blown down to me by the wind. I caught it and thought, *this leaf never touched the ground, since I caught it.* I held it and walked on. Right away these ideas came to my thought: "I died and I never touched the ground." Around me were all the fallen leaves from earlier events. "I died and I fell to the earth." And then, "I died and was reborn," settled into my awareness. These are the three possibilities life offers. We can drift; we can merely fall to the earth and die; or we can fall to earth and be the soil for rebirth.

In the first, many live and never become grounded in life. They have all the thoughts, actions, and expectations to be, do, and have. Even so, they never really contact the source of life; never connect with what is real; never contract with what mystery, depth, and greatness there is. They stay forever in the abstract, not the theoretical, and completely float through the one life there is here and now. Believe me, there is no judgment in this. It is just observable.

There are those who do fall to earth and it is merely that. They go through their lives as if living were a chore. Well, I'm here, so what? Let's get on with the absurdity. Oh, my. No big deal. Most of this doesn't matter, so why worry about it? It is presented in the play by Thornton Wilder, *Our Town,* where love is expressed only after people you are close to are dead. Too late. The most important point is communicated after the key people in your life are not here to hear it. Great eulogy—too late.

To live is to die. It is a fact of living. I will spend more time on this later.

To be in the kingdom of God, you experience change. There are two ways this occurs: traumatically or by insight. There is no reward for this. No rewarding gold, money, wisdom, enlightenment, Nirvana, Satori, heaven or such. To see the kingdom of God, you must change. Oh, and here is the catch-22. No one is forcing you to join up. There is no draft or conscription. You get to decide. It's your choice, your call. There is a proclamation though, if you want to hear it. The kingdom of God is about changing your heart, mind, and beliefs. This is the new and the good. It is all about the depth of God, and this is a big space, a kingdom. God's kingdom is immediately open when the choice is made to walk through the gates in this moment.

Well, I am no closer to answering the *why.* It is about living, really grappling with this, now and forever. Right in the process of living is an answer. Moment by moment. Then it is your kingdom; you have arrived and are with God.

Jesus Shoves Off (Mark 1:14–21)

The words of Mark don't state a location where Jesus proclaimed the gospel. Jesus's proclamation hangs there like a mirage in the desert from which He came. He shows up and tells us to change, and from there He shoves off toward the Lake of Galilee. He walks around the shore, and He sees two fishermen. Now, this is also strange. The land around the sea is studded with towns, fishing villages, and hamlets, no doubt. Looking at the map in the book, it seems not to be a large body of water. The amount of fishing carried out has to be big, because it's both a source of food and part of the business life, I suspect. Two men are named of the many; they are called Andrew and Simon. Fishermen are like loggers, shepherds, farmers, herders—they all work close to the land or, in this case, the water. Simple people, I dare say approachable and unpretentious. Odd that Jesus chose them. He could have used other workers, scribes, merchants, businessman, or tanners, or smiths. He could even have chosen higher nobleman, Pharisees, government officials. Why not these? Why fishermen?

Were they merely handy, right there in his path? Simon and Andrew were casting their nets in the water. Witness that image. The nets were cast and in the nets were *fish*. At this point Jesus had no followers. Not even his mother, Mary, was called or invited to join up. Of course, women were not of the stature as today. These two men were the first ones. Amazing. The fishermen use nets to catch fish. They mend the nets and fish some more. The nets may or may not bring in the fish. Their life is tenuous in a real way, yet Jesus says, "Hey, drop your nets and follow me, and I will teach you to catch men." Wow. We don't know if He even knew them from before this, and He asks them to catch men, which are equally as hard to catch as fish. "At once they dropped their nets and followed him." At once. This is called immediate enlightenment, satori in Buddhism. It applies here well. I have never experienced this type of event except when I was invited to a party for which I dropped everything to set out with those going there.

He invites a few others a few moments later, James and John, who leave their father and follow Him too. Again, since there is no hint of prior acquaintance, He points them out and away they go. Now we have four who are enlightened. Well, maybe not. Have you ever been moved to drop, stop, and go in this way? What was the spark?

I believe this is a metaphor. Of course, this happened. This type of metaphor is acceptable in the New Testament, and it is frequent. It is an image of selection that shows the power of Jesus. Jesus has a character that is unstoppable. He invites them to be fishers of men! And as far as we know, this is without previously hearing a word of the Gospel. Maybe they were baptized by John. They came on Jesus's invitation alone. Could they have been so dissatisfied with the lives they were leading to follow Jesus on this call?

To catch men. For what? The kingdom of God. You have to run this around your head a few times to appreciate the gravity of the event. Stop what you are doing and follow me. This borders on the senseless, as these men were nothing if not rational.

Most of us are in our gerbil wheels. See it? It's there with your name on it. Fill it up with the important things you are doing. Now stop and get off. Leave the scene and go, follow. "I will teach you to catch." Teach me what? How? Who are you? You'd have these questions and more. You'd most likely blow off the invitation. After all, this is not an invite to a pot party like in the 60s.

Pretty blunt stuff, really. This comes after the paragraph of proclamation. Recall the call to change hearts, minds, and beliefs. This is the play-action. Your playbook as a usual game book is different, slower, black and white, while this is in 3-D and up to date. Only we see the whole play in action all at once. The moment—the second—has arrived. Stop. Halt what you are doing, and in the stop you are responding to the possibilities of the moment. Herein you can change your life. The teaching is to apply it to what you are doing now. Only do it totally, fully, and really. Fishing is, well, easy. Men, this is the kingdom of God. Take it to another level, like the electron. Don't be a zombie and act by rote. Be a fisher of men, and I will show you how.

Now we follow Jesus. Is it Him or is it God through Him?

I don't think that matters. As I think, we have the Trinity at play already. Reading and pointing back to the baptism, the affirmation is in. The road of Jesus is with God and the Holy Spirit. As a matter of fact, their heeding the call to follow is probably the work of the Spirit. The four got it, responded to it, and did what they decided was right. The new apostles looked, were silent, witnessed their experience, understood, realized, and did what was in accord with being itself.

Answering a Question with No Answer

It was bound to happen. In a brief discussion with a friend he said, "Well, you mean to tell me there is no answer to *why change*?"

Yes, Ralph, there is no answer.

And so, I am going to try to answer, "Because." This is the pat answer to all *whys*. Having said this, I know there is a road to the horizon that stretches forever. And this question has a forever answer. Yet there is a kind of, sort of, maybe, I think, answer.

This takes us off topic only a little. Recall the earlier chapter where Jesus shows up seemingly out of nowhere stating a change has to happen. The kingdom of God has arrived. *This* is called a "kyrotic moment." This is a moment heavy with meaning, and a moment outside of time. It is unrepeatable. I say that Jesus is not the kingdom of God or that He did not see Himself as a savior. A salvator who yokes the four corner boundaries is not so negatively self-conscious as that. It is a sin of pride to hold yourself inside as some sort of savior. It is not at all godly, and may be evil. Why, then, did Jesus say you have to change. Really the question is why *change*?

By the way, how to change may or may not be easier once there is an answer to *why. Why* is infinitely difficult.

Let us assume you want to change. Then it seems there is no problem. A "natural course" of change takes place—bad habits end, outlooks shift, projections cease or are withdrawn, character or ownership commences, humility builds, love functions, responsibility for yourself and to your brother grows, and empathy is developed, which has been called fellow feeling. Negatively put, you stop being the center of your own world. There is more, I am sure. These are necessary conditions.

And what if there is forever resistance or mild resistance? Well, to repeat myself, you can go through life just the way you are with minor wellness and never come to the peace that passes all understanding, peace beyond the common sense of that word. You too are saved, I am told. But what is the big deal about the kingdom of God. Isn't that the land of milk and honey where money grows on trees and you are all the rage? This is the peace that comes from the flesh, from the marketplace. And it needs to be fed, don't get me wrong.

There are moments in our lives, all of ours, even the lives of Hannibal Lector, Stalin, Amine, Mao, Hitler, Hussein, etc., where there is a crossroads. It's a place where for an instant, you see you have a choice to say, "I am responsible." And you go away by turning away. You turn back and you end up where you are now forever. Or somehow you fall into the abyss at the crossroad. And in the fall, through the flight going down, which is not one bit enjoyable, you cannot say, "This too shall pass." It just goes on and on. The pain in this is large, dark, immense, thick, choking, and complete. This is the dark night of the soul. Sometimes there is a moment when grace strikes. Grace is "a unification of that which is completely broken and torn or separated." (Paul Tillich) You cannot make it happen. It happens or it doesn't.

Saul's conversion to Paul was such an event.

There is a one-word answer for the *why change* question: *choice.* There is a choice to go another way anywhere and anytime in the process of living. Where that leads is not to talk about now. "Come, I will make you fishers of men!" Come I will make you able to offer the moment of choice to men, right now. This is the kingdom of God: living in the choice.

Going After the Cadre

These last periods have been distracting, and I have not had the peace and quiet to compose much of anything with meaning. I have been reading and thinking, however, of the immense power of Jesus and his selection process. The vignette runs barely ten lines and Jesus chooses four apostles. Boom! They are signed up to go for broke and over the cliff if need be. Mark says it that way. "Come and follow me, and I will teach you to catch men." Like, one, two, three, it is so easy.

The part that is making me go wild is "I will teach you." If you look above this line, you will see the power line, "The time has come at last—the kingdom of God has arrived. You must change your hearts and minds and believe in the good news." I see that the teaching will be how to change the hearts, minds, and beliefs of every man to feel, know, and understand the Gospel. I notice that nowhere in this line is there anything about behavior, acting, or doing. It is *internally* that the gospel is grasped. No jumping the establishment or Pharisees and killing them. No jumping the Romans for revenge. No jumping the tax collectors for retribution. Yes, there is the action word *catch* in use: "catch men." Still, there is the absence of catching something for the purpose of being an apostle, disciple, or believer. Jesus did not say to catch men to be a Jesusian!

Again, Jesus did not say, "I will teach you kung fu so that you can beat those so and so's to the punch." Is the gospel a socio-political message or a message to help you get that the kingdom lies within? Not merely piety either. A big space this kingdom of God is. And certainly not a political power! This may be a thirteenth-generation fruit, not an immediate ruler, Jesus, rather a teacher who recruits fisherman to catch men. Whoa!

Let's look again at the chosen four. As I wrote in a previous chapter, fishermen are a pretty simple folk—down to earth and in touch with all that are natural and real. I do not think that you could pull the fishing nets over their eyes or heads then or now. If they just dropped the nets and had immediate enlightenment and later illumination, they were compelled by the invitation to act and to follow a teacher who promised nothing more than his teaching, his talent, and his ability to catch men for the kingdom. These four were not even baptized, so to speak. Jesus did the (in the moment) baptism when He called them. And when they responded, they were baptized.

MISSION IS LAUNCHED (MARK 1:21)

I have not penetrated much of the gospel thus far. I am only into the twenty-first line of the first chapter of Mark. Many words, yet I am still on the first chapter. In Mark 1:21, Phillips starts off with, "Jesus begins healing the sick." As the title to this section, so is this the mission getting set into action. Jesus is in the trenches right away, so to speak. After leaving the sea of Galilea, his troop, composed of Simon, Andrew, James, and John so far, heads to the main town, Capernaum, or thereabouts. It appears on the map to be merely a few miles to the town, perhaps a day's walk, about twenty-five miles. This is not much to these folks as they are stout-hearted men who are used to a trek, unlike us!

Again, Mark's delivery is stark and to the point. Not a bit of extension of words, merely, they arrive in the town and they go to the synagogue, as it is Sabbath. Now, if this is like today it is night, or it could be the day of the Sabbath. They would not do much on the Sabbath, so they go to the center at or before sundown. Jesus walks in and starts to teach, "They were amazed at the way he was teaching for he taught with the ring of authority, quite unlike the scribes." Jesus is teaching to recruit? Or is Jesus teaching the kingdom? And where were the Pharisees? Were they not available, or was this too far from Jerusalem? Interesting that out here on the edge of Israel, away from the center of power, Jesus begins the teaching. (Teacher means *rabbi*, my master.)

This is not the real point. The point here is the difference between Jesus's teaching and method and the scribes' teaching and method. Can we break it down?

Jesus walks in and starts to teach. Bam! No fear, no beating around the bush, no worry, no self-doubt, no hesitation, apparently just clarity. (I asked a few Jews about the ability of a layman to do this and received no insight. Maybe I'll have to go higher to a trained rabbi.) What could He have taught to get a response like "wow, far out, righteous"? Speaking with authority is being able to deliver your thoughts with such a force, such an impact on the listener that it affects the person on a non-superficial level.

Going up to the previous paragraph, Jesus's words had to have been about changing your heart, mind, and beliefs, for this is it—the truth is at hand, the kingdom of God is here and now. Jesus delivers the good news in such a manner that it rings with his being so that it brings the audience to reality, the Transcendence, or brings them to the Source of Life. He spoke so that His words moved them to change their hearts, minds, and beliefs.

I have been to talks that moved me. So have you. They had the ring of truth, and thus authority gives power. Jesus spoke with a sense of what He was talking about. He was inside God's kingdom. He had firsthand knowledge, but from where? Well, those forty days in the desert deepened the baptism experience; He was with the Source of Life.

How do we know that He moved the people?

Well, it is right there. A man in the synagogue in the grip "of an evil spirit, shouted out, 'who do you think you are, you bum? Why are you here telling us these things? We know who you are, you are God's holy one!'" Ha! He said it in so many words.

What is a vocal evil spirit doing in a synagogue? Isn't that a holy place, a sacred space? And this spirit derogates Jesus by calling him a low-class no-body, one from down south, Nazareth, a no-place.

"Have you come to kill us?" This is a chilling thought. Jesus speaks with so much power that a person from the congregation stands up and hurls invective!

Who is the "us"?

This congregant is so deeply upset that he taps momentarily into his unconscious and says, "I truly see you as you are, a Savior." Called "God's holy one."

And what is your mission, Jesus? What have you got to do with us? Why are you here telling us and teaching us to change our hearts, minds, and beliefs? We are just fine in this congregation, thank you very much!

I am sure you have run into these types before; they are possessed and they are deranged! But listen to them, as they offer clues to us about what state we are in when it comes to salvation and being on the road to God's kingdom. They are the canaries in the sub-luminary world; they are calling from the underground. Metaphorically, it is the "making public" of the non-conscious.

A Digression

One inception of this book was being struck by the need to pray years ago. This was not a usual condition for me at that time. Really, except for the many formula prayers I learned in school or church, prayer never entered my mind. I found these prayers out of touch with my existence. But I had no clue even how to form words into meaningful sentences to convey the myriad experiences I have had or was having at the time.

I did, however, have my mind on a reworking of the "Our Father" prayer. It struck me, and perhaps you, that this is a powerful prayer and it needs a bit of rewording to remain true to the intent of the prayer. This statement is audacious, but that is a common word these days.

I am merely trying to de-reify the words so that they speak to me.

Here it is; see what you think:

> God, Father/Mother, which is in heaven, on earth and in our hearts, everlasting love is Its integrity. We are awe-filled and acknowledge the Queen/Kingdom's majesty which is unfolding throughout time, space, and beyond any dimension. Thank you God for everything being as

good as it is. God, do not forsake us when we are up against You; do not disappear and forget us when we quake, wish us well, and then drop us into the pit. Please champion us as we venture daily to incarnate into spirit Your mystery, depth, and greatness. In humility, responsibility, and joy, we unceasingly pray. Amen

This is perhaps still too pietistic, I don't know. Too personal as well?

A Confrontation (Mark 1:21–35)

In my last section I struggled with Jesus's selection of the first four to be his apostles. Jesus clearly assumed that they were free to choose to be or not be part of the team. Second, He assumed that they were free to choose to change their lives, minds, hearts, and beliefs right there on the spot. The example to us is that the four had heard or knew none of what was to come; they got the invitation on the spot, in the moment. They witnessed Jesus as the One who was grounded in the Mystery which captured Him and, through Him, them. He had the authority and they acted on it. And again, they took this step outside any of the typical pleasure-pain categories we know of today.

Mark's gospel tells the story of Jesus in action at the synagogue in Capernaum. He tells us that Jesus is teaching His way and a man begins being oppositional: "You are God's holy one!" This is not so bad, except that as a kind of group spokesman he is definitely hostile, stating that Jesus's teaching is going to kill "us." People are taking sides against His amazing way of teaching even this early. This suggests to me a teaching that confronted the men in the synagogue with core questions or challenges to what was. Or did Jesus so startle the members of the synagogue with His words that some became followers on the spot?

Thus this sermon was not an abstract pie in the sky, but apparently moving enough and challenging enough to evoke an evil outburst calling Jesus a blasphemer! Thus the foregoing line, "You are God's holy one!" Now how did this evil one know?

Next, Jesus interjects, "Hold your tongue and get out of him!" I read this as "I've got your number! You are diverting us from the message I have to deliver." From here there is peace and quiet. The members are "astounded," murmuring among themselves about how Jesus manages even to control "evil spirits" with his "new teaching." It has oomph!

Bare bones, this synagogue scene.

What might this mean or suggest to us?

This is a powerful opening sketch just after the apostles' draft. Here in the Capernaum synagogue, echoes of what is to come later in the story of Jesus unfold. To kill something is to forever change its and the killer's compositions. Assuming that the man shouted something to this effect in the congregation, this could only mean a powerful confrontation must have been delivered or felt to be so. Remember that what is felt is the preliminary and initial reality. Then we rationalize it, some say. To kill is also a wish by the "speaker" for total control and to psychically pass into another realm as a shadow metanoia. It seems that Jesus's power called forth the hatred. Second, Jesus's powerful teaching also prompted action, the shouting out. Third, the shouter spoke the insight, "I know who you are." The sentence suggests a parallel, perhaps a projection, as in the phrase, "It takes one to know one."

Faced with the truth, what is our reaction? Anger, hatred, mayhem, negated insight?

Or is it awe, astonishment, thanks, wisdom, pause?

Finally, Jesus speaks to the evil spirit in the man, not the man, saying, "Get out of him." This is a bit different and may be a pattern to pay attention to.

Tackling a Big Question

Are evil spirits convulsive?

First, what does *convulsive* mean? A dictionary definition, please! It is a spasm, jerking, from laughter—here not so funny—anger and rage of a high type; the body shakes, rattles, rolls—yes, like that—agitated, to shatter or tear loose and then to irregularly or involuntarily quake with grief or pain. Phew. Epileptic shock? Well, later there is an epileptic, and whether that one is an extension of the oral tradition, I do not know. There is a clear collision between Jesus and this evil spirit.

These are strong words with a visual quality and immediacy that few other words have. The evil spirit is strong and did this to the man; Jesus casts it out. What does this mean?

In less formal words, He said, "Get out of him." Jesus rebuked the evil spirit by telling it to, "Hold your tongue." Let's see, this is a direct, active command. It is not a please, would you be so kind as to consider leaving? Pretty please, with sugar on top? Let me be sweeter, oh, you are so bad. I'll check back tomorrow and see if you are ready to leave, okay? I'll go now, good bye.

Boy, I wish I'd been there to see this. Jesus just tells the evil spirit to *get out*! Notice as well, He did not say, come follow me. *Get out* was the command. Can there be another way, a nicer way to convince this evil spirit to leave? Evidently not.

Second, what is an evil spirit? Have you ever encountered one? Or is this just some dumb Mark tale about Jesus being nasty in the congregation of Jews?

It is time to try to tackle this question of evil even though there is later chapter just on this. Evil is described here as a spirit. It is a strong adjective, a word that conjures up centuries of discussion and debate and judgment, and still there is more to reflect on about evil. I will try from afar to add to the enormous conversation. From afar because I too have only a small clue. You will have to sort this out on your own, too. I will skip the general dictionary definition, except for this: it is considered the "most comprehensive adjectival expression of dislike, disapproval, or disparagement as in unskilled, defective or cruel." Thoroughly clear. If we separate the word from spirit, we have an individual who is listening to the sermon and becoming absolutely "emotionally tied up," bound, and totally shut and resistant to Jesus's message, "The time has come, believe the good news." The man has to say something, and in the delivery he is torn and riven with angst and has to speak up. What comes out is evil. And, in fact, the story says that the man calls Jesus out. The man knew what was being said and that it was the truth; the evil spirit in the man could not handle it. In the face of utter, pure insight, the man goes to the opposite extreme, spiritually evil, and becomes ever more constricted. The man goes out and the evil comes in. I will not use the common word, "darkness." This is an intense state of prideful power which stands before the soul and blocks the affirmation to reality. It has also been called the D-evil. Was Jesus casting out Satan? Yes, an aspect of the Fallen Prince. It would not be too uncommon for it to be resident in a group of believers.

Kierkegaard suggested the possibility that the deeper the faith, the deeper the fall from grace. Thus, for the man naming Jesus, his state of panic may not have been too far-fetched because of the man's possible former faith. Second, speaking a little bit intellectually, the word *Satan* was not used in Jewish circles until much later. Here it is merely an "evil spirit."

One last thought, a small one perhaps. In the last line of the scene, the congregation kept saying to each other, "Why, he even gives his orders to the evil spirits and they obey him." Three things strike me. First, His orders, like an officer in the army; the evil spirits do what He tells them and they obey Him. Jesus is the ruler of His kingdom; second, Jesus is portrayed as having power over earth and the beyond; third, the passage almost fashions Jesus as a magician. Only a magician can do that. And, at that time, the worshipers saw that as great power because, as it was told, He created awe. You see fear and fascination all at once, but fulfilled with love. Love would call forth from a weak one a rageful convulsion. The greater one, Jesus, judged it and cast it out, here is the love. It left the man, though with a scream. The judgment was the purity of love.

The man was free in faith at last.

What Is Healing? Part One (Mark 1:27–35)

The next short section of Mark's gospel takes up the situation concerning healing. It is a timely topic for me personally, as my wife is healing. Healing offers up a hard though awe-filling period in life. It is said that every breakdown is a potential breakthrough, though during the breakdown it seems quite the other way around. The healing period is a bummer, a downer, a shattering or shaking of the foundations, as Paul Tillich suggests. Many of my phony beliefs were offered up for my observation day by day. Faith eventually surmounted the struggle, but only after ordinary hope and emotional love were pulverized. If there is such a thing as normal, a state of balance or equilibrium, it is momentary. I walked from point to point on the road of life in a type of balance. If you notice, walking occurs when a slight off-balancing of the hip that starts the motion going. Walking is initially hard for children because they don't have the knack of gliding with their hips and their legs are too straight at the knees, although they are ready to walk at birth. (Intense biological development is going on that eventually manifests itself in the first step!) They plop often until they can handle the slight imbalance. It is fun to watch, though a bit scary for the parents, but kids love it afterward. Healing was a state I prayed for always in that time, as I felt just about crushed by the weight on the way to it.

Thus, the section I see here starts with a feeling of a rush, urgency, like something is awry. Jesus has just had a bit of an affair at the congregation with a wrathful individual. There is a line following this scene that is also a bit urgent. His "reputation spread like wild fire in the region," which feels out of place, like a later add-on. Anyway, "Then he got up and went straight from the synagogue" comes across to me as urgent. I see Jesus sitting and teaching, then He gets done, wraps up the service, and boom, He is rushing off to the house of Simon who has told Him that his mother-in-law is ill. Why leave so promptly? Answer: someone needed healing.

What is healing?

A healing takes place in the house after Simon "lost no time in telling him about her." She has a high fever and Jesus gets her up and running, "and she sees to their needs." Okay, a healing, but in Mark it is not called a healing. What is this healing, then? There can be a few interpretations, surely. It strikes me, though, that Jesus again does not say anything, but takes her hand and raises her up and the fever leaves her. I like that ending phrase, "and she began to see to their needs." Jesus brought the mother-in-law back to herself, which meant "seeing to their needs." Sexist though this is now, this was the reality then. Elevated, it means that Jesus healed her so she could be herself, be normal, not ill at ease, she possessed herself. This is a crucial point to me.

I am always, we are always, seeking things that are not so. Wishing that matters were otherwise, we work ourselves into a lather about matters, things, sights, sounds, and feelings that move us away from reality, awareness, suffering, high fever, the way life is in this world. Just let me lie down, let me dream, hallucinate, get into a trance—anything just to make it different, an illuminating story, a mountaintop experience, a final blessedness. God, please, get me out of the limitations of this fever. I feel ambiguous about this fever, this world shows me suffering and death. Can I blot out the awareness and anxiety with this fever and see some other kind of world? Hope for change.

Jesus takes her hand and helps her up and she attends to their needs. This reality is simple. What are their needs now that she "lost" her fever? Dinner? Serving bread and wine? Hanging out with her son-in-law? Your guess is as good as mine, yet, she is active and the fever has left her. Is she healed? She inhabits reality, I think she is living her life. The fever is dead and gone, she is ready for more life.

"They knew perfectly well who He was."

WHAT IS HEALING? PART TWO (MARK 1:27–35)

Healing is an important part of everyday living. It seems to me that we know very little about healing and much more about sickness, disease, affliction, and inner and outer disorders overall. How much of our lives is about healing? I suspect that it is minimal because if you consider the multiple Physician's Desk Registry revisions, and its size, medicine and the health sciences spend more time on identifying X than attempting to heal X. (I speak personally. I have deep respect for the medical profession. Yet, because of what happened to my wife, I am suspicious about proper etiology in her case.) I guess identifying the thing leads to healing, right? Healing is complicated, and perhaps these comments are too inattentive.

So a vast majority of life is either an effort to heal consciously, or it is an effort to live as best as you can unconsciously. After all, the driving of Adam and Eve from the garden in Genesis suggests a breakdown of life. However, that is not the only way to read it, though the literal line is a powerful, evocative tale of why our life is the way it is. So what is healing? How do we heal this original sin? I want to return to the scene in Mark where Jesus heals Simon's mother-in-law of fever. I want to focus on the line that jumped out at me as I reread the passage two nights ago in an attempt to fathom the scene.

Jesus must have been prompted by Simon in the synagogue about his needs. It must have been almost like, "Well, Jesus, you are doing good here with the healing. Could you please help me at home? Seeing as you are helping these strangers, could you help me with my wife's mother's fever?" If He was not prompted about the fever at Simon's home, was He acting like God and knowing where to go next? Though this is my sense for what could have happened after the service, thus the urgency to get there. And what is a fever anyway that it is so necessary to heal? She is in bed. This seems serious, seeing as the level of medical care at that time was nil and not of the sophisticated level of later centuries. It is serious, therefore important enough to involve Jesus and not the local "medical man." Also, it may have been costly since, like today, some fell outside the health system. "Okay, let me take the matter to Jesus," thinks Simon. Really, I am kidding here a little. Jesus is surely not an alternative medicine man, so there has to be another way to see or interpret this matter.

The fever might be metaphor for the mother-in-law's state of being. Maybe she struggled with the meaning of her life, depression, alienation, needing support, or maybe she is agitated. The definition of fever stretches from these to ecstasy, heat, and desire. Fever is a powerful state—being on fire, full of nervous intensity—and she is in bed, an unusual state considering the day. And since nearly everything in the home was carried out by women, this must be a real disappointment. She is abed with a fever; she is lying there "out of it."

Fearing no contagion, Jesus reaches over, takes her hand, and she gets up and goes about her work as a woman to serve the men. The fever is removed; it disappears. Jesus resets her fever to normal and she becomes as she was—healthy. The fever was a barrier to fully being there, a real, present mother-in-law. She was called to live, to be. The operation of healing by Jesus—the act of healing by him—merely set things to "normal" for the mother-in-law. The fever left her, it stayed in bed and she got up invigorated.

This scene recalls to me the power of touch described in a short article I read decades ago about a monk who was able to tell the diseased person merely by touch, feeling the pulse. By doing that he apprehended what the matter was and what was not working. The pulse of the person suggested to the monk what to do about the illness. Perhaps Jesus reached into the mother-in-law's fever with his hand, showing no fear of the fever. After all, what is there to fear? Easy to say, hard to grasp. The correct touch is also important. Recently, my wife had a serious operation. Afterward I attempted to hold and rub her feet. Again, the important action was in the way this was done. Jesus had to have touched in such a way as to heal. To be able to do this suggests an eternity inside that he had found and fostered.

Finally, in bed, she is in fever. The bed: what is that? It definitely is not a Tempur-Pedic mattress of today. It was likely straw and maybe a clean sheet, but not too much more. The bed was flea-ridden no doubt. Thus it was not like the clean, spotless affair we generally repose on at night. The bed is an image of our life. All the jumble, dirt, junk, baggage—you name it, it is there. Jesus touches her hand and the fever of her life and living leave her. She gets up to what is so, "to see to their needs." She was healed.

Healing, Continued

I remain with Simon, the apostle, at home with his family. His mother-in-law is ill with the fever. Jesus heals the fever, cures the illness, mends the disease. Jesus brings "wholeness" to the mother, and she returns to her daily activities of living. But, there is more: He mends the person and eradicates the condition she is limited by.

Ruth, my wife, was ill over a long period, and due to the care she received she is well, cured, and healed. What is worth studying more is the process: how did this happen? As a common matter, how does illness happen to us, to me? The doctor made it clear from the beginning that there was no commission or omission in my wife's case. Her neuroma had been there for a very long time, thirty years or so. There may be a few items to note for cause, but they are really not certain. It just happened. Many forms of illness are caused by doing or not doing something. You know what I mean. Smoking, drinking, and various other vectors and addictions can be included. Not eating right, sleeping poorly over a long time, and driving like jackasses are some of the preventable things we do. At the end of it, my wife declared that she was a healing machine, and so it is.

We have heard, "healer, heal thyself." Rurh was a healer, and it took a momentous event to begin the healing process she is still completing. Faced with mortality, some can change. Others continue to cling to vanilla ice cream shakes when they know they will surely kill themselves. So how is it that some hear what there is to hear and others turn a deaf ear? That's the question for the ages. Wait for a moment before I attempt an idea or two.

I have been accused of being judgmental and a know-it-all. Let's stipulate to this. I always consider the source of the accusation or the agenda of the speaker. Healing will only occur when the diseased one wants to heal. Oh, yes, there are addictions that make it doubly hard to stop the behavior. Yet even with the worst addiction there is an opening for wholeness, a cure. What genetic or social or psychic push initiated the disease? I do not know. I just know from personal experience that the cure can be long, deep, and risky.

What made this small event at Simon's house so important? A fever, as I said before, is nothing. Surely, it is survivable! There must have been a deep desire for a cure in both Jesus and the mother-in-law. Well, there was a deep desire to be cured in Jensen. She initially set out on a very metaphysical route to achieve the cure. It came, just not in the way she or I expected. Here is the crossroads. She was able to discern the healthy route to take despite many around her pointing to a metaphysical application which contrasted with a practical, medical route. There is the yin and yang here—there is no clear exclusion of anything helpful. There is a rational, soulful, sensate, and emotion process, all at once and to various extents which were incorporated. What is seen on the outside is different from the internal process. This is the sweet Mystery of Life.

Jesus healed the woman in a sentence. He held her hand. The writer knows, we know, I hope, that the point is profound education. The point is to teach us. We are all on a bed and we are sick. If not now, we were or will be. The power of Jesus is shown in the mildest touch. We all want to be healed, cured of our fever and brought to "normalcy" so we can go about our lives restored, well, and active. Why did Jesus do this? If I may, to show it can happen. And Jesus did it all the time. It is normal to be sick and to be cured, to be a healing machine. You have to get up and go. Healing is "right-minded action." It is the individual's special liberation. Here, Jesus is the catalyst.

And the Healing Goes On (Mark 1:30–35)

The exemplar is Jesus. Mark and his sources were clearly stricken by Jesus's ability to live his life meaningfully. As the central figure of the four gospel writers, Jesus, in the next paragraph, goes on a healing frenzy, it seems. It is almost as if He were possessed. Jesus did not stop when the sun went down. He responded to the demands from the town's populace. Were there that many who were ill? Just imagine a town bringing its sick, ill, and such. How many? Well, the whole town's population was out there at night getting "well." And again, Jesus expelled both evil spirits and healed the sick. There is a difference, it seems to Mark.

What can we make of this event?

"For they knew perfectly well who he was," *they* being the evil spirits and the townspeople. The sentence is vague about who knew him perfectly well. How can an evil spirit know perfectly well? This seems a contradiction in terms, an oxymoronic phrase. A deranged person who knows perfectly well is, well, not ill. *What is going on?*

May I go down the rabbit hole here with you?

First, maybe they were not evil spirits. The sources of this story saw it that way and it held up as a good tale. So the story is sort of not true, a little for dramatic effect. If you are in need of healing, well, then you are sick. What if the people merely wanted to be touched by Jesus as a hero? Who would not want to be close to a celebrity. Mark's source and the community gathered saw Jesus as all-powerful. He could heal the scariest evil spirits! The story is an embellishment. Not everybody in town was possessed by evil spirits. How many is many? I am not doubting the text, rather it just seems questionable.

Second, "They kept bringing him all who were sick or troubled by evil spirits." I think no one in those days could tell the difference between a sick person and one with an evil spirit; too much superstition. A wound, leprosy, and clear illness were evident later on in the gospel.

Here, I believe, we are in a state of *trance*—an altered state of consciousness. Not mass hypnosis, but a holy state of possession, a state of awe. Synonyms—alarm, amaze, bewilder, fascinate, fear, fright, intimidate, overcome panic, quivering, *mysterium tremendum*— all describe a state in which you sense the divine. The Godhead is close. Eternity is present. The onlookers were stricken by the unfolding events, transcendent mending was taking place.

Third, Jesus says to those He healed, "Say not a word." This is a paraphrase of the expression to those with evil spirits and to those who witnessed the mending.

Here is the message I believe. Jesus implored the healed not to let the healing go to their heads, not to become inflated in their well-being, nor to let their newfound circumstances make them become prideful.

"Be not proud, your new well-being, it is merely a start of your gospel road. And, we share the same God. Avoid all inflation. I am God's tool for good, I am not the end. We serve the same Master."

The sin of pride will come later as a topic. Here, I see Jesus's humility fully. All of the good works and healing, and not one word of satisfaction. There is no big deal. It is all in the course of living in the moment, the kingdom at hand, doing what is required. The compassion here and the love of the people regardless of their status are amazing to me.

After a Lot of Hard Work (Mark 1:35–40)

It is currently Holy Week. It is Good Friday eve and Jesus has died on the cross. He has been cleansed, buried, and put into the tomb. Joseph of Aramithea has offered, and the family has accepted the offer for Jesus to be interred there. Precisely where is unknown to us.

As a boy, I used to sit in the services of the cross amazed and totally oblivious to the suffering Jesus had to go through. Later, though, I had an experience while gazing at the cross with Jesus hanging on it and suspected the pain. Some events later in life have approached the level there, maybe. What has been missing for me is the divinity part, the majestic and incarnational sense he must have had, of which I can only suspect.

I ended the last section with Jesus healing far into the night. In the early morning, after some sleep, He leaves to go pray by Himself. He goes to a deserted place. I see it as isolated, away from people. Jesus meant to be alone, wanting to pray by Himself. Praying at night or in the early morning when it is still dark is different from praying in the synagogue surrounded by a crowd, and it implies a deep state of meditation. It is just Jesus and God, one to one. The ritual of the synagogue or church is a group act with all the power of the whole community behind it. Here the power is self to the Mystery. It is a prayer of a solitary one to the sky in a deserted place. It echoes Jacob climbing the ladder to the heavens in the desert. It also echoes the desert after Jesus's baptism by John at the beginning of Mark's gospel.

Why go off to pray alone? Why does God need to pray? Why does God need to recharge or communicate with Itself? What is happening here?

Humans need this. Jesus is evidently in need of reflection on what is going on. Healing, creating from the center of being, requires power. As it unfolds in our souls, prayer is a grounding experience. Jesus balances the power of His healing by grounding into His heart with prayer. Jesus may need to thank God for Its help, as well. Jesus certainly mediated the Almighty, brought the Mystery of Life to his hand, for it is this that heals, not merely Him. The prayer in the dark morning is a prayer to the Almighty that is near and far at once.

Simon, that busybody, perhaps hearing him leave, panics and rushes out. Oh my, where is the boss? He manages to tow the others along as well. They search. Can you see it? Which way did He go? This image makes me laugh out loud. They must have thought that He split. Where? Everywhere!

"Everyone is looking for you." Exclamation point! Who is this "everyone," the apostles or the town? We don't know. Boy, the apostles thought He was popular.

Jesus gives, to my mind, the exquisite non sequitur: "Then we will go somewhere else, to the neighboring town." Really? "So that I might give my message there too; that is why I have come." Bam!

Jesus came to deliver a message of healing to their synagogues. That seems funny to me, that phrase. It seems like it was added later or something. Is it not his synagogue too? Jesus was a Jew. And they go off to the rest of Galilee. The healing must go on.

In closing, healing is a little resurrection. The wrong is set right, the weak made strong, the part that is dead comes alive. Easter, the rising of Jesus from the dead, is the ultimate life over death symbol. Is it a physical event? I faith not, and I part with many of you on this. The event is not a repudiation of physics. I don't think the Mystery wants us to be psychotic. I also sense that God's ways are Its alone. There are miracles. There are asynchronous, nonlinear events. The magnitude of Jesus's resurrection is not impossible to me. What about calling Lazarus back to life? This "event" is not in Mark, so others will have to go over the other gospel writings. Jesus was always about not creating a scene. Do not make a big spectacle, keep a low profile. Jesus is described differently in other gospels.

Did Jesus know that He was going to rise from the dead? I posit that the resurrection event was the rising of faith in "the after-death community of Jesus Christ." Among the apostles, disciples, followers, and many, many others, Jesus is alive and well. He is among us, God be with us. The good news is still at hand despite the death of Jesus.

Matter and Incarnation (Mark 1:40–Chapter 2)

As you may suspect, writing is autobiographical, either a little or a lot. It doesn't matter what type it is, whether hard science or poetry, poetry being the most autobiographical. The process of writing is taking internal thoughts and objectifying them with a form. Each category of writing has its own vocabulary and intonation. Creativity is the stringing together of words, ideas, groups of thoughts, and in the end the chain becomes an article or more, a book. This effort truly has to emerge from a spot where I can connect with the gospel and soul and witness the lines as they flow on the page. This next section was challenging and involved a different set of perceptions than the other ones. The previous chapters almost rolled off my mind to my fingers and awareness. This one was more impenetrable. My fingers had to pull the thoughts to my mind, consciousness, or insight.

This section is a famous one for many. It involves the leper's healing.

While preparing for this fragment, I had somewhat of an insight, or a least a change in viewpoint, about the section before me. The typical view of most gospel interpreters is Jesus's actions, behavior, and thoughts. Some clouds parted as I looked at the leper story, and I saw the story from a different angle. Let me show you.

Mark brings forth the leper after the many healing events Jesus is involved in. Jesus was on a healing spree, it seems, virtually from the time He selected the apostles up to this event. The leper approaches Jesus, Jesus heals the leper, the leper goes off and spreads the news of the healing far and wide despite Jesus's admonition to go to the Pharisees according to the law of Moses. These are the steps to the vignette. Time is most often spent on the healing and Jesus's power to heal. We know this. This is not news, it is a bit of a carryover from the previous healings in the gospel so far.

What does the leper represent? Leprosy is a sickness of the skin that makes the skin like the scales of a fish. Like scales fall off, skin falls off and the victim suffers a horrible bacterial infection that also looks ugly. The afflicted later dies due to the infection. It strikes me how virulent the disease must have been at that time. Anyone infected would seek a healing. Mark barely portrays the leper. He approaches Jesus, falls on his knees, and says, "If you want to, you can make me clean." His act of obeisance on his knees before Jesus is striking. In humbling himself on bended knee, the leper lowers himself before God, praying to be healed. The leper could not be lower in society. He is a walking sore, a diseased one who could contaminate the populace. Therefore coming before Jesus is a great act of courage. Please heal me. Last best hope, Jesus, please.

What is most amazing is the materiality of this scene. Most people are repulsed by it. They turn away, look away, run away, float away, delegate away, anything but *deal with it.* We look down on the body with contempt at the conscious level. We abuse it; we make fun of it;

we do not understand it at all; we desire to get away from it or mortify it; we unconsciously behave and call it Brother Ass (Nikos Kazantzakis, St Francis); and we think that by doing these things, by being this way, we are being or becoming spiritual.

Perhaps an answer is the inheritance from the Aristotelian Greeks of a mind, body and soul duality. "The Aristotelian slogan: Nothing in the intellect except through the senses" (Stephan Hoeller) separated the integrated mind-body and kept them apart throughout history until recent times. The body is like the donkeys that carry tourists down the trails to the bottom and return topside at the Grand Canyon. This is the way many use their most valuable possession. An over-emphasis on the mind, effectively downgrading the body to it, leads to a type of sloughing off of physicality.

And then some hunger for the Deific. We reach and reach up and up and up and up, and we can almost reach God's ankles. But we can never quite touch It. We reach some more and more and more, and we climb and soar and soar and soar, and we almost but never touch the sky, the ankles of God. By our own power we can never touch the hem or God's ankles. God is beyond our reach.

The leper comes humbly—not hungrily, not possessively, not grasping. He does not want to swallow Jesus, he kneels. The leper freely, consciously, deliberately wants to give himself to Jesus, stopping before him to—come what may—lose himself. "If you want to, you can make me clean." He says this short phrase and no more.

This is a correspondence that is foreign to us. Inside of this leper there is something to be healed, and the inside is good. There is nothing purely spiritual here. Jesus loves this leper. He loves the leper as a material being. This love of matter is a stumbling block for many among us. It is a love of biology. Jesus loves this man, and Mark says, as if he knew Jesus's mind, "He was filled with pity for him." He felt compassion, sorrow, at-one-ness, commiseration, and He felt pious-piety, as if He were in the presence of the Almighty. At His core, He identified with this leper.

"Of course," He says, why not? Amen, "Be clean." Clear, pure, be like your inner self. Be humble before life. And he is back to his original self, clean.

What happens next is a bit inexplicable. The leper is told by Jesus to follow the law of Moses and present himself to the powers that be. The leper does not. He goes around like a disciple telling all about the healing. Why did he go against Jesus? This is difficult to say. Yet, this is a bit amazing. So full of himself and full of the event is this ex-leper that there is no need to follow the law of Moses. And this is as it should be. No one has to sign off on the event but the man in it. I don't think I would have done it differently.

Wrapping up: the leper was humble before the mystery of Jesus. Life, as it is, is best served with humility. It takes a great deal of courage to ask for healing. The leper trusted the Man of God to see him as healable. Jesus recognized this posture in the leper. Jesus's love was apparent, so He did what God wanted him to do down on earth, in the material world: He healed the leper.

It was God in the leper. It was God in Jesus.

Encounter With Powers and Principalities (Mark 2:1)

Mark ends the last section with the line, "Consequently, it became impossible for Jesus to show his face in the towns and he had to stay outside in lonely places. Yet the people still came to him from all quarters." Why is Jesus avoiding the visible sites and staying in the remote spots? Well, if the message was getting out and being heard, and he was being seen, noticed, and listened to, the commotion must have been big, causing much attention. Were matters getting too hot? Was His presence making Him a pain to others? How?

The events at Capernaum were a bit of the answer to the question of why Jesus behaved as he did. The events materialize into a startling conclusion. Starting this paragraph as he usually does, Mark shows Jesus teaching. The crowd is large enough to choke the street and block the doorway. Who could allow this to happen in or around their homes? We are not told. Anyway, a group brings a paralytic to Him, but they are blocked at the door. They open the roof and drop him down before Jesus on the pallet they brought him on.

Jesus comments on the faith of those who suffer this process for healing. Seeing the man's faith, He says, "My son, your sins are forgiven." First, the man was paralyzed. Something was broken and holding him back from living. The man was unable to act, was not in control of himself, a part was lost to him. Maybe it was a loss of sensation or mobility; he was powerless. And in the midst of this situation he wants to get well, to regain himself or, for the first time, to be who he knows he can be. And he knows Jesus can do it. Nothing new so far.

But…

In the crowd were scribes "sitting silently." Oh, my. What are they doing there? It is as if, out of the blue, they are dropped into the scene, like beamed up or down. Zap—there they are. I find it unusual. For the first time there are aliens among the people, powers and principalities. The power structure shows up to see what is happening. *Que pasa?*

Silently thinking and noticing that, my, my, this man among men is a draw!

Asking themselves, "Why does this man talk this blasphemy? Who can forgive sins but God?" Is it a sin to be paralyzed? I never knew.

What they are really asking is, "How does He do it?" Theologically speaking, they are neatening up the confrontation, if you know what I mean. Jesus, not missing a beat, catches them with, "Why must you argue like this in your minds?" He got that they were covert! Saying, "Your sins are forgiven or pick up your bed, walk and go home." Well, which is easier, saying it directly or invoking God?

Okay, let me try this on for size, says Jesus, "But to prove to you that the Son of Man has full authority to forgive sins on earth, I say to you…."

The scribes were sent to trip him up. Calling someone a blasphemer was a serious indictment in those times. I believe the sentence was death. Under Jewish law or even Roman statute, this was serious. This was a curse to God, and it ignored the first commandment. Clearly, uttering it means Jesus assumed that He was God. Third, He was irreverent to the powers that be, and the Jewish laws and the scribes would know it. In terms of Roman laws, He was superseding them due to his utterances. Bad on many counts.

Now, was Jesus saying He was God? The Son of Man appellation is strong. It suggests he who is fully, really, in the moment, living in the kingdom. He is at or in the source and in complete relationship with His Self. This is one who, at the center of being, comprehends this. And, He is one who can forgive sin and reunite the brokenness. Are the two alike, Son of Man and Son of God? Parallel they are; they are alike only for Jesus, and it is on earth as it is in heaven.

Here Jesus peers into the scribes' hearts and sees the fear and distortion of their minds, hearts, and souls. He was not sent there to manipulate them, but to get the job done. Heal the paralytic. And the man was and walked away with his life on his hands as everybody watched! They were wowed. Then Jesus again went outside to a place of deeper quiet, the lakeside, and continued teaching them.

The Inside of Followership (Mark 2:14–18)

We read about a tax collector sitting at his desk when Jesus abruptly invites him to "follow me." He is named, so he must be well known, and he is a "sinner." Is Levi a sinner because he is a tax collector?

Jesus did attend, and at the dinner at Levi's house "other tax collectors and disreputable folks" were in attendance as well. His disciples are there too, and as before there are (by chance?) scribes and Pharisees hovering. They grumble, almost in dismay, as to why Jesus is eating, breaking bread, and drinking with a bunch of lowlifes. No doubt the scribes and Pharisees, who see themselves as the "real deals" are not respected and do not gain a single bit of time with Jesus. I see a bit of jealousy around them.

Shocked! We are shocked and have to ask the big *why* question?

Jesus nails it. "It is not to the fit and flourishing who need the doctor, but those who are ill. I did not come to invite the 'righteous' but the 'sinners.'" Oh, boy. This is certainly a big line. However, I believe there is a hidden angle of some import within this scene.

Question: Are all the apostles, disciples, and followers of Jesus sinners and ill?
Recall that He issued the same stark invitation to them, "Follow me."
Question: Do you have to be a sinner, ill, or an outsider to follow?
Question: How deep an outsider do you have to be to be an apostle, disciple, or follower?
Question: If you follow, are you healed?
Question: If you are righteous, like the Pharisees and the Scribes, are you excluded from the kingdom (e.g., the Pharisees and scribes)?
Thought: These people perceive themselves as righteous.

Jesus chooses the tax collector as a follower. This is not an idle choice, I believe. Even then this function of tax collecting is a low-status job, not well liked. The tax collector was cut off from others. He was unloved! The tax man is your enemy, enemy even to the power structure. He was turned away. Here is a partial answer to the above questions. Jesus acted as the yoke between ordinary everyday suffering and the kingdom, in this case the deep life of unconditional love. Come follow me. There is no condition on that.

It reminds me of the words, "Marry me." There is a lot of breaking of vows, agreements, pledges, and bad behavior in a marriage. It is healed by enduring, unconditional love, among other truths. Real marriage starts with and evolves to that. And yes, if you follow, you are healed. Instant healing is the ability to see the possibility of life in the moment you are asked. Come follow.

Now what about that last question? If you are righteous as the Pharisees, are you excluded?

I believe so. What are you excluded from, however?

You are excluded from the glorious association with sinners, tax collectors, fishermen, and all the other followers. Why?

It is almost impenetrable. Jesus characterizes and graphically shows us how to relate to God. The Pharisees and the righteous, for example, are caught up in the externalities of countenance and ritual, form, scripture, and internally smug, prideful, soulless, and blind to their illness. Jesus, as the doctor of the soul, went where no one else would go—to the loveless—and invited them to follow his way to reality, to the Godhead. He pushed the faithful, the scribes and Pharisees, to see more than their little righteous selves and world. This was not something where Jesus despised the world. Instead He went into it, and not as a half-wit. He went whole hog into the ditch with "such people" and had dinner with them. Hard stuff this, no armchair theorizing. Follow me unto God. And this is not social action. Follow me to God's face then, as now. This is practical charity or creative morality toward such who have illness. He did not change Levi, He merely asked Levi to follow Him to the most obvious thing in the world: God.

Three Dimensions of New Living (Mark 2:18–23)

And so, we go from who is a follower of Jesus and determining his or her bearing to deepening our understanding of who we are.

This section has the very often quoted line regarding wine skins. New or old? Paper or plastic? Saved or damned?

I said in an earlier part of this work that the gospels are not a road map to Atlanta, Jerusalem, or any place, time, space, or realm. The words of any gospel will get you in deep trouble if the literal or initial words on the page are taken to be "true." I am not an Evangelical, as by now you may have guessed. I am not a typical Roman Catholic with a deductive approach from the church above via the priest, either. I am not an agenda-driven thinker who takes pieces to support my agenda. I am not an updater either, one who merely fast-forwards the words into today and disregards context. I am trying to follow the art-form method which combines or utilizes a four-step deepening process going from the terrestrial, temporal, or superficial to the ontological, the Ground of Being, including the psychological and psychic in-between.

This section has three layers, I think. They build on the previous section in which there is a big question about who are the ones Jesus seeks to reel into the kingdom, so to speak. Just why He reached out to the sinners (as described in that section as tax collectors and outsiders) tips the scales massively. He wants them, not the others. That is a total affront to your "holiness," as you are not a sinner (to yourself), an outsider, or a tax collector. *Oy vey*!

Reread the last offering, it will rekindle the scandal. The scandal continues a great deal more.

This is the first dimension. Why are you all so different from us, and why do you not fast when we do? So say the followers of John and the Pharisees. They are not bad boys. They, in the case of John's followers, were there undoubtedly when Jesus was baptized on the shore, and they experienced the awe of the event. They knew the power of Jesus from that experience. So what gives? As for the Pharisees, they represent the power structure, so to speak, of the Jewish community of the time. The priests, who were the arbiters of right and wrong, good and bad, were in charge. Why aren't you folks fasting? Are you boycotting?

They had to have been fasting for a reason. A holy day? Could it be something like High Holy Days? Or was it just another type of day that required fasting?

Now, this business of fasting: a purification, self-abnegation, asceticism, a desire for transcendence, a denial of bodily satisfaction, an offering for a cause, a ritual to eat sparingly or just a certain kind of food, preparation for something, or a religious discipline. None of these are bad on first blush. These steps seem to make you holy. They are carried out for good reasons. This fasting is kind of visible. When you fast you feel so holy, special, chosen, called to be in the caravan, one of us, getting closer to God, leaving this terrestrial veil behind, elevating your awareness and meditating on what is realer than real. Is this bad?

The Pharisees and John's followers think that Jesus's group is too good to fast with them. Not fasting sets Jesus apart from them. Whoops! But Jesus's followers are too few as of yet to get away with this. They get called on the carpet and are subjected to questioning.

Second dimension, why did Jesus say and respond by pointing out, "Can you expect wedding guests to fast in the bridegroom's presence?" Stop. This is so painfully obvious. If you are at a celebration, like a wedding, you do not fast. You celebrate. Everything going on is about staying "in the moment." The guests do not brood on the meaning of life just yet. Later, maybe at the toast, but not now. Now you are too happy to think. You are overflowing with joy. (Oh, and the question of who the bridegroom is, well, I will leave that to the scholars among you. Who among you really thinks that Jesus is calling himself the bridegroom? This reflexive tone is impossible to imagine for Jesus. It had to have been added.) This is a great metaphor for being in the kingdom, in the moment with what's so. Later you will brood on the meaning of life and your salvation and what your vocation is. Today, eat, drink, and be merry. Why is this upsetting to the Pharisees and John? Don't sinners have to be purified? And fasting is the way.

In so many words, Jesus says, "To party or not to party, that is the question." Well, He did. He used the most common event for all to relate to: a wedding. What happens there if not inebriation, fullness of spirit, and total abandonment to the moment. Well, some still fast at weddings. Too bad. It is a happy occasion. Fast later to gather yourselves up and recollect what it is you are about. For now, party. Enjoy!

What is the meaning of this? Surely it is not this silly? The righteous cannot see because the law blinds them to what is right before their faces. Their pride prevents them from seeing. They see commandments, the Torah, the definitions, the rules, and some cannot behold the spirit. They are also blinded by their brokenness, their sin, which they do not see, feel, hear, or touch. You do not get to God by doing. You do not get to God by not doing, either. You get to God by being. Seeking God is like looking for light in the darkness with a candle in your hand. You do not find the kingdom with your nose plunged in the Scriptures, by fasting nor rapture, various intellectual idols, or creeds. All of these only suggest or approximate the Ground of Being, the reality of God. Please do not misunderstand me. I am not suggesting not worshiping at the altar.

The third dimension is in the last paragraph, which has the wineskin line that has been quoted so many times to explain just about anything imaginable. Yet I feel this verse is deeply powerful for us today and eternally. It succinctly holds the best guidelines for salvation, for inside the words are the way we are to proceed to "enter" the kingdom.

Starting with the rhetorical line, "No one sews a patch of unshrinking cloth onto an old coat," we have no disagreement. Right? It would be very stupid to carry this out. Meaning? To repair a coat with old cloth would leave you worse off than without repair. We do this a lot. I recall my efforts to overcome my addiction, to forestall the effects and grapple with my life. I attempted to get my stuff together, but no matter how hard I tried it was to no avail. Though I had fallen and could not get up, pride still held me in its grip. At the bottom of the well the water was not killing me, pride was. I kept sewing the old pieces together and "hoping" for warmth from this coat of pride. I was worse than ever. I wish there was a moment when … well, there wasn't. It came over me in time like a slow-motion movie. Staying present in a time of deep trial; praying "small wise" for guidance; reading and applying what I read in spite of no guarantees; being thankful for what was, whatever it was; looking through to the nether shore while being alive; and turning down the false light of pride. I became thankful for things being as good as they were. Here I suspect I have found my coat for the many cold rivers to cross.

Now what about the good wine to celebrate? He says, "New wine cannot go into old wine skins." Seems true, no? Wine in old wine skins is worthless, tainted, impure, fake, inauthentic. Maybe even satanic, a wolf in sheep's clothing. Yes, "new wine into new wine skins." Clear? For wine to taste right and be true to itself it has to be pure! For us to enter the kingdom we have to be new inside and out. It is not a special thing to get or enter into the Kingdom or Queendom for that matter, the kingdom is the phrase for beholding the Reality of God and the process is the correct planting, growing, harvesting, crushing, vat-ting, fermenting and cleaning, all of these under the proper conditions. Then new wine comes into existence. Who would ever put it in old wine skins to harm it? Bad wine will make you ill. Follow?

Thus from not fasting, to weddings, to new wine, we have in this section a very potent call to us about our lives. The kingdom flows with new wine.

More reflections on this section are necessary. There are three distinct images here: the fasting of John's followers and the Pharisees, the image of the wedding or bridegroom, and then the final image of the wineskins. The joining of these three is mysterious to me. Within these paragraphs there is the query to Jesus as to why He and His followers were not fasting. Jesus presents parables about the bridegroom, implying a marriage celebration as the answer to their question. And, of course, there is wine at a wedding. Taken one by one, fasting and marriage are opposites, as are fasting and wine; they are at opposite ends of the ritual spectrum. They are contradictory in nature. Fasting is for purification, usually done maybe as a community rite. It's a type of asceticism versus the joy of the wedding event. It is a solitary experience versus the union of opposites, a man and a woman. Fasting is solitary worship versus the vows spoken by the man and the woman carried out by a priest. Fasting may bring about a new you, whereas the marriage truly is a new unit that, if attended to, will surely bring about a new man and woman and new birth—the children of the union. Fasting is no such thing. Finally fasting is asexual. It may be carried out prior to an event, again as a set-up of the body, spirit, and soul for the event, but still you do it by yourself.

Tying it together, a marriage, bride and groom, is a new venture versus fasting, the purpose of which is just to slough off old stuff. There is the suggestion, I believe, in the phrase "new wine into new wine skins" that points to a union of opposites, like the sun and the moon. At the wedding, in truth, you shoot the moon, and the shining of each partner seeks the kingdom of God.

A KOAN (MARK 2:23–3:7)

This section in Mark's entry about Jesus is peculiarly hard to title. Philips calls it "Jesus rebukes the sabbatarians." In my work and reflection on the writings of Mark, I have come to see this as well and a few other parts as a Christian koan. These stories do not, what shall I say, flow. They appear more and more to me as that—a type of koan as in the Zen meditation practice. Perhaps this section will give more sense and credence to this notion.

A koan is supposed to produce enlightenment. Repeated enlightenment as a perpetual state becomes illumination. It is a figure of a scene, something like this:

> Zen is like a man hanging in a tree by his teeth over a precipice. His hands grasp no branch, his feet rest on no limb, and under the tree another person asks him, 'Why did Bodhidharma come to China from India?' If the man in the tree does not answer, he fails; and if he does answer, he falls and loses his life. Now what shall he do? *(Adapted from Zen Flesh, Zen Bones, Paul Reps)*

A paradox, indeed. Like last time in Mark, there's wine, marriage, and superseding the law—three veritably incongruent things, yet in the kingdom, much is not what it appears to be. Oh, and the "answer" to the koan, well, let's hang with that 'til later.

We have a type of layer cake to cut through in this section. It seems again on the surface as an "us vs. them" style of show. Us, the followers of Jesus, and them, well, you know who you are. Opening with a super line, "One day he happened to be going through the cornfields on the Sabbath day." *Oy vey*! What? Piece by piece now: he happened .... When does God ever just *happen*? I laughed out loud when I read that. God happened to be walking through a cornfield on the Sabbath. This is a joke, right? A rabbi walks through the cornfield on the Sabbath. This is a non sequitur. Sorry. Okay, okay, this is divinely inspired, right? Jesus is a bad Jew, has to be. Jewish rabbis do not walk in cornfields on the Sabbath. Okay, let's say this is so. Next, they begin to pick the corn to eat it. Raw? Yes. They were hungry. Stupid! *But...*

First, it strikes me that the Pharisees are there following Jesus and the apostles. Then they say, "Look at that. Why should they do what is forbidden on the Sabbath?" Here it gets very funny. First, the law makers don't get angry because of *stealing*, no, but for picking and eating corn on the Sabbath. Jesus aligns himself with David and supersedes the Pharisaical law again.

Jesus says, "The Sabbath is made for man's sake; man was not made for the sake of the Sabbath. That is why the Son of Man is master of even the Sabbath." Thus, is it good to observe the Sabbath or to eat corn when you are hungry?

Is it okay for us to steal? Is it pre- or post-services? It appears very Zen-like herein, like first there is a mountain, then there is no mountain, then there is … it's hard to follow. *But…*

There is a lot of talk about the spirit of the law. We are called to that, and spirit supersedes the law. Hm.

Let's go back to the hanging man and Zen above. I like that image. It reminds me of Cotton Mather and the spider thread, a great echo of the similar theme. Over a precipice you are focused, aren't you? You are very focused. Your whole life is in the moment. You are not scattered. You are right there concentrating. You have to pay attention on an unroped free climb or you will fall and hurt yourself or die. This is scary and full of toil. The plan for survival is staying focused. You hold on with sheer force of will. I hear that later you and the mountain become one, according to mountain climbers. In order to achieve that level of the "spirit," there is and has to be a close adherence to the laws. Then you become free in the midst of the climb. Great skill allows great risk within the moments of the climb. The upward push to the top is the only right answer. Now, the question posed to the hanging man requires an answer. And the Pharisees require an answer. The lawgiver in the moment is you; on the mountain climb the lawgiver is you. All is in the context of the plan; all is within the context of the Sabbath. You are the decision maker in the moment.

In an earlier comment I suggested that the state of "bliss" is one in which the lawgiver springs from the spirit within; you are the lawgiver. This state, however, is pretty delicate and deep. This is not random, nihilistic, opportunistic, anarchic, let-it-all-hang-out, relativistic, or any other kind of synonym. However it is not perfection, either. The law from within is substantially of the holy kind, arrived at from the discipline of effort and reflection with very little ego. Rather, the self is at work on itself. This is beyond mere emotion. The state combines or bridges the heart and the mind. There is a bit of hearing the call or cry from a vision of the Godhead, urged on by a soulful push for more consciousness. It is like the saying, "Boy, that took a lot of heart."

The Sabbath for the sake of man is not a twirl on words. Recall that God created the Sabbath in Genesis. After the "work" was the condition of Sabbath. This work was immortal, being was created, a lot of "something out of nothing." So, just there, it was "in the moment," Sabbath. What Jesus is getting at is the mere form of the Sabbath, all the outward stuff absent the grace, the holiness, and the fullness of being in the presence of awe—in the presence of God, well, that form was not enough. And finally, being in and one with God, well, the Sabbath is a movable feast in that "the Son of Man is the master of the Sabbath." This is not to blow off the event but to infuse it with more meaning.

The hanging man on his way down answered with a happy grin and said, "Because," to the question. I think in exact words it is, "Mu."

Jesus brings his humanity forward more in the last part of the section. A man with a shriveled hand seeks solace on the Sabbath (continuation of the day's story) in the midst of services from Jesus, asking, "Please heal me." Here, too, Jesus goes beyond the law and reaches out to the man and heals him of his affliction. Of course the Pharisees are aghast. Jesus is deeply hurt by their inhumanity and angry with their superficiality. The Sabbath *should* be a time when the attendants touch the holy, a time when they move closer to the reality of life like the sick man to the kingdom within. So He takes the man outside and heals him there and then. The Sabbath is about the healing in life, the deep healing we need. The Pharisees run to the Romans via Herod so they can remove Jesus.

The sense of a koan may seem blithe or irreverent. Yet, these stories about Jesus are stories full of mystery, depth, and greatness. They lead to greater grasp of what life is and corroborates the kingdom at hand, right here and now. They point us to our moments of human encounter where the spirit supersedes the mundane, goes to the heart of the life we inhabit, and deepens life ever more.

Enormous Popularity (Mark 3:7–13)

Jesus retires to the lakeside, but not to swim or relax. He is there with his disciples, and a large crowd from all over northern Israel has been attracted to Him. The areas the spectators traveled from are listed. It was quite the gathering designed to give the impression that He had a big group, an encampment by the lake. Galilee? Not specified. Still, Mark means to imply a large mass, so this section is meant to show Jesus's "popularity." I guess He would be popular! People are always looking for the newest thing, and the time was ripe for Jesus. There is the thought among some thinkers that when times are ripe, fruit is produced—some good, some bad, and some glorious! Jesus was meant to be. So in this short section the masses are in step with him to the lake to see something come out of somewhere. "This vast crowd came to him because they had heard about the sort of thing he was doing."

What, pray tell, was He doing? "So Jesus told his disciples to have a small boat kept in readiness for him, in case the people should crowd him too closely." This was a strange line in the midst of an ordinary description. Jesus, according to Mark, was concerned about his safety! Why? The people were pressing him so as to "touch him with their hands." Pushing forward, I guess, into the water. Jesus was concerned about his safety; this seems a bit inscrutable.

Purely human. Did Mark interview Jesus? "Well, how did you feel when you saw ten thousand there before you on the shore? Were you a little unsettled? Can you tell us?" There is the feeling that Mark was "reading into the event," wouldn't you say? And what is the problem with touching Jesus? Why care to the point of caution?

We also have the repetition of the line, "Evil spirits, as soon as they saw him, acknowledged his authority and screamed, 'You are the Son of Man.'" But He warned them repeatedly that they must not make him known.

This seems screwy on so many levels. Was Jesus viewed as a *magister ludi*? A chief magician? What authority does Jesus have over them, the evil spirits? And then to say, "Hey, but don't tell anybody." Wink, wink; nod, nod! "I don't want to be known."

This goes to the question, *what is the essence of God?*

If you or I see an evil spirit on the road, what do we do? Please leave, we say. And we likely keep the experience to ourselves! Jesus asks sternly that they not make him known. Jesus's presence engages them. For them to see Jesus as the Son of God is like the shadow noticing the substance, the head seeing the tail in a coin and just not saying that they are related. Jesus dissuades them from naming Him. This is observable, Jesus casts them out in public. It occurs before a crowd, people witness it.

Sorting this out is a challenge. Another Christian koan, perhaps? Or is it the mysterious essence of God? Being hidden, exhibiting humility, atonement to God, God Itself keeping a low profile, all suggest a Son who wishes to serve with no pride or ownership. To be known is to be objectified, to be identified, to be typed. All this makes for being pigeon-holed and over looked or projected upon by all who "see," yet do not.

To cast out screaming evil spirits authoritatively exhibits a kind of love we barely grasp today, perhaps ever. He exhibits the love of the evil not as an emotion but as an action of casting out. The Son of God, the Son of Man, will not name the evil, He merely ends it. The possible gnostic interaction is present. The presence of God casts out the evil. End of story. Yet I have a question: I get that Jesus talked to the evil spirits, but why ask them to collaborate with Him? What do you think?

Jesus was enormously popular on earth, in heaven, and in the crowd's heart.

The Twelve (Mark 3:13–20)

This part was written on Yom Kippur. This is a holy day for Jews throughout the world. It is part of the High Holy Days cycle that includes a religious New Year celebration. It is a bit sideways to mention this here, yet it is meet and right.

How deep is your sense of recollection? Not memory, that is easy. Rather, here I use the definition of the Roman Catholic tradition. It is withdrawing from the external matters of everyday life, going down to the soul and looking around, and asking if God is here. It is deepening the soul life, interior space, and solitude. For almost every man recollection is the experience of being up against the wall time after time. Your nose is pressed against the wall; there is no space behind your eyes, as Caroline Myss has said. There is no sense of recollection for most. I offer this as a recollection to the Yom Kippur Day of Atonement, which is interesting, at-one-ment with the Mystery, Ground of Being, God.

Okay …

The question we ended with (which is truly the only question) is, "What is the essence of God?" It is a thread spun out of the last session with Mark and Jesus, and evil spirits evacuate the scene as Jesus stands present. To be a Son of God is to be at-one with God. In this posture, evil spirits flee. They recognize the state of affairs, the way it is. In God there is wholeness, not brokenness. Evil is aware of itself as broken and runs. But evil can be "saved" or healed. More on this later.

After the mob scene at the lake, things evidently go so well that there has to be a team response to the masses that cry out for health. Can the twelve do it?

The twelve team is called forward out of a group by implication in line one of Mark. He summons the men He wants. A selection. On the hillside, up in the higher levels of awareness outside of consciousness and unconsciousness, the twelve are summoned and named. Surely, from the lakeside and the waters of the deep consciousness, there is ascent to a rarer plane, a space of altered consciousness. These men are the ones called to know more, see more, feel more, and be more. How high is "onto the hillside"? Well, maybe just high enough to get away and be apart, alone, with Jesus. Here He changes Simon's name to Peter the rock; He calls two to be the "thunderers"—they are the most impetuous. Driven to work the crowds, you needed a loud voice to be heard, and only two more had an appellation: Simon, the patriot, and Judas Iscariot, who betrayed Him. Judas also kept the money bag. A fascinating thread of thought could be developed here.

An aside:

- Twelve is a numeral in other religions and a belief set.
- There are twelve tribes of Israel.

- There are twelve imams of Islam.
- There are twelve minor prophets of Judeo-Christianity (there were three major prophets).
- There are twelve signs of the zodiac.

These chosen were his companions, comrades in arms, *compadres*, soul brothers, or his squad. Their mission was to cast out evil spirits and to preach the gospel.

We all need a community, these men were his. The disciples were close; these were the closest. They perform like him, almost in his place, as Jesus does, preaching the kingdom at hand and driving out the evil spirits. They also seem to be a diverse set of believers; you'd need this to talk to the many kinds of listeners who they would attract. Many of these show up as the leaders of the New Testament. For now, they are there to support Jesus's vocation action.

Perhaps the question and issues of community must be answered at a later time.

WHO DO YOU LOVE? (MARK 3:20–31)

"Then he went indoors …"

After the 'mountain top' experience, for all—apostles and disciples—the scene suddenly breaks to another place—indoors. There is no transition to the scene. It is almost like the end of a scene in a movie, black and then the next picture. Then, after the magnitude of the apostolic selection and the impressive event of being chosen to be one of the insiders, it ends there without elaboration.

It feels like a big break for two reasons: first, the suddenness of the shift to the town of Jesus's birth, Bethlehem; second, the graphic event with Jesus's family.

Here, "When his relatives heard of this …"

Here, "The scribes who had come down from Jerusalem …"

Okay. Jesus again attracted a crowd so large that "they could not eat a meal." Not such a big deal. It has happened before, so the team makes do. This time it upsets the family! The relatives evidently wanted to be with him exclusively, (wouldn't you?), and it freaked them out to such an extent that they wanted to put Jesus away, "To take charge of him." They wanted to commit him, to lock him up. This seems to be strong language.

Then the scribes are there; how? Down from Jerusalem. This could only be if He was in his ancestral home, Bethlehem, visiting the family. Yes, Jesus did have a family. How did the scribes know He would be there? Well, even then word passes. They had a question, of course.

Again, the decision to commit Him in order to keep Him safe is startling. Why would He need to be kept safe or be protected? Take Him into custody? To whom would they give Jesus over? Here, early on in Mark's gospel, chapter three, we see Jesus's family upset and ready to try to halt his vocation. I don't think they were happy. Too much notoriety, attention, and exposure; this is unlike today where some seek notoriety willy-nilly. People are saying He is mad. Hm, I guess casting out demons, evil spirits, and so forth is way too much for the relatives. There is the reference that you had to be mad to contact the evil spirits. You had to be off to be able to communicate with evil. People are saying, "He must be mad." What a thing to say about your son, he who is your flesh and blood. Of course they did not know that they were talking about God, about their Savior, just then. They labeled Him mad, as in, "You are possessed of an evil spirit yourself." Is this not betrayal? And from whom? Your loved ones. This is not too surprising. After all, family can be the worst.

The realm of madness is interesting. In those days no one really grasped what mental illness was. Being under the spell of an evil spirit was the best explanation. To witness what Jesus did surely implies madness in his behavior. And the opposition would normally accuse you in the vilest terms available. Jesus is mad, meaning possessed. More correctly, He is committed to God in Him. And in His hometown, well, He is just the son of a carpenter, not God. To save face, His relatives do what relatives sometimes do: they act as His enemies. Of course, you readers do not have this kind of family, the type that would lock you up in an institution.

Then, to add to the mayhem, the scribes gathered and accused Jesus of colluding with outsiders, a believer of Baal. Translated, Beelzebub is lord of the flies, and those who follow these beliefs are in cahoots with evil spirits. A lot of heavy accusations are really flying around. Relatives and scribes are ganging up to wage formidable two-fronted attacks on Jesus's person.

Mark says Jesus relates a parable to them all.

Well, not really a parable. If you read it, it is more like a wise reply. It is too long to reproduce here. Jesus's reply goes along these lines: There is no way to be a part of Satan's team and throw out evil spirits. It is not consistent. Evil spirits honor one another by allowing each other to exist. They do not fight against each other, otherwise they kill each other off. Okay, now that that is settled, "I am Jesus and not in league with the evil one," He says.

Who am I? Jesus doesn't say or ask this. It is implied by the final lines of the section.

Listen up. Sins and blasphemies can be forgiven—all of them. What cannot ever be forgiven is a sin against the Holy Spirit. "That is an eternal sin." Singular. Jesus comes as close as possible to saying He and the Father are one. To grasp a sin as an eternal sin, one against the Holy Spirit—not just a little old blasphemy against a minor god, Baal, or any lesser symbol—Jesus posits the Holy Spirit as alive in him. Yes, and alive in the world. These four short lines set us to consider his way of preaching the gospel. "There can never be any forgiveness … that is an eternal sin."

Jesus states that the sin of blasphemy against the Holy Spirit is forever—forever and timeless. Such a sin is beyond time, it is ontological, having to do with the nature of existence. This sin is another way of thinking, doing, or being. It may be the true evil, something apart from reality. This sin against the Holy Spirit separates us totally from God, life, the Ground of Being. This is "real madness." Psychosis—this is the best word I can use to describe made-up reality. Being empty of the divine, denying its action in our lives.

Here is the first time, I think, that we see the something we call the Trinity, the three faces of God alluded to in Mark's gospel writing via powerful meta-languaging. We have Jesus in life walking, breathing, in all the facets thereof, totally related to what is so: God. And this relationship becomes holy. The Holy Spirit is anchored in their dynamic, Jesus's and God's. This is an eternal state. The sin is in the denial of the fact that it is and can be. Jesus held his atonement to the Mystery of Life—God—close. It is a power, a force, and it enthralls the person fully. Jesus wanted and chose this. The choice is ours to make as well.

In closing, Mark says, "He said this because they were saying, 'He is in the power of an evil spirit.'"

Jesus was possessed—possessed by God. His actions were from this core position. It is not an evil singularity, it is not a reduction. It was beyond duality to unity with the Mystery of Life. Jesus was not dependent on symbols, so He cast evil out. Jesus was not dependent on images, so He preached "the kingdom of God has arrived, it is at hand." There is no monkey business—none.

Jesus realized and acted always on the inescapable presence of the Mystery of Life, the here and now of His union—nay, unity—with the Ground of Being. God was present in His life; He knew it, lived it, and loved it. The kingdom was at hand, here and now. In this sense, yes, Jesus was the kingdom. His power came from this relationship. The Holy Spirit was there beyond time, space, and dimension. So too was God, and thus Jesus. The brokenness of life in the poetry of evil spirits was cast out eternally. Jesus was mad with God.

COMMUNITY (MARK 3:31–4:1)

A while back I said we would have to discuss community. I know nothing about it. Many purport to, but I have very little firsthand knowledge of it. I will try to direct my mind to this nevertheless, as this section of Mark deals with it metaphorically.

I did have a chance to read part of Dietrich Bonhoeffer's *Life Together* long ago. I also had an experience of community because of my affiliation with the Ecumenical Institute, Institute of Cultural Affairs, from about 1968 to 1980. During that period I was part of the group and a functioning leader in various capacities for about seven of those years. Thus, I have had it, a group experience. I also was part of a Hungarian community in Minnesota for the first twenty-three years of my life, because I am Hungarian. Also, as a married man for more than twenty-five years, I have been in the community of my wife, who is Jewish, and we go to most of the celebrations of Jewish life. These three facts are more or less community experiences. This is all I know. I wish there were more intellectual depth to me about this, there isn't. Using these three, and perhaps a dictionary and a few looks at Bonhoeffer, maybe there will be a breakthrough for me and a grasp of the section now. By the way, I left out the question of college community and other groups of which I am and have been connected to. This includes Roman Catholic schools and the church as a child.

It just depends on how deep to go into the question of community. In the end, we are utterly alone. Or to put it another way, we are utterly alone in the end. These two seemingly identical lines are the poles for the discussion of community, for we are alone in a community as we are in community. And we are a community of the alone. The dynamic of the two poles is only as strong as the link, the individual, the self. The individual and "its" depth occurs when in discovery and authenticity, the individual is there in the group, wherein there is respect and fellow-feeling.

Among other things, a community is about something. It has either a mission or an awareness of being a group. In this sense it is a "chosen one," whether by self-selection, by necessity, or by election. The apostles were chosen, and they were attracted to Jesus. I am sure that they, in some dimension of their awareness, knew they were special—the chosen ones. It was not just a sham to hide from the shame of life and sin, but their state of being pure of heart. The apostles had character. They were a community of characters gathered around Jesus living in the kingdom, a big fat now. One of the group. What a gas. No disrespect, and I am sure they felt at times very cool and at times, "What am I doing this for? And, why am I here?"

Naturally, because this was a Jewish group, there had to be a sense of chosen-ness. It was in the law and Old Testament. They received the Tenach as the ones chosen. It was in the culture of the people, passed down through the mother's milk and the father's heart. Their life together was, I am sure, intense, close, and contentious; it had to be. We never see them or know of their exploits except as we see Jesus, but too bad. Their acts carry out the story! Also, the epistles of Paul, though later, point to community of early Jewish Christians and Hellenic Christians too. I am less aware of this, and that epic has been told better by others. Staying thus with the twelve apostles attached to Jesus portrayed in Mark, there are but glimpses of their time *together.* This is one.

We see them listening to Jesus teach; we read of them getting assignments, a mission, orders, directives, asking questions and living and eating together. Did they have any family? I don't know, it is never fully revealed. We know that they were sons to some fathers. We do see Jesus with his relatives, and when they connect with him it is a time of testing the boundaries. What a strange scene Mark describes.

A seeming repeat of the earlier section about casting out evil spirits, this seems to be the positive side if the previous section was the negative, in the context of Jesus's community. They arrive, mother and brother, seeking to be with Jesus or at least listen in on the teaching. Yet they are left standing at the periphery of the large crowd gathered around to hear Him. They send a message, written or verbal, we do not know: "Jesus, can you come to see us out here." Pretty normal, but maybe not. In the last section they were ready to bind Him over to the "powers that be" since He was mad in their judgment and assessment. Clinical? Perhaps. Here it is, "Come out, come out. Your bothers and mother are outside looking for you."

Putting myself there, there had to have been a pull. Imagine a family member's call. Even if you are the worst, like Jimmy Cagney in *White Heat,* who plays a small-time bum and thug (a movie well worth the viewing) Jesus cracks wise—almost. Who are my brothers and mother? Indeed, who? Mother, birther, succorer, nurturer, trainer and teacher, friend, confidante, and much more. It's the same for the sibling(s), more or less. The reply, "You around me are my mother and brothers, those who are here." Unbelievable!

To say that the new tribe of believers is more special than the tribe you were born into, well, this was really something for that day. The community of followers and apostles was more important than His family of origin? This is a hot knife through the butter of convention, of tradition, and the way things stood. The roles of mother, brother, sister, and father by implication are all resident in this group and do not originate at home in their birth towns down the road in Bethlehem. Ahem, "Can we talk outside for just a second?" Just what does this mean?

It means that in the chosen group called by God, named by a decision, they are in a new tribe of believers unlike anything heretofore. Jesus called them to Him. They are selected at that moment and become the chosen ones who value their community, who want to extricate themselves to a new way of thinking, interior knowing, doing, and being. They were different from the usual roles of being mother, brother, and sister. Better, not superficially, better for the road taken. They were called to be mother, brother, sister, and father *to each other*. Standing before God in relation to each other, there was Jesus as the one who went before to do God's will. In this they were first among equals—brother, mother, father, sister, one to another. This is the rule they acted out: "Love one another as you love yourself."

Their relationship to Jesus was Jesus's relationship to God and vice versa. "Anyone who does the will of God is brother, sister, and mother to me." Anyone! This is the trick. To get to Jesus, you pass through God. The sequence of the sentence, if I can say this, is clear. God's will first, then to Jesus, who is already there in God, in readiness. God in the moment, the eternal now. No monkey business, it just is. In the beginning was the Word. The will of God is active, the verb of Jesus, and *is* Jesus.

God's Will (Mark 3:31–4:1)

Recovering from minor surgery, I have not focused on my journal regarding the Gospel of Mark. Not that I was uninterested, just off the beam, so to speak. The respite gave me a chance to see what is essential in the gospel. So I am back to this. A rest from the pressure of writing is good; going unconscious and absent is not good. Every day is a now, never to return.

This reminds me of a book I am reading. It is the Odd Thomas series of Dean Koontz, a remarkable chain that is introduced with a graphic comic. The most recent installment asked three questions, "a burning philosophical thing: What's wrong with people/humanity, what's wrong with nature (as in floods, earthquakes, fire and ice), and what's wrong with cosmic time, as we know it, which steals everything from us?" Stated by the author in the negative, these are eternal, enduring questions we ask in the midst of an event or at night. Right there they roll off the tongue. They do have a bit of victim-ness in them, yet they demand a response, no? In the EST training, they said that, "The world works when you follow the rules." It is axiomatic—follow God's will and all will be, have, and do as it "should." There is this issue called sin, however. We live in a fallen world. No? Jesus was in this world of the fallen. It is said that He was sinless.

Thus, what is God's will? It has to do with the here, the now, the kingdom or queendom. This is not a time thing. It is not temporal. It is beyond time, space, and any dimension. And it is not metaphysical, either, not preternatural or supranatural. It is best described as an active receptivity leading to responsibility, a tension between freedom and duty, a combination of heart and mind, attention and action. Jesus was in total union with God—living in a state of grace here and now. Recall, "You must change your hearts and minds and believe the good news." Preach and heal the sick, cast out demons and follow the will of God.

Still, what are we talking about? We suspect at times that we are basking in the love of God. It is unfiltered, unblocked, unencumbered, untaxed, poured out. Our job is to go with the flow of love.

Repeating, what is the will of God?

It is something to contemplate, this question. I don't believe there is a pure, simple, or direct answer. Bonhoeffer offers a scientific method.

Observe. Judge. Weigh up. Decide and act. At that point we follow the will of God, giving up the ability of knowing and letting the knowing go. (An older meaning of "let" is to contract or assign. Think about that in relation to the Mystery of Life.) It is, however, nowhere near the thoughts of Kazantzakis, who states, no less, that we are God's eyes, ears, nose, and throat, that we look at the crimson line behind us and know that we are on the march with It as It struggles for awareness and the transubstantiation of matter to spirit. I prefer the "soul." Kaz's work, entitled *Saviors of God—Spiritual Exercises,* is truly amazing. It runs about one hundred pages, and after reading it you are never the same.

Back to Mark. God is there in the community of believers, the mothers, brothers, and sisters. Will suggests action; will offers a force with a direction, a power moving in time and beyond it, as God is at once close and far, on earth, in heaven, and in us. To get to will there has to be *a priori,* forethought, or readiness. In the beginning, the Mystery of the eternal now was there, here, and ready.

I finish with this: "Use human means as if there were no divine ones, and divine means as if there were no human ones." *B. Gracian, circa 1570.*

What Does It Feel Like to be Hit with a Parable? (Mark 4:1–21)

Parables are a big thing in the New Testament. Jesus uses them frequently. Mark comes now to the parables that are biggies, the ones that are called on often as teaching aids by ministers, priests, and other interpreters of the gospel. In a way they are cudgels, verbal hammers used to beat people over the head to get them to wake up! I aspire to go in another direction.

Parables are metaphors by definition. They are allegories, stories, teaching tools, similitude, and the like. In the Old Testament this type of "story" was a proverb. Skeptic that I am—not a doubter, rather a friendly inquirer—I have a few questions.

First, who is the audience? Was there more than one? What is the context versus content? What are the origins of the parables we read in this section or any section of Mark? What was the purpose? What was Jesus out to have happen to the audience? Are the parables at all transferable to today?

Before we look at the parables that follow the last section of Mark, I am impelled to brood on these questions. I think they are very important and may go to the center of gospel thinking and interpretation.

The audience was right there, so it seems, the folks on the beach and the apostles in the boat. I ask again, who is the audience? Who is listening to the parable? Let's look at the scene objectively. In a boat, in weather, rocked by the waves, at a distance from the shore, Jesus speaks. Who can hear the parable? Oh, maybe a few deep. The rest: "What did he say?" Truly, the parable is hard to hear above the crowd. Ever been in a crowd outside? Who can hear? Recall that there is no sound system. Thus, the message is barely intelligible. Sorry. Yet, here is a record of that event. Myth?

Was there another audience? Yes. The apostles, who are ostensibly in the first row. Right? They are the real audience. And then the word spread as a chain of talks, no doubt. For example, the radio station I use for a show has a group e-mail server where the news is disseminated. I posed an inquiry about how clean the microphone was and asked if someone could hose it down after ten years of dirt, breath, and dust. By the time it got to the last of the members, cleanliness was not the issue. The issue became whether it worked in terms of bass and treble frequency. The last member did not get the initial issues, but got the issue from the person before in the chain of emails. Are things any different from us two thousand or so years ago? Maybe, maybe not. The parable the ring-siders heard was different from the one we read today. We are another audience.

Can a parable be so changed and still mean anything remotely like the one heard at the time? We are faced with an oral tradition in the gospels.

There were no scribes scribbling the words in the moment, real time, were there? Mark, as the first gospel, appeared about 60 AD. Imagine retaining oral tradition for that length of time. The parables would have to start somewhere around 31 AD. It is clear that they had a lot of time to be altered—forgotten, remembered, added to, subtracted from, and so forth.

The context was a speech before a mob of people, "A bigger crowd than ever collected around him." I wonder if Jesus projects correctly. Where did He learn public speaking? Is He sitting or standing in a boat? Waves and water riff again. We have to assume that someone kept the boat steady. I am sure that this was not a short discourse, somehow. Sermons sometimes run long. Is it morning, afternoon, dawn, or dusk? Who knows?

Where did these parables come from? Maybe they come from Jewish sources, as there are a few parables in the Old Testament. However, there are no parallels between those and the ones in the gospel. Stories are often ways to teach and engage. This one is engaging. So what is the point, the purpose? What is the message, and what is the intended effect on "us"?

This parable is not breaking open very well even after a month of reflection. I looked at an atlas of world myth by Joseph Campbell to assist me and really came up with little. The geography of Hebrews was mixed, so in between there was planting, herding, and some commerce and fishing, of course. This is an agrarian motif, however. The sower sows, so the parable goes. Not a fisherman, no politics, not a jot about sheep or goats—seeds instead.

You know the parable. Sowers sow seeds and they fall in four places. Good, bad, ugly, and neutral but ultimately bad, where the seeds die. Only the good seed that falls in the right spot lives to grow. What type of seed is like this? It took my non-agrarian mind to get it. *Wheat!* All others that I can think of have to be planted in rows: corn, soybeans, vegetables, tobacco, and so forth. Wheat is the staff of life and can be like a field of hay we see when we ride through the countryside. Wide stretches of fields were unlikely, more like a few acres. Bread is made from wheat, so there is an immediate connection. It gives life, meaning it is the source of daily sustenance.

This parable is often shot at you assuming that the sower is Jesus. Who else? Your mind goes there easily. I believe not.

There is a natural flow to that option. Jesus is teaching, so who else can it be about but Him? Well, I think not. If this were about Him, He'd be out of character. It feels unlikely that He would place Himself at the center of the guidance. He is not the subject and object of this lesson at once. To think otherwise is an error in reference for the parable. Jesus would exhibit too much pride, an almost arrogant bearing, and make the presentation too complex. I think it is simpler. The sower is the source of life. It is the Unity. It is God as It sheds light on us.

Yes, Jesus and God are one. So, in the absolute sense, He is the subject and object at once. Something like this: one is one; one is many; many is many; and many is one. Work with that and see if you can make a case. However, the listeners aren't able to make that distinction as much as we are. This is simply an unsophisticated awareness for the time. The ancients drop pearls for us to nudge around with our noses, and often we get it.

As I start the New Year, this is the third or fourth time I have tried to break open this important topic. There have been some technical difficulties. I repeat, this is a hard piece of Mark to work on. The more I work with this, the more the question of just what the parable or moral teaching is escapes me. It is as the title suggests: I find this parable to be impenetrable. I honestly don't know what it is about.

Yet here is a try at interpretation.

This sower parable is about the kingdom of the Spirit. It is about seeking reality. A man sows his wheat and it falls hither and yon, everywhere. The man is an image of God. God throws us and sows us all over, and four things can happen when He does. First, the "message of God" can fall by the side of the road; second, in the weeds; third, among the rocks; fourth, on good soil. That is all. Okay? Now what?

The message is scattered almost randomly. It falls on us where we stand, sit, or run. As some of us are by the side of the road—at the edge, the periphery—naturally any of us will understand just a bit and be swept away. This correlates to the image of the birds eating us, as the effect or message is lost on us. Or, more forcefully, Satan whisks us away to its definition of light. Some of us do not even have a chance. So it goes, and there is no avoiding it, it seems. It is as if you were a deer running from the wolves. The others fall among the rocks. You hear the message, but you don't prepare your soil. You cannot drive down roots into your life, and your character never gets developed. You don't get how hard it is to grow and, well, you die. Those among the thorns are beset by life's prickles. "It should not be so hard, this process of growth, this rooting goes too slowly, the leaves and stalk are too weak, with not enough nutrients." You are effectively distracted by life's smoke and mirrors, and the kingdom of the Spirit. Well, it is just too hard to see. Some, though, push and grow where they are planted. They have good soil and they grow into bushels of wheat. These transform the spirit into flesh, into wheat (food), and offer the sustenance to all. "And there are some …."

Thus, there are options. If you are by the side of the road, move to the road's center. Now, don't wait. You will hear the message better out in the open than at the edge. If you are among the rocks, make it your own quickly with the little bit of soil so you can mature. If you are among the thorns, the hardest spot, pay attention to the message, love it, love the spirit, love awareness, and take nothing for granted. And if you are given this setting make of it what you can.

Grow on behalf of the others who may not make it. Own it and be bountiful on their behalf. This is the possibility of everyone who looks around and witnesses. The secret about the kingdom of God and life has been given to you.

And the Parables Just Keep On Coming (Mark 4:1–21)

Here is a famous parable. J. B. Phillips calls this section "The truth is meant to be used." Apt.

Not much intro here. It feels like a continuation of the last session's doozy, "Then he said to them …."

What?

"Is a lamp brought into a room to be put under a bucket or underneath the bed?"

Not if you don't want to start a fire!

In two paragraphs, Jesus, in fifty words, utters a koan of immense proportions.

First, right off, the question is totally rhetorical.

Duh. Not really a good idea … under a bed? Imagine a kerosene lamp under a bed. Ding, ding. 9-1-1. Right now, a two-alarmer.

"Surely its place is on the lamp stand." Right.

Whatever are you getting at? This is normal, standard operating procedure.

"There is nothing hidden which is not meant to be made perfectly plain one day." Oh dear, whatever does this mean? Can't you be clearer? Next it gets really good: "And there are no secrets which are not meant one day to be common knowledge." Secrets about what? We will know who killed Kennedy, then?

Hey, Bozo. "If a man has ears he should use them." Are you talking to me?

Who doesn't?

"Be careful how you listen." Is there any other way to hear than to hear?

"Whatever measure you use will be used toward you, and even more than that." So If I behave poorly, act out, menace, blah, blah, blah, this will fall back on me? Are you calling me a retard?

"For the man who has something will receive more." Oh, great, again with the privileged few. The rich get richer and the poor get the gas.

"As for the man who has nothing, even this will be taken away." Nice, real nice. The downtrodden get the shaft again.

There you have the entire parable. And, what does it mean in context of the kingdom of the Spirit in the universe of life under the stars?

Beginning at the beginning, then, we have a lamp, a simple image of light. It should give off light from where it can be most effective, unencumbered, and visible to all who need it. But there is more. It is the light of God we are offered as the theme of this parable. More, it is the light of your life, soul, and spirit. Let me use them interchangeably for now. The inner light that is illuminating your *life*—what is it? Is it visible or is it underneath the salvage of your existence. If so, then it is under a bed. Think of your bed. What goes on there? Is your light hidden by your mess, your messy mind, your too-large shadow, your complete unpresence to living, to others, to the ground of your being? Is your life a small or big litter basket?

Light's place is, of course, on a lamp stand. If you are truly in the moment with your real and true self, the glow is unmistakable. I suspect this is a state of grace, a state of union with the one, others, and you. And, if you're a schmo, well, everyone knows. I don't think it is necessary to be liked by everyone. I suspect it is a realness, authenticity, integrity, character, and presence suffused with love, power, and delightful bearing. This is necessary. In this frame there are no secrets. Secrets in this context are not its common definition. Secrets are the projections we carry. Here, there are none. You own all the projections. Then you see, hear, and witness common knowledge. No artifice or trick to hide yourself from life, others, or God—there is light.

From the internal, the shift to the external, "Be careful how you listen." Once you clear your insides out, well, it is easy to listen. Still, every day is a new day. It is a challenge to really hear, to be ready for the other person, for yourself, and for God. It takes great awareness and sensitivity. In a way, life is circular. Our projections tend to bring with them results we'd rather not have. Force will be met with force and so on to a greater extent. Does this suggest we should keep our own meditative council? Perhaps.

The answer lies as a mystery in the next lines. "For the man who has something will receive more." What is the something? And what more? The man who has light gathers more light. It is a law. Light, a source or power, brightens what is. The something is the inner light of the kingdom of the Spirit. The something spreads, grows, and effuses the surroundings. The surroundings change forever. The light never ends. Well, in physics it can run out of energy, but in the soul it glows on. It glows on and it is reflected in the surroundings—all the greater. And the opposite, those with nothing lose the nothing they have. This is scary. As so many will die and leave nothing. Is this an issue? This is between the Mystery and you.

The Classic Parable (Mark 4:26–35)

Mark comes now to describe the third parable in the series with two parts; maybe they are related, maybe not. The first part seems like a repeat of the previous parable. This happens often, almost a rephrasing of a previous event or, in this case the "sower," which was first in the line of parables. Again, it is a motif of the scattering-of-seeds theme. However, this shows the sower in a seemingly more passive role, emphasizing him and not the result of the seeds' locations. Yet this is a simile, too. "The kingdom of God is like …" The crop is corn. The parable is perfunctory, almost formulaic but for the opening line. We are imaging the kingdom of God, pointing to the seeds' process of growth. What is the kingdom of God like?

The organic production here is natural. It is pleasing to the farmer to see the development of the land. His crop is well, he will eat, his family will have food, the order of nature endures. The process seems naïve, "though he has no idea how it happens." This is the mystery of life, the universe showing its beneficent side, the goodness of earth, the union of heaven, earth, and sower. "For the harvest has come." To the farmer, then, it was a full-on miracle that the earth worked well to his benefit "without any help from anyone." It is God's will, in a manner of speaking. The man got out of the way and participated in the expansion and result, over which he had no control.

What is like the kingdom of God?

Trying to be as clear as possible has stumped me a bit. I was at a Kabbalah session where the speaker outlined a type of art form, and I guess I should have used this to plumb the terms of this parable from the beginning. Kingdom is clearly a political term. It also connotes a space. It is clearer when we look at the farmer as the king of his field. He is the king of his kingdom, his space. The land he tends is his kingdom. Kingdom of God is a field of God; it is all that God is. It is seen and unseen, known and unknown, felt and unfelt, bounded and dimensionless, full and empty, void and dynamic; we are inside and we are outside God. God and man, It and us, in us and without us, in time and out of time.

The farmer is the king of his space. The seeds are spread by his hand and are released like we are released from the Mystery of Life. We are born into and from this world, and we grow as if by magic. Overnight we sprout and off we go, growing where we are planted. "The earth" as a metaphor for the kingdom of God shows how easy the realization of growth is. It does it "without any help." This is how easy the process of capturing the kingdom is. What does this mean, to capture the kingdom?

Since we are in the space of God forever, Its kingdom can be had by acceptance, by absorbing it. The growth and harvest show the fact that we have absorbed (took it in, a state of readiness) the kingdom of God as our own. We have won the chance to be in the kingdom.

This is the mystery we face daily, seeing the kingdom of God naturally and easily, without a bit of difficulty.

Turning now to the mustard seed parable, this is another classic. I include it here because it flows from the previous sower parable. Jesus continued, "It is like a tiny grain of mustard seed." Mustard, like salt, gives a stoutness to flavor. Mustard seeds pickle. Mustard seeds also have some medicinal qualities. A little bit of seed goes a long way to get the results, one way or the other. Kingdom of God is both small and everywhere.

Here, too, the ease with which the mustard seed fructifies in the earth is mentioned. The kingdom of God follows this pattern: it grows and spreads, if allowed to, with many ancillary benefits. Even the birds live there freely and have shelter. The kingdom of God is as it lives in us, helping us be the real characters to life in all ways, times, and places. We are the seeds of God's kingdom on earth.

The section closes with, "although in private he explained everything to his disciples." Hm, the secret teachings, no doubt. Really. The secrets were shared in private. What could these secrets be that they have to be withdrawn from public sight or knowledge?

Do You Want to Know a Secret? (Mark 4:26–35)

"So he taught them …."

As I read this last paragraph, I think there are again two audiences: the followers and the listeners or readers, then and now. The line strikes me as revelatory because it raises the question of hidden meanings, secrets passed between Jesus and his followers and apostles. But what does "in private" mean?

The audience is two groups—us and them. We are composed of the listeners now and the listeners then. The teaching was done in parables, but only the followers received the firsthand interpretation in private. Mark communicates it as if he were there. He was not there. Someone had to tell him that there was such an event, or it was assumed.

We who are not there are left to our own devices to interpret what "this" is. What does Jesus tell them about the kingdom of God? He is the guru, they the disciples.

The disciples are the initiated, the listeners, and we, the readers, are not. So there is an element limiting the information to a few. "Although in private he explained everything to his disciples." The word *everything* is an all-encompassing word Mark used. This had to have been handed down to him. What is so beyond understanding that it has to be confidentially shared among the initiated?

Parables are delivered as metaphors. They are offered to point beyond to the deeper strata of life, to suggest meaningful characteristics where they are not apparent. To then go to the next level among the followers, I have to notice the layered message. Multilayered, maybe? This bops the scientific worldview hard in the twenty-first century where rationality reigns as the *summa cum laude* of most life. Where the rub is today is that it suggests that the disciples were treated a bit differently from all others, including us. The in-sies and the out-sies, hm. This chaffs the supposed egalitarianism purported or proposed by some about early Christianity. It hits at the possibility that some get it, others wait to, and some just do not. Am I missing it here with this interpretation?

The tradition of teacher and student is a long one in religious studies. Eastern thought is passed forward in this way. Of course, the father-son teaching and the mother-daughter teaching are given in this one-to-one, slightly intimate fashion in all societies. Why not here? Given this fact, and since religion is often best transmitted when done one-on-one, the question is only a *what*, not a *why.*

During these quiet times, Jesus had to have talked personally about God, his relationship and insights, and readiness regarding the ultimate mysteries of life. For sure Jesus was bearing His soul. They were all friends, some relatives, and closer than most. Intimacy was there, everyone guessing how special and yet normal this man was. In private, where it was safe, Jesus explained. He was a rabbi; they listened to His sharing.

The three previous parables were so simple to read, yet hard to pierce to get to the core thoughts and images. I believe to get there you have to have an insight not commonly appreciated today. You have to be anchored, as Jesus had to be, in the Ground of Being, God. Yet, you must also be able to walk in the square among the people and tell parables. The divine and the practical were therein the parables He taught them. If there was a secret it was and is the nature of God's being in the world. And this is up to us to uncover, realize, experience and know in our life daily. "with many parables such as their minds could take in." Yes, be ready.

Resting After a Busy Day (Mark 4:35–5:1)

After a long day of parable-izing, Jesus wishes to relax. I would too. It is hard to know the size of the crowd He addressed for the day. I know exactly how I feel after a long day in front of people—shot down to the bone. Recall that He spoke by a lake, on the water's edge. He says, "Let us cross over to the other side of the lake." Whatever could there be on the other side? Somehow I feel it is not in His character to go have a tall cool one in a lakeside tavern. Kick back and debrief the day with Peter and the team.

What we have here is another story woven with deeper meaning than it appears in Mark's telling.

The evening, well, that could be after sundown. Really, who would go out in a boat at that time? Purpose of the trip? Who knows? Jesus wants to go, to cross over. The way the term is used today is maybe a bit different from then. It strikes me, though, that a crossing from one space to another, a leaving of one spot to venture out, a bridge to another side, all imply a break with the day's activities and adventures to seek another frame of mind.

How do you send a crowd home? "Game over," losing side buys, gets to forlornly leave. "See you tomorrow in uniform at 1:00 p.m." Crowds leave, I am sure, sad. The team gathers Jesus up along with other small boats and they go to the other side. En route, a storm pelts them while He sleeps. They are terrified and beseech Him to do something to prevent them from drowning.

"Master, don't you care that we are drowning?" Whereupon Jesus stills the storm and wind, and it is quiet. And Jesus asks, "Why are you so frightened? What has happened to your faith?" They were awestruck and said to each other, "Whoever can He be? Even the wind and the waves do as they are told?" The end! All is well that ends well.

What a wonder. But first…

Jesus is sleeping on a wave-tossed lake. Amazing. Can you? Are you so at home in adversity that you can settle into being? What is the lake anyway? Water? How about this? The lake is a stretch of unconsciousness that we all are in and cannot float on. Jesus, unlike us, is at one with life and being, so what is there to fear? What is there to be or act afraid of? The elements are not a problem or a worry. The storms of living are no issue. I recall the feeling of dread around any authority figure at a point in my life. My life was in turmoil.

The Buddhists have a great saying: "There is no wind, the flags do not flutter; it is the heart of man that is restless."

The seas of life throw us to our effective death. It seems never ending, relentless. We bob in the pitch. We cannot seem to get ourselves or acts together no matter what. Joseph Campbell said it well. There are four things you can do as you try to grapple with living: 1.) blow it or yourself up; 2.) succumb and live a quiet desperation—give in; 3.) stay alienated; 4.) begin your inward journey. Jesus sleeps on the cushion in the stern (in the back), mind you, through all of the natural tumult. It is calmness of being, not inattentiveness. I think you get the point. There is a deep equanimity from having "crossed over" long ago, not temporarily or briefly but soulfully, in and toward God.

"Master, don't you care?" It appears that Jesus is oblivious, dead to them, unaware of the excitement. Well, how many times have you felt that no one cares? Especially that a key person to you doesn't care? The followers are no different in this event. We scream out with our fear, "we are drowning!" Is there any help around? Could there be anyone in the small boat of life we are floating on? After all, I am in danger of dying. I'm near death's door. Where is God when we or I need a hand?

Jesus awakes and calls the disorder to order: "Hush now. Be still." Is it not the way you talk to a child? Who is Jesus talking to out there? Since Jesus is not a magician, He is talking to the apostles. Some have said that He is, in fact, talking to nature to be calm and still. Oh, really? Could be. However, if God is life and being, and Jesus is not the one upset, in danger, or worried, and God and Jesus are one, the only reason this is "conjured" up is as a lesson for the apostles. He asks, "Why are you so frightened? What has happened to your faith?" All this occurred after He explained the parables and the private time they had after all his teaching to the crowd. You would guess, suspect, and hope that they got it. And the followers were swept with awe again, and they asked, "Whoever can He be?" Duh. Wasn't it just a little while ago that Jesus shared about life and all its charms on a deep level?

Yes, awesome it is. There is so much here to reflect on. It all happens out in the depths of life the opportunity to grasp the mystery of life and being. Jesus clearly demanded a teaching moment about faith. Faith can calm anything. Have faith in the mystery of life as we are tossed about and try to cross over to the other side, over the waves to reach the nether shore. How often we only want to escape—to go anywhere, but not stay where we are thrown? Here there is the peace in the moment that passes all understanding, so it is said. Standing before or riding the waves is our lot in life with the mystery of Jesus on board. Life is perilous. Jesus is not going to save us, per se. In faith there is nothing to save. Coming out of the parables, we can see that we are in the kingdom even on the raging or calm seas of life. After all, suffering, which is what this section points to, occurs just as we seem to have reached a certainty and meaning about life and ourselves in it. It is a little boat. We are bid to the kingdom of God in it.

A Remarkable Conversion (Mark 5:1–20)

(This fragment was inspired and completed during Easter.)

Happy Easter to all. At the end I will consider the Easter holiday. Some prefer to say Happy Resurrection Day because Easter is an echo of Ishtar, and I don't mean the movie.

The section is another hard one. Please read it before proceeding. I will not be quoting it much. Are they ever easy? The superficial items are clear: there is a healing, there are witnesses, there are a few thousand pigs, a burial ground, and more. Philips calls the man a lunatic—insane, unsound mind, reckless behavior, daemonic, and moonstruck. Such a nice man, this one, or is He really an everyman? The passage says as much, that he is possessed of many "devils," a legion of at least six thousand. I believe that any more than three of them and we are living with the Devil. But wait …

"In the grip of an evil spirit." If anyone lived in a graveyard, they would be called "one who is in the grip of an evil spirit." But this man is also gripped by more than that. He seems superhuman in strength because the chains and ropes cannot bind him and no one can restrain him. He howls, screams, and cuts himself. He is out of control in the most and worst way. It is amazing that he is alive, living as he does. Plainly, he is off his rocker. Today we would say he is psychotic and drug him. As a metaphor it is compelling.

Mark portrays him vividly and adds a piece that makes it even more metaphorical—the tombs. Live among the graves and you will have a very different frame of mind or vision concerning what life is about. Here is a man who is outside of the "world" of the day. Only a person beyond the pale, an outcast or a shaman, could get away with this. Why is he even alive? Plainly he is dead to the world and dead to the Jewish community of the day. Maybe this is why Jesus was going across the lake. This man is way beyond alienated. Let's say he is there for a "reason," or that he secretly wants that graveyard spot and is trying on his own to rejuvenate himself but made a wrong ramp choice on the expressway of life and ran into a pileup of wrong-headed knowledge full of a legion of devils. He could not distinguish day from night. He howled at the moon realizing his situation and cried out on the hillside, "woe is me" in associated pain. Been there? I have screamed as much as anyone, "What have I done, why me?" This is an everyman set of circumstances I offer.

Mark says that the lunatic runs screaming to Jesus. Every man would. Jesus's reputation precedes him, yes, but more than that, the lunatic sees salvation. Not the chance for easy living, but rather the chance for conversion.

One of the facts I found to be true was my own complete self-involvement during the worst of my condition. Because I felt like a "cold turd," I guessed mightily that this was the condition of the world. The way I felt was the way the world was—life was meaningless—not seeing that the statement was meaningless too. I saw things in my dysfunctional way as reality. This perception *did not mean that they were so.* Recognizing that fact, I had a chance to see what and who and how it really was. I had to step away from self, to die to my false self and loosen the grip of my ego, to understand that I was living among tombs but really was death. My life was torturing me, killing me. That the world revolved around me and only me was a lie, I had to admit. And, I had to admit that I was a victim.

This man kneels before life, humbles himself, and sees the reality of Jesus as the one who took a relationship to life fully. This man knows that he has to die in order to live. He lives right then in the moment as a son of ultimate reality. This man begs not to be tortured—a peculiar way of saying, "Let me live. Let me lay down my chains and bindings of life, let me release the ropes of mere existence and be free at last." Well, not precisely in these words, but in the spirit, though.

It is a bit magical after this. The legion leaves and jumps the pigs and awe is all around. The pigs are a fine image for the results after the event. It is an awe-fully big event when there is a conversion. A change of heart of this size because of the man's visibility has to be followed by the disaster of the pigs. This man doesn't hog the show anymore. Jesus sends the man home to his people, telling him to spread the word about the reality of his rebuilding, his newfound life wholly from his conversion which was, of course, due not to him, but Him. And this is called the kindness of Ultimate Reality, God. "All were simply amazed."

I am not done.

What does a changed heart entail or mean? The next chapter carries on. Meet me there.

A Redo, though Still in the Same Place (Mark 5:1–21)

I have reread the last offering and reflected on it some more. I liked it in some ways, and on other terms, it is not so good.

I wish to try again. I think this is a very important section in Mark.

This place across the Galilean sea, in the town of Gerasene, around Decapolis, has a man possessed. Could this man be well known, with a reputation preceding him so that Jesus wishes to address him? Heal him? The description of the possessed man is vivid. Mark describes him as having a home among the tombs. He also wounded himself. Others tried to bind him to no avail, as he seems to have abnormal strength to tear the chains and bindings off. A man who has this bearing has to be widely known, at least to the immediate area. Now then, "possessed by the Devil" is a metaphor for being dead. This is also underscored by the life among the tombs, self-inflicted semi-suicidal behavior—all point to no life. There is no living here, only deep delusion. He is a man stuck in the underworld. The man is attacking Jesus, provoking him (subtly begging him?): "What do you want with me?" As if he were the point of Jesus's visit, and maybe he is.

In despair we often have grandiloquent notions, as would he, secretly hoping to be somebody when we are not, at least not under these circumstances. Perhaps Jesus is totally aware of the desperation in this man. In desperation, I have cried, "Why am I not understood? Why does everything go wrong for me?" I, too, have thought that life was torturing me when it was not. Here is a man who is dead in all respects. The man is self-involved, self-hating, self-destructive, and self-centered. The etiology is not the point. In the moment, Jesus calls him to live. Imagine not a psychological healing, but rather a healing of the real self, not the self of the tombs but the self of God.

The words are, "Come out of this man," and here is the kicker, "you evil spirit." Its name was Legion. It seems that the violent man picked these evil spirits.

Come clean, be clean. After the abnormal self is gone, what is left? After the evil spirit departs, you have emptiness. You can have a life of immensity. Why all those pigs were the external sign of the size of the death and self-possession. Legions of pigs were run off the cliff. And the man becomes well. From death in the tombs to life among people—what a relief.

This is not a social or psychological healing. Jesus is not a master therapist. I use the word *healing* as a metaphor for living in and before un-shrouded reality. Perhaps unshaded light of what is so, an image fully realized, seen, un-blinded by Legion's illusions. And this is "kind," as Mark says in the second-to-last paragraph. It's really a different picture of God. And to share this picture of God is really a gift to be shared that is worth six thousand days of reality, release, and readiness for God's kingdom.

A Story in a Story, and Event in an Event (Mark 5:21–6:1)

Many of us have had experiences where two events unfold. Maybe there are multiple permutations in a scene. In this section, one story is the main event while a smaller, equally impactful event happens. Individually, each can stand alone. Together it makes for great "theatre."

The thread with the previous story is short in that it says Jesus crossed the lake to the other side. Change of scene or scenery occasions an event of huge proportions. A leader in a synagogue acts as a supplicant to Jesus regarding his dying daughter. He "faiths" that Jesus can heal her and pleads his case, fervently hoping that Jesus will act on her and his behalf. Wasting no time, they leave with the crowd close on their heels to see Jesus's power over death again. You can sense the intention in the passage among the believers as they go to the synagogue leader's home. It is most interesting that a president of a synagogue would humble himself by kneeling before a "rebel rabbi" just as the lunatic in the previous reading did. Whether high or low, many saw Jesus as the court of last resort for their struggles.

In the press of the mob there is a woman who is also very ill, hemorrhaging blood with no possible healing. She got no help from the doctors and is penniless—a pauper in earthly terms—bereft and getting worse. To whom can she turn? Merely touch the hem of Jesus's garment. That will be enough, she thinks. No. She really, truly decides that there is nothing more that will work. She approaches from behind, too despairing to look face-to-face with life itself. Coming from the rear, this is all she can muster. She succeeds in touching His garment and, lo and behold, she is well. Her trouble is over. Hallelujah!

The gospel says that Jesus, sensing or intuiting, stops. Who goes there? The apostles and others say, well, there is such a press that it could be anybody. He looks at the people's eyes and sees her. She is afraid perhaps of committing a crime, a misdemeanor. No one touches such a powerful man's garment and lives to tell about it. Confessing the action, she throws herself down in front of Jesus as the culprit. No worries, woman. Your faith has set you free of your malady. Another act of faith that achieved the desired end.

Meanwhile, the leader's attendants run to tell him that his daughter has died. Jesus says to hang in there, don't worry, "just go on believing." The leader's home is in bedlam as Jesus arrives. Everyone is in grief except Jesus. He even says, "Why are you making such noise? The child is not dead, merely sleeping." From the assembled crowd a derisive laugh comes, where upon Jesus turns these out and proceeds to minister to the leader's daughter. "Little girl, I tell you, get up."

And she does. Happiness prevails in all there, and Jesus again tells them to keep all this under their hats and asks that food be given to the risen girl.

There you have it. On the surface it is just another death-to-life scenario. Jesus is acting the part of the redeemer. It echoes earlier events in Mark's story of Jesus, the gospel of living the kingdom.

There is more. Both of these people are at their wits' end. The synagogue leader's most cherished daughter lay dying on a bed at some distance. This man has nowhere to turn. Certainly he is a man of power. He is not another rabbi, but greater in stature. He is the president of the synagogue. His desperation is palpable. To believe with this strength in Jesus is real. The laying of hands is a small way to heal. "She will get better and live." He says that to Jesus, and there is no hesitancy in the articulation—no maybe, no perhaps, no let's try, give it a go, old college effort.

Also, there is the power of the hands, its presence. So we all know the power of touch, closeness, and the need for it. It feels as though the whole passage has a sense of closeness, the jostling crowd, and now the woman. The woman is in awe of Jesus. Twelve years of pain is no short time. This is a chronic thing. This woman symbolizes the total abjectness of life, penniless, helpless, and she is a woman, no less. She is fearful of being rejected. If she could quietly touch and go, then disappear. She does not want to cause any attention to be brought to her. Anonymity! I would. Who would not?

Jesus intuitively knew. What a $640,000 statement.

Who said so? Mark—right there in passage 5:26 or so. Well, this is the living end! Here Mark spills the beans that Jesus had an interior life. Do you? What is it like? Can you feel the touch of someone's pain so you can make it all right? Perhaps that is too much.

Anyway, Jesus stops because he is so in touch with himself that he knows the need behind him. He reads her face, her eyes, and sees the aftermath, the result of her action. He does not claim it as his own; merely that it is her faith in action. "Go home in peace as you are free from your trouble." She even tells him her story, all he wants to say is "go in peace." It is *your faith*. It is *you* who has healed yourself. Oh, my. You are released from your sickness through your faith. I have been the Salvator, not instigator, for your health. We could spend a year meditating on faith as a means to heal. I leave it to you to figure the path for yourself. It is not belief strictly in Jesus. You need to ponder your faith in the Mystery of Life.

The next scene is the dying daughter. Here, too, is the faith action and the hands of holy touch. It also illustrates the need to have a peaceful arena in which to act. Notice the quiet around the action of touch. It is peaceful, not intrusive, around the little girl. It is almost a circle of attention, a loving posture before the situation. Holy space and awe.

The healing is spoken in Aramaic. Mark uses this word for the first and only time. Words are important in the holding of the little one's hand. "I tell you to get up." This is a very direct statement to her being. Again, no pussyfooting around. Bam. But gently, "I tell you to get up." Joy explodes when she arises. And tell no one what had just happened, merely get her some food. So down to earth. Stay humble before this event even if you are healed.

There is a great deal of food thought in this section of Mark. The reflection has to be on faith and its effect. Yes, love is the greatest of all virtues. However, faith opens us to the Transcendent. It gives us the freedom of action. Abraham's faith is immense and empowers him to face God's demand. Faith is an enormous invention because it sets us as legitimate followers of Jesus, as we are indubitably invited to be. Later we will talk about faith as it plays out in Jesus's words.

You Can Never Go Home Again (Mark 6:1–6)

There are barely four paragraphs of text in this section. It is full of information about Jesus as Mark sees it. After many miracles and profound events, Jesus journeys home to His native ground, His nativity. There is no mention of where this place is—Bethlehem, Nazareth, or elsewhere. "His own native town" is how it is phrased.

Of course, the team is there. His followers and disciples know. They play no role except as silent witnesses to the events. They follow Him.

They probably hung out a few days prior to the Sabbath. When the day arrived, as Jews, they go to the synagogue for the evening. The service on Friday is a relatively new event. At the time of Jesus there was nothing like what there is now, so I can only guess that on Saturday, some type of Torah reading went on with some kind of interpretation among the congregants. It is here that Jesus, according to Mark, gives his "lecture" or had some "input." Boy, what must that have been? There was astonishment, harrumphing, surprise, offense, maybe displeasure, resistance, incredulousness, taunting, and likely hostility. "Where did *He* come from?" Or, as Marks relates, "Where does *He* get all this?"

In this passage, we find out that Jesus had a family. Though there is no mention of Joseph, there are four brothers, unnamed sisters, Mary (mother of Jesus) and the fact that his job was carpentry—many facts to ponder.

A fairly large family, in my opinion. The brothers are elsewhere, says the passage, and the sisters are there in the village. It seems to be some kind of homecoming event. Was Jesus invited to speak? Likely. He is now famous everywhere, so this could be. This would explain the tart comments of the villagers to his words. "Where does He get all this?" Yes, indeed, where did he get it? This is the million-dollar question. The passage suggests that the words are full of wisdom, along with his miraculous actions. They called Solomon wise. But Jesus was "only a carpenter's son!"

There is a big difference between wisdom and carpentry, so they were deeply offended by this man of the village who was virtually a nobody but who was renowned. There had to be a bit of tension because Mark says, "No prophet goes unhonored—except in his native town or with his own relations or in his own home." This is His home! Some words, no?

The resistance is so immense that he can do no good there. He neither heals nor changes the hearts and minds of the villagers. Some welcome!

It's a very interesting passage in that it says so much about Jesus—his outlook, the reception as a tableau, an image of his self-perception as a prophet, their sense of Jesus, his "anger" at their resistance, and his relationship to his family. This is a goldmine of information—a mother lode.

"Their lack of faith astonished him." His expectation that they would be otherwise is exceptional. And why could He do nothing miraculous? Remember that this is God-in-man. Why do those who are the closest seem so hostile and resistant to Jesus, their flesh and blood?

In the mingling of God and man in Jesus, we have a likeness of something, a sketch of what is so ultimately in the kingdom of God. This sounds more Platonic than it is, meaning that in the day-to-day struggle of life we can image the kingdom to those around us and still get zilch. God is imminent in Jesus and the people are upset. God shows us His face and we run, we hide, we lose our faith, we fear for our lives, we call God out in offense. And then, when God is transcendent, we get scared, we get upset and feel alone, we dishonor the facts, the truth, and generally act small. We throw up all barriers to God, to Its grandeur, horror, and mystery. We want it simple, easy, and by 5:00 p.m. Yes, it *is* easy. "The time has come at last, the kingdom has arrived. You must change your hearts and minds and believe the good news." This is up to us. There is no recourse but responsibility, the tension between duty and freedom.

But why is there no miracle in his village? Why is there no transformation? God is God, after all. All in all.

Something like this, there is no plug-in. God is there, but the people are elsewhere. There is no connection; there is a cord, just no connection. They are not ready. And God made Its expression felt and moved on. You are dishonoring me and yourself. *I am astonished.* No harm and no foul. God goes on. This recalls the sower story. There are people who will never get it. There are people who get a bit of it, and there are a small number who may see what God is through a darkened glass. And even in the flesh, right there in Jesus, they behave weirdly.

The tension between God's immanence and his transcendence continues today. God is close by and far away. Yet, we are never bereft. It is up to you; it's all there to see when uncovered, when you are ready. The villagers, however, lacked faith. And you?

It Must Have Been Hot and Dusty (Mark 6:6b–14)

It must have been hot and dusty.

This paragraph is another whopper in church history. It is a biggie. Yes.

But first, a detour.

The previous passages are as personal as you get with this gospel. I cannot speak about the others. We see Jesus actually evincing a personality. He is upset, as he should be, with the people of His village, His birth place, totally blowing Him off. A prophet is never welcome in His own land. Such a mild way to say, "You don't really accept my teaching, even if I am one of you." This is the first time the line, "If you saw Jesus, would you know him?" is portrayed in between the lines of a true story. The folks of his village are not impressed by his appearance or his communications.

We know the phrase "you can never go home again." It is a fact, since all is dynamic. He is not a carpenter's son anymore; He is deeply "other" to them. For me, this is a pity. It is a shame. Here is God in your midst and you know Him not. "Here is for whom you really are waiting, expecting, and hoping. You Hebrews are in the midst of oppression and you get whacked out," I say. Pretty sad. This must be the offense many speak of. Jesus offends the villagers. Since we are not sure what He said, as it is not communicated, I can only guess. Maybe: 1) pick up your bed and walk; 2) the kingdom of God is here; 3) if a person has ears, let him use them; 4) I came to invite the sinners; and so forth. Jesus left in peace, I am sure.

Following this, we have almost a reaction. Well, if you cannot accept me, then I will send the apostles out to the hinterlands, beyond the pale, and preach and teach to those who are fresh and know not, those without preconceived notions, expectations, and pretensions. "He summons the disciples, the twelve." Out with you by twos, "giving them power over evil spirits." How do you do that? How do you transfer the power you have to friends to control evil spirits?

Okay, let's think of this. Jews today do not proselytize. They did not at that time, either. An immense departure, the twelve truly believe. Next, they are to go as mendicants, with nothing. They can use staffs. They are pilgrims. No food, bag, or earthly possessions. No money! He instructs them to wear sandals and a single coverlet, nothing more. They project poverty. They fit in as the dispossessed.

This is the army of God's kingdom.

Pretty flimsy. A very simple group, and not the kind of messiah's team anyone wanted then, or now for that matter. Pomp—none. Spectacle—nada. Power—zip. Yet powerful enough and tough enough to expel evil spirits. Very Zen. And the specific instructions, "Stay where you are, in one place." Stay put. Get acquainted, know the host, I guess. And if the people there are not hospitable or attentive to your presentations, "shake the dust off your feet as a protest." I guess that is as close to a curse as you get in Mark's gospel lines. Just turn your back on them and leave. Don't beg, don't plead, don't stalk, don't do anything, but leave them to their own devices. So long, good luck, and good-bye.

This is a bit, hm, harsh. Yes, it is. If folks do not want to hear from you about salvation, what are you going to do? If you offer them the good news and they turn you out and do not welcome you, this is harsh on their part. Where is the other cheek here? There is none. Dust your broom and leave. There are others who might want to know and hear.

And the good news is what? "Men should change their whole outlook." Think about that. What is life, anyway? It is about finding out. And if you choose not to love consciousness (reject finding out), well, here again, eventually you reap what you sow in life. You have the life of everyman in contradiction with "to die is to live." You don't have a commandment for this; it is not in the Decalogue. Why? It is because this is a fact of life behind the ten laws. Healing evil spirits is this and nothing else: to die is to live. Evil is thinking you are everlasting, that you are your personality, and that you are your ego forever. It is rather the pertinacious process of looking again, again, and again at you, others, and the Ground of all Being. The Mystery summons us always to change our whole outlook. Being in the kingdom is not some woo-woo stuff. Simplicity itself—because it is grounded in life. It is in the particularity that I discover divinity, in the actions with others, myself, and the Godhead. Great news. Now you (apostles) can cast out evil, heal the sick, and provision the poor in body, heart, and mind by absorbing the pain and insecurity of living. This was second nature to Jesus; He did no less.

Mark's Pulp Fiction (Mark 6:14–30)

This section of Mark seems simple, yet it was one of the hardest to fathom for me. Again, like other parts of the gospel, Mark plops in a non sequitur. The flow is drowned, it is flipped out, and I am left scratching my head. *Whah?* If you ever saw or heard of the movie *Pulp Fiction* you get what I mean. This section is angular, sort of circular. What is the point of it?

John the Baptist (JB) is beheaded. So? What? Gruesome, yes, but how does this fit into the good news narrative, except to answer the question, "Who is Jesus?" Well, not Him, that is for sure. He is now dead and buried, hopefully with his head on top of his neck. This is the only other execution death in Mark's gospel. Jesus is the other. And the circus around his death certainly foretells the bad craziness around Jesus's. An echo.

As readers of the gospel, we are treated to an inside view of Herod's court. Pretty messy. John acts as Herod's confessor while in jail, here echoing the role that Joseph played in the Old Testament. In the end he is a pawn in the power play among the family who wishes for his death, not very unlike Jesus later in the gospel appearing before Pilate. An echo.

So?

Jesus is in the big time, not a little play for Herod. Sometime in the past, John the Baptist was killed, and later many thought that Jesus was John arisen. No, that is an error. Jesus has a bigger drama to play out with the Hebrew Herod, a paltry appointee of Rome. You see, no one thinks that Jesus could be anything but a facsimile of the truth at the time. Not *the* truth. Jesus was thought to be John the Baptist, Elijah, Isaiah, et al., not the *truth* about life.

In fact Jesus was after higher stakes, plunging or plumbing a deeper well.

Yes, who is this Jesus? His reputation grows and he gathers more followers by the day. Remember, the twelve are out spreading the good news. And even though the news travels slowly, the walls have eyes and ears. The powers that be are worried and afraid. It must be a risen one, a walking ghost of John. Therefore, we can dismiss him as a fake. We have no cause to pay Him mind. You wish.

This section is sandwiched between the "send out apostles" section and the return to "report their experiences." This may have been an interlude to let the audience unconsciously ponder what happens and the effect on the apostles during their journey to their center so that they could heal the sick and tell the masses about what they found within Being Itself—Jesus.

I suspect that the storytellers wanted to stuff JB so there was no later confusion about his relationship to Jesus. Jesus is another person altogether. He is the anointed one. JB is special, but not the one. Jesus is the first of many brothers.

Readers are left with the story of John's beheading, which closes the tale that started with his baptizing of Jesus. Still, the question stands, "Who is Jesus?"

A person I know said, "If you get what God is, Jesus is easier." We are about halfway into the journey through Mark's gospel. This phrase is what I will try to address and tackle from an essential, existential, and phenomenological point of view. Yes, it can be done because, absent some handle on the Ground of Being, we are all lost.

THE MEAT OF IT, PART ONE

Since the last chapter, I have been thinking about the phrase I mentioned—if you get God, Jesus is easier. Of course, what I mean is the question of God followed by "an answer" will open the gates to a better, clearer grasp of Jesus. I think.

God is not dead. There are no atheists or agnostics. Pretty uncompromising and arrogant on my part, I suppose.

There are two classes of people: those who wish to engage with the question of God and those who do not. Yes, a choice is what is at hand. We all have made it. If you are conscious at all, you may remember when you made it. If you are not conscious, well then, you still made it and did not notice, did not see, or chose to avoid recognizing it. Life is different with the awareness of the choice. Your life is different, and so are your relationships. But I am ahead of myself here. All of the engagement regarding the question of God is a deliberation. It is about self-knowledge, esoteric thinking, looking internally, and looking down and around in your own catacomb of the soul. It's a bit like looking into a cave underground, not like Plato's, but dark with just a bit of a light, even if only from the glow of your bacteria.

The major "problem" is often expressed, "Well, you cannot see God." Yes. However, the deeper issue is not the seeing, it is the doing, and it is about the action. Truly, the initial stumbling block is detecting the miraculous. A rational, intellectually acute person does not believe in miracles! Yet, Mark's Jesus is full of miracles. It is childish from an earthly, terrestrial plane, a physical causality perspective, to imagine the supernatural. Aristotle said, "Nothing in the intellect except through the senses." We are earthbound, we do live in a universe, not a heaven, hell, or whatever else from some old, leftover worldview. It is sort of said this way, right? "What you see is what you get."

Again, it may be more elaborate for you. Or a bit more nuanced or not even expressed, or just—you go about life, life is a bitch, and then you die.

I am not here to uncover your way or story about living. In a small sense, I don't really care. In a bigger sense, I pity those who do not get it—the Meat of It (God), as my title says. My hope against hope is that there will be an event in your life that calls to you and you go on finding out more, and more, and more about the Ground of Being, the Mystery of Life, the Higher Power, God.

Returning to miracles, to dismiss them is the pretense of knowing. (This is not like believing in UFOs, either.) This leads me to the point that with the universe, you could say that it is all God. This is easy—it is totally pantheistic. Or that it must be willed by God—theological. And neither is the case. The easy part is the bridge or step from the universe to God. Why, look at the stars—wow, surely God. I ask how? The harder and more important step for us is from God to the universe and back to us. Why is there the universe, why is there us and this phantasmagoria? God's will, creation in seven days, and so forth—why? Perhaps I am rushing a bit? Am I too blithe?

What is awfully hard, I repeat, is this part: from God to us, how does that work? Did it ever? Whoa! This is where the breakdown occurs; the brain's axle will not hold up under the weight of the question. The limits of earthly logic cannot hold, carry, or imagine, the holy irruption into a limited plane—three-dimensional plane at that—full of contingent sets of rules-based experience, the something "divinely natural" which is not limited and noncontingent, not even dualistic. This is what we are in Western culture, though not to our detriment because it is merely a single purposeful mode of perception that we apply needlessly to everything to get along and survive here in the sub-luminary plane. Thesis-antithesis. Either-or.

An additional issue for many, me too, is the question of suffering and evil. *Why?* Because there is no easy answer, if it is phrased this way, to the why, the response is, "There must be no God. Or else how could 'He' allow it to be so?" You can imagine how this goes as well as I can. Go to it, start spinning.

God is obviously dead! Rest in peace. Who said so? Always consider the source and destination of the message.

The Meat of It, Part Two

What is God? If, as I stated previously, he is not dead—despite the internal and external statements by you or others' beliefs, positions, recent books by very well-known authors, and writers of the past as well, who run on for more than I will—then where do we go? We have centuries of authors including the Bible, saints, professors, theologians, ministers, etc., etc. Is it a Mexican standoff? Is it all relative? Up to you—your call.

Except in John's gospel, Jesus never states, "I and the Father are one." Does this say what God is? What does this tell me? It says to me that if you wish to know Jesus, know the Father. In the Old Testament, it says, "I am the Father of Abraham, Isaac, and Jacob." And Jesus's God as well. Again, consider these Old Testament characters and then you will apprehend Me. (God appeared frequently in the verse and text line of the Old Testament versus the gospels.) I suggest for this discussion not to parenthetically raise the question, "Are these 'men' real or merely composites or metaphors for people's relationship to Ultimate Reality?" Yet the God of both documents is the same. This begs the question, what is God?

I tried to say in the first part that consciously or unconsciously, we struggle with one thing only: God. Choose or don't, which is still a choice. In the Old Testament, Jacob wrestled with the angel, Moses went to the Mount and wrestled with God, and Job did the same. Jumping forward, Jesus did not apparently have any of this type of struggle; on the cross he plainly addresses God. Yet Jesus was tied to God all along. No doubt. Would Jesus have carried out his vocation or mission absent this binding? Yes, He was called, chosen, anointed, and in the last, ready.

God is that which drives us into life and limits us. In the midst of our preparing, procuring, and providing for the means of life, our daily bread, we encounter a limiting factor that shows us up short. It may present itself in the form of a person, thing, or place. Poetically, God is sometimes the Holy Other. This perhaps seems a bit weird for those who see God as the throned presence in the upper room and in the realms of the cloudy universe. God is totally out there "in heaven" for some.

In a search for the "relationship" of Jesus to God, there are many citations, of course. Yet amazingly, in the citations, at least in the gospels, there is no overt definition of what God is. There are images, however, like this: "Don't call me good, for only God is good;" "have faith in God;" "with men it is impossible, but with God it is not;" "God sent me." These phrases do not define God. Such as A=B. Thus the effort to get to what God is leaves me and you in a quandary: *What is God?* I repeat, the gospels are only marginally helpful in answering *the* question of all time.

We have all heard that God is love. This is a temporal definition of a "divine activity." The definition of love is something you do, not something you have, and second, that the act of love is transformative;

these somewhat suggest what God's love might be. After all, God so loved the world and Jesus loved us such that he died for us. These are beatific thoughts and worth deep contemplation, yet do they get us any closer?

Jesus repeatedly invokes the kingdom of God as a functional image, a picture, a terrestrial phrase, earthly in that everyone then was familiar with a kingdom. And, well, a kingdom is large. To a peasant-everyman, it is enormous. As I said in the last chapter, God as the universe is awesome, and a kingdom is the universe to a small man. This idea of space as an analogy for God suggests something powerful, laterally, though, and not vertically. And we all know that God is both vertical and horizontal. As above, so below, say some. Thus, God is in heaven, on earth, and in our hearts.

The Ground of Being, Higher Power, Mystery, Divine Providence, Supreme Being—as you can see, there are many names for the Godhead. (Yet, the descriptions are not better or helpful for the death-of-god types out there. Their negative words are just as squishy.) We can look at It in a few ways: God as a spatial being, a temporal image, or a spiritual force. I think these factors describe the many ways man has tried to articulate what God is and was. But It is more, because words cannot describe the Being of God.

God is immanent and transcendent, omnipresent, omnipotent, and all knowing. Some refer to It as absolute infinite perfection. There is the Trinitarian aspect to ponder, all for One and One for all. And to say something I said earlier, the one is one, the one is many, the many is one, and the many is many. All this is great poetry. The struggle to know It is lifelong and a relentless, and in equal measure mystical and theological or exoteric—external and rule-based as well as esoteric-internal. It is also a soulful event to encounter being. Sometimes it is a flight of the spirit, an upward experience. Sometimes it is downward. Finally, It is not that, the *via negativa*. By cutting away all that God is not, we are left with the perfect sculpture to experience.

I leave this discussion and return to Mark next, but not before these points. Here, as best I can manage, are my reasons why people do not believe in God:

1. sloth or laziness
2. no belief in miracles
3. no grasp of suffering
4. no available explanation of evil
5. evolution is beyond doubt
6. we live in an age of relativity
7. a feeling of conceit, false authority, pretentiousness
8. alienation, desolation, and despondency

I am sure you can add another. Please try.

In closing, the terror of history, as named by Mircea Eliade, lurks in the background of these reasons. The solutions to the terror are stagnation or faith. For the answer, I return to Mark's Jesus, who excoriates the terror of history.

FEEDING THE MASSES (MARK 6:30–45)

Jesus debriefs the disciples by taking them to a quiet place, to no avail. They rest there and talk of the trips they were sent on. Actually, they try to avoid the masses that were, not surprisingly, incessant with their demands. This level of demand interferes even with their meals together, probably an important time for collegiality, asking, and taking advice. So they try to hightail it off to another spot on the shore. Jesus is touched by the disciples' ardor for truth, and so he teaches them again as he gets off the boat at another part of the shore. The followers' constant pursuit is not surprising since John the Baptist is off the scene, or actually off with his head due to Herod's action. Murder one, more specifically. The crowds must have gotten larger and larger. Their devotion to Jesus was growing. Thus the line, "his heart was touched with pity for them because they seemed to him like sheep without a shepherd." Jesus feels their hunger for comprehension of his message.

The masses are out in the wilds, a desolate area, with no food or water. Perhaps Jesus had a long day of teaching, and they have not eaten; everyone is most likely famished. They are in no-man's-land far from their homes and families, and they are in rapt attention to Him. This was a wilderness experience for the gathered crowd. The apostles are probably hungry, thirsty, and tired like the rest. They ask Jesus to let them all go home and rest, get to the places of comfort and familiarity. This led to Jesus's phrase, "You give them something to eat." You all are capable—create something. You are my chosen, right? The apostles remonstrate, ah, what are we to do? We don't have any money as per your instructions. And, like, where's the Wawa? The Wawa doesn't and cannot feed these masses! This is the multitude that we are seeing here. It seems to me that there is a bit of upset, discomfort, paralysis, and confusion. I am sure the apostles have no clue. This is too big a job to execute for them. In this situation, in the midst of these circumstances, what do you do, feel, have? Anyone would be at a complete loss. "We have five loaves and two fishes." And we are to feed a mass of people, including us?

This is so real. When you are over against the facts of life and you do not have a plan, you come up short—5/2, that's all I got! Five loaves, two fishes, and I truly need a running ton of good ideas, actions, effort, and execution. But I have come up short. Lord, help me!

Jesus "orders" them, strong medicine. Jesus takes command, organizes, arranges, creates the rules of the game, conducts, and ordains that they sit down "like beds in a garden."

This is when we see the miracle happen. Jesus prefigures or echoes the last supper. He takes what is right there and magnifies it from his heart into a satisfying feeding of the body and soul. He feeds them fully from himself. He feeds them *because* He is full of life. Now, whether they are eating "real" fish and bread or are fed the word of life, God's life, we don't know. Fish and bread are symbols of Jesus, and the masses are satisfied! This scene of a supper feast shows the crowd consuming the Word of God. And only because Jesus is wealthy in life and could feed everyone to satiation. He does not feed because it is a rule. Jesus feeds because he participates in the life of God. He feeds from his own satisfaction and fullness, so to speak. And in the end there is plenty left over as, of course, it would be. He loves God with his whole heart, mind, and soul. And He loves His neighbor as Himself. First, he loves God. Then, His neighbor can be loved because Jesus is right with God. The neighbor is fed since He is able to feed; it all comes from God.

LESSON OF THE LOAVES (MARK 6:45–7:1)

This section is rather famous. Who walks on water, after all? Philips calls it "Jesus's mastery over natural law." This is a great title, as certainly Jesus did. As God, he did demonstrate mastery. Of what?

As previously, of course, when you change the minimal into the multitude, five into five thousand loaves, you have power over natural law as well—period. As I said there in the previous topic, it's about a miracle whose proportions are large. Looking, though, into the mystery, we have not a literal, but rather a profound sign of giving to life your breath, strength, will, and mind. It is love of God that makes it possible to feed anybody, here shown as feeding five thousand. It is the feeding of starving life for soul or spirit.

My title, though, is the essence of this key section in Mark. And Jesus thinks so too. More on that later.

Here there is again a bit of a confusion for me. First, there is the boat going to one side of the lake, yet they seem to end up where they started, and it happens overnight. It appears to take place throughout the small hours of the morning. No one gets any sleep, and they are none the worse for it. I really suggest you read this section and see if you get it, the coming and the going, and coming. I cannot, for the life of me, see how this works logistically. It is perhaps not important how it works, as it is in the realm or space of the unconscious. Okay, what does this mean here in the gospel of Mark?

Surely, we can assume that such did exist even if it was over two thousand years ago. Human development was a given by then. We had already seen other major leaps of awareness. I do not mean this in an evil sense. I mean it in the deepest sense of the self as shown to and by the apostles. They were grappling with the earlier day's events without awareness, like we all do when we cannot get it in the moment. We get it later like a flash of lightning—ah, that is what it means! It took this long to get it. Well, let's let the story continue to unfold.

Jesus directs the apostles to go to the other side of the lake of Galilee. He sends them off while he disperses the fish-and-loaves-fed crowd, five thousand of them. After they are all gone He goes and prays alone on a hillside, and he must be there a long time because it grows late. *Dark*. Meanwhile, at the boat, the apostles seem to have hit a snag. The wind is dead against them, and it is the wee small hours of the morning. They are rowing for their lives somewhere out there in the dark, scared, alone, pulling for all they are worth. In predawn morning, Jesus decides that they have had enough and makes for them, walking on the water to lend them a hand. Hm. Think of this as a holy life saver. Imagine their surprise, 3:00 a.m. or so, rowing, pulling, heaving, the weather whistling, and here comes the Man Himself to offer a hand. Well—? They think he is a *ghost* and not a holy life saver, spirit or such—just evil, a phantasm, a dybbuk. They scream. They are absolutely terrified. Speaking softly to them, "It is I myself; don't be afraid." Phew, we are relieved! Not. *Who are you?* they think. "We are scared out of our wits." Mark writes, "They had not the sense to learn the lesson of the loaves. Even that miracle had not opened their eyes to see who he was."

This section is about that phrase, the lesson of the loaves. First, symbolically, the waters of life, as they bob along out there, are hard for them. Jesus is amazing for sure, but still, they who were initiated needed a bit more enlightenment and training. Second, as he prays, going inward to the Almighty, Jesus knows they need more facilitation. Third, when you are frightened, surprised, or astonished, think about where your awareness sits. It thinks it is elsewhere, not in a state of attention regarding what is up with you, others, or the Mystery of Life. You are, in some way, out to hunch, lunch, or absent from the scene of your existence. You are not dead, just in rigor mortis, frozen in a pall of smog. It is as if you are in a trance. I say this knowing the ramifications of the state, having been there, done it, and not seen what was going on before my eyes. On the seas of life or the darkness of the unconscious, you forget a lot.

Fourth, the apostles *just* saw a massive gift before their eyes. They saw the miracles of Jesus giving of His life in the form of loaves and fishes, the staff of life, the matter of His Being. This is also the Man that can conquer both the seas and the movement of the seas. Fifth, this little spree or episode reinforces Jesus's attachment to them and his mission on earth: to walk on the waters of life and not drown. Jesus, as the Exemplar of Being, shows them they have no wind in their face, since the wind stopped as he got in the boat. It is "natural" for there to be no worries.

I am reminded of a story from long ago. There is a drought, long and very dry. Finally, the farmers call the rainmaker for his help. Arriving, he goes into a hut and closes the door. Time passes and they wonder. After a long time, it rains. They are curious to ask him what was up, how did he do it. He answers, "I did nothing; since the country was in disorder, I had to wait four days until I was back into the flow of life and then, naturally, the rain came."

Mark ends the section again with Jesus healing the sick where ever he goes; giving life to all who want to have faith and to touch the hem of His garment. The flow, the fullness of life, is in Him. Here is no ghost or projection of fear, worry, or harm. Jesus causes no alarm. He came to help them by transmitting life abundant.

What's the Ugliest Part of Your Body? (Mark 7:1–24)

Before I embark on the final installment of Mark's adventure with Jesus, I want to revisit two sections back, where we read of the feeding of the Jesus movement. I am a bit incredulous about what I am going to write. The feeding of the five thousand was, I think, an event in the sense of a real happening. Many of the other stories I have my questions about, but this one I feel is real, though clouded in the symbols that Mark uses. By this point in the story, there had to be a significant group of followers: a movement of the spirit, if you will, around Jesus. This gathering, described as a teaching experience for them, is too large to blow off. But how do you portray it so that there is no hubris in it? Well, you shroud it in the way Mark does, as a feeding miracle. No doubt about it, the feeding miracle and the mythos around it are perfect, meet and right; if it were left completely as a movement event, there would have been trouble. And there was enough trouble already, as we will see in the next section. Looked at from Mark's point of view, he had to shift the lesson to feeding and not a socio-political gathering of some magnitude. In the end, the beauty of feeding has a deeper ring than a movement event on the shores of Galilee.

OK, then the meaning of the following event matters and makes more sense. Here come the Pharisees from Jerusalem, which is a long way away from this place. They are big guns of rabbinate, Jerusalem! Why? Well, the event of the feeding and the ongoing healing are enough to attract the attention of the powers that be. This is another time when Jesus gets a bit hot under the collar with the Pharisees and scribes. Not for the first time, either, except that by now more of his reputation is out there for Jerusalem's rulers to be worried about.

It is pretty simple, really. The team is absolutely not following the laws of ritual cleansing. They are not *kosher!* Oh my god. *What is happening here*, my dear boy, you are *two rows short of a crew!* Jesus quotes Isaiah as a way to indict them as mere men and not the big-time people they think they are. Hard stuff when you call up the head prophet, Isaiah, to rouse a bit of wrath. And, more so, that they have made these laws "their tradition" and ignore the will of God! Swat. And, by the way, God is larger than your tradition. A bit harder swat.

Just so the Pharisees do not get to him with their henchman, Jesus calls the crowd close to him and says, "Listen to me now, all of you, and understand this. (Here is the big idea.) There is nothing outside a man which can enter into him and make him common. It is the things that come out of a man that make him common." And what is the definition of common? Perhaps vulgar or base might do here.

What a teaching.

Jesus profoundly says that it is the life inside that matters, and what is inside endures as the most important piece. He goes further in his description for the apostles by stating categorically, it is from inside that evil thoughts come and not from whether you wash your hand before you eat or not! Mark lists the "sins." There is not a one that is uncommon, yet there are two particularly surprising—folly and arrogance. Could he be saying that the Jerusalem crew, the Pharisees, was arrogant and folly-ridden? Hm. The rest of the sins were, as I said, easy enough to get.

Here, though, there is a change or shift from the traditional way of thinking of sin. We all know the Eden story, but there is a sense in it that there was something external that drove Adam and Eve to be banished from the garden—the evil one, the serpent. Aside from the Gnostic issues around the serpent, let's just say that it was portrayed as a thing outside of them. Jesus has just relocated the issues as internal to man, no more victim-hood here. Got a problem? Well, look to you, yourself first. Look to your hearts and minds. Go there and see what is or is not going on and unscramble the type.

This is a revolution in consciousness, I believe.

"All these evil things come from inside a man and make him unclean."

I'll leave it at that.

Jesus Visits the Gentiles (Mark 7:24–30)

This chapter was composed during Christmas. Christmas is truly a multimedia time of year, when the sad and the glad and more nestle in with all the visitors and watchers, all seeking the star of wonder, as the hymn goes. Mark doesn't say anything about this birth scene. As you recall, Jesus shows up at John's baptismal activities in the beginning of the story, His gospel. This hits me as being correct. Jesus is ready to assume His way, life, and light. By then it is about the year thirty, as the guess goes. He is mature enough to get it on with the world as it is and take on God's mantle in the marketplace. Jesus has cleared up the issues of his life, the underbrush is gone and He can see the trees. By now Jesus knows what is important. The baptism sealed His calling.

We now have a jump in space and time; the coordinates move dramatically to Tyre, about forty miles to the north of the Sea of Galilee. Well, God can jump like that, can't he? Look at a map. See or look at the distance; one day Jesus is here, then, the next moment, He is there. Snap. What is truly strange is that He trudged there to get away! To be alone, to retreat a bit, ponder the day, the time and the future, and what is on His soul. The gospel says he wanted to be hidden. Hah! At this point, the chances of that are nil. And who wouldn't want to get away for alone time. Big things had happened, and big events were up ahead. Why, other than this, is anyone wanting to be alone?

No luck.

He is found by a Greek woman with a sick daughter. This sounds familiar, actually. Very much so, as this is a repeating theme in this gospel. And why a gentile? Perhaps to prove that Jesus is not following in the steps of other rabbis in his message. This is a message to be heard by all, yes, even the Greek who had a sick daughter, an evil spirit. It is a fact that at that time, most sickness was supposed to have been caused by something from the outside, like the evil eye. There was much superstition about sickness then.

Well, she implores Him to help her daughter. Yes, even she knows of His abilities. Yet, this interchange is a bit loopy for me to get my hands on. Reading it repeatedly, I have not a clue about it. Read it yourself and tell me if it makes any sense. Yes, she showed incredible faith in Him. Yes, she finds Him, not an easy feat.

Jesus's response to her sounds truly weird. Does the woman mistreat the child some way? Does she not nourish her? Is there abuse? Food is the point in the discussion, thus there is a possible effect that produces the "sickness." Again, is she starving the child due to their poverty? He says, "Let the children have all they want first?" I thought there was only one daughter to heal. Children are innocent. It is the parents' responsibility to satisfy them bodily. You cannot ignore them and pay attention to lesser demands like feeding the dogs with their food. She replies, "Yes, Lord, I know, but even the dogs under the table eat what the children leave." He is satisfied with the answer and sends her home to a healed daughter.

Let's look at this obliquely, a metaphor. Jesus is in the Greek part of Palestine offering aid to an outsider, a non-Jew. Obviously there is no barrier to His helping her or going there to seek solitude from the crowds. Even Greeks can have faith in His powers. Maybe I am wrong and there are more ways for the Jews to interact with outsiders. Certainly He had no issues and did not look down on her. Jesus had more trouble with His own Pharisees. After all, God is God to all, and Jesus came to share His message with anyone who was ready. They were fed and enough was left over to feed "the dogs." Thus if the Jews are not at the table, well, maybe the Greeks are just as entitled to the gospel of healing.

Healing and Feeding Again (Mark 7:31–8:11)

Why would Jesus want to hide out? Mark 7:25

Why did Jesus repeatedly ask the ones he healed to say nothing? In the Mark 7:31 section, though it appears earlier as well.

Why does Mark seem like it is repeating itself? Two feedings of the masses. Mark 8:1

Why does Jesus imply that the apostles are possessed by an evil demon? Mark 8:11

Jesus sighs a lot. Why is this?

This is a long reading to take in; please read it in order to follow along.

The sections after the healing of the Greek woman's daughter feel like repetition, like a circling back. Recycling, we'd say. There is another healing where Jesus tells the man to not even go into his village, followed by Peter's statement to Jesus's question about what the people are labeling him. Peter answers with the famous line, "You are Christ."

I have to mention another run-in with the Pharisees such that he scoffs about the need for signs. Want a sign? Well, there is none. Next.

These all go by fast, and I sense oral tradition here, meaning Mark had a lot of chronicles available to him and he wanted to fill out the picture of Jesus. Or course, the team that selected and repeated these stories did not guess that I and tons of others would look this closely at them with faithful eyes and see the "rambling" going on.

The healing of the deaf and dumb man demands a thought or two. (Mark 7:31) We notice Jesus trying to be alone with Himself, and in this case He takes the man away from the crowd. If, in fact, this is correct, we have a significant occurrence told firsthand. Yet He is alone with the man. Perhaps the man tells the story of his healing later because of its totality. Meaning the mystery Jesus shares is of such seriousness that he has to tell all, thus us. Additionally, Jesus is revealed to speak in Aramaic. So? It seems odd that this is mentioned. But, Hebrew Scriptures were in Aramaic. As a rabbi, Jesus had to speak it. By implication then, Jesus was imparting some sort of scriptural message to the man privately.

What is set free here? What is opened up? If you are allowed to speak for the first time, would you not tell a story of your freedom with amazement? Also, if you are healed, do not return to your old stomping grounds, keep clear of old haunts, and hue to the new path you are on. "Don't even go into the village." This is clearly a command to stay private from the community of nonbelievers because you have been given a gift of "sight" that has to be nurtured and protected to remain open.

In Mark 8:11, Jesus is hounded to give a sign, do magic, be a sorcerer, as many were in those days. Well, he does not—period. He does not rise to that bait. "Now the Pharisees came out and began to argue." Deep sigh from Jesus, as if to indicate, my God, why have you put me into this? It is fair to ask the Almighty for a sign. Haven't you? This, however, is a trap set by the powers that be to catch Jesus up in a head trip, like, prove to us who you and others say you are—the Messiah. After all, you just fed the multitude of followers a good meal. Jesus or Mark moves on without more words as if to say "stay tuned." But I do want to zero in on the discussion on the boat about bread, yeast, and the apostles' thickness.

On board the love boat, Jesus feels empathy for the hunger of the followers gathered there. He sees them seeking His Truth and wants to sustain them in their path by feeding them. What happens is a repeat of the earlier repast. "They ate and were satisfied." They got fed to overflowing. Perfect. Away all boats.

What gets interesting is the short course in the boat to the thick-headed apostles. "Keep your eyes open." Good advice, that! See things as they are, not your projections, hopes, wishes, desires, expectations, or impressions—be aware of them. Next, "Be on your guard against the yeast of the Pharisees and the yeast of 'Herod'!" They then go down the rabbit hole and talk bread! Well, Jesus chides them again to be alert. Such great poetry. What is this yeast? Well, to simple fisherman, they thought, for sure, *bread*. Literally. Like a few people today, who read this as if it were a road map to Atlanta, not the holy story or the metaphor it is. Jesus says by implication that they are possessed of an evil spirit like the many he healed who were blind and deaf. But again, what is this *yeast*?

It is the pseudo-esotericism of the Pharisees. They are all about the externalities, the jot and tittle; this is the yeast, the binder that blows up their lives and defines them and makes them what they are. They are killers, like Herod, "ignorants" whom the apostles need to guard against and protect themselves from with the life-giving word of thanksgiving. Jesus does not say some of the Pharisees, or Herod had a bad hair day and he has to be given a break. No, he says the "yeast of Herod" almost like a curse. Their yeast kills, while the spirit gives life. They are all about the externalities, the outside, and the warped letter of their laws, the surface and the superficial. And this becomes the internal yeast of their lives. Jesus says watch out for this; otherwise you will be blind and deaf. He impressed it upon them, that they say this to no one. Right. I cannot say I am Christ. Nor can you. You can think it, live in the spirit of the kingdom, and let it fill and inform you, just do not say it to one person.

Next is the great "What's my Line?" tale. If there is any part of Mark's gospel that shows Jesus's humanity, this is a key to unlock it. For the troop is walking to a village and out of the blue comes the question, "Who are men saying that I am?" Here I read men as the "everyman," both the powers that be and those he just fed. It strikes me as a bit narcissistic. Yet, He asks. There are a few answers offered up, turning to them, Jesus waits and Peter says it bluntly, "You are Christ." Or, you are the Messiah. And tying this back to the earlier question about the signs, well, there is none. And there is not a Messiah, either, and keep this fact to themselves, a secret. Then, if Jesus is not the one to take them, the Jews, out of Roman captivity, what can be made of this circumstance?

"And he began to teach them" (Mark 8:31). Jesus breaks open their reality, their cosmic egg next. Up until now it has been sort of easy going, not too many confrontations with the Pharisees or other powers. Yes, they were sent out to teach by themselves. No record of that in this gospel, which had to have been challenging. Jesus's words tell the future plainly in these paragraphs. Anyone can guess it, yet the apostles are thrown back on themselves. Stunning words from their leader scares them to death, so much so that Peter calls Jesus to task about His communication not in parables, but in words that ring as fact. I will be killed and die, but will rise again. Huh? Well, Peter the Rock doesn't want any of this talk. Jesus nails it. He curses Peter out and tells him to go inside himself and recollect His message about the kingdom. Get right with God.

Jesus lays out precisely the vocational path that they are on in the next five lines. After Peter's weak-kneed remark He tells them what to do in order to see things from God's point of view.

1. To die is to live.
2. You will carry a cross too.
3. Live a life connected to God.
4. Tender your soul to God alone.
5. Love God with your whole heart, mind, and body.

Saying it is one thing. Doing the divine action is another.

THE MARCH TO LIFE BEGINS (MARK 8:31–9:14)

I struggled with the title to the last section, and still feel it has no real title. Perhaps I'd call it "Transition," as we are in that phase now with Mark's gospel. The episodic or incidental and incremental stream comes to a turn here. Until now Jesus was wandering and healing the sick, deaf, dumb, and blind, healing the senses that were blocking reality for the common people; He was bringing freedom. These disabilities were associated with externals. When restored, their senses allowed the healed to begin their journey pondering the significance of their lives now that the disabilities were lifted. Thus a journey to inner sight, hearing, speaking, or dwelling could take place. The physical release allowed them a transcendent and intrinsic experience, which is most of what life is about, as in the "unexamined life is not worth living" (Ascribed to Socrates by Plato). Life is not merely the externals, the mammon of the outside. Jesus was all about the Spirit of life, the soul, the esoteric in distinction with the exoteric law and the Pharisees. Paul said, "The law of the Spirit of life in Christ Jesus has made me free from the law of sin and death" (Romans 8:3). Jesus pointed to the kingdom of God, meaning the space of holiness we "can" inhabit; this is what he brought to us and to history by his discipline. Because he used the word *kingdom*, there is confusion as to what that means, as if it were something beyond us. To me it is "God's kingdom" that we are in. Here you have to decide what God is to you, your life, and your future. As I said before: "If you get God, you get Jesus." From this can flow many, many actions and thoughts.

(Reviewing Mark 8:31) Jesus tells of his impending death. We could spend a lifetime in Mark's preceding line. Jesus earlier hears Peter say He's the "Christ." Jesus immediately tells them to "tell no one." Keep this a secret. Hm. For Peter to say this is not a declaration about Jesus, it is a statement of faith. I faith that you are the Christ. (This is deeper than a belief.) The one we are waiting for is here in you, Jesus the Christ. This is a massive statement. It comes after so many events that Peter's line spills out as a culminating line in a play of events to that point. I am avoiding the whole issue of translation, tradition, and training. Peter blurts out a faith-line. Blunt and true. Why? Let me say that the times were full of Messiahs, Zealots, Essenes, John's, and more. For Peter to recognize Jesus as the One is an internal statement and says that he is the one to follow and is first among equals.

I cannot forget to mention that Jesus calls Peter "Satan" to his face. (Mark 8:33) In addition, He says that Peter has to see things from God's eyes. This point of view is startling to me and had to go over Peter's head as well as others. What could this be pointing to? Jesus takes this up in detail below.

At that time every man madly expected the "one." Jews and Gentiles alike were "awaiting what the stars would bring." As I pointed out before, people were primed for someone to make sense out of the moment. Do something for me, my community, or us. Jesus's 'correct' role is the representational activity "on behalf of" or acting for us. This was not what every man was looking forward to.

And in that present, Jesus acts with full awareness of the fact that He will die, ignominiously, horribly, and fully in the moment, living the now with no clear *future* in mind about his efforts. Meaning is in the moment chosen freely. This is the kairotic moment, a full experience. It is not, however, the exact action every man was desiring.

We are now in the thick of human emotions. In Mark 8:31–35, Jesus tells the apostles about what will no doubt happen. Peter freaks out and acts as every man might when he hears that Jesus will die. Jesus rebukes him totally and actually calls him Satan. Phew. From God's point of view there can be no other end. The powers that be will kill me. Get it?

There can be no getting away from this. Where have you been, Pete? The reality is they will kill me, wake the — up. Don't you see who I am to them? Or something like this: Ultimate Reality rules.

Following this is the inner reality of life the *secret* of it all, if there ever was one.

Read 8:35 to 9:1 to yourself again. The heart of the matter is here—all of it. The terms and the words are thick with resonance. Here again we can spend a lifetime reading and pondering the meaning of this archetype. *To die is to live.* To live today you have let go of the past, it is approved. To live today you have to let go of living in the future, it is not your business to know it. These are all deaths to unreality, step by step. Life is living today in the kingdom of God, meaning the interior castle of the spirit. And no, you cannot expect food to just fly into your mouth because you have faith.

The paragraph that Jesus utters is meaty, big, and full of truth (e.g., "take up the cross and follow me"). I read this to mean "follow my path as a spiritual creature." The cross is the sign pointing above to transcendence, and below to the terrestrial world we live in, the horizontal, filled with soul and spirit. The mammon of existence is worthless in comparison to the interior life. Mere externalities are unfaithful and sinful. Calling these your gods will lay you low. Again, if you behave and believe (be-live) as a fool, a clod, you cannot expect to have a full life now or ever. There will be no mercy on your soul when push comes to shove. Oh, and if you think I am fooling, just wait until things are at the twelfth hour, when it will be too late. No quick and last saying of the perfect act of contrition. You are down the drain if you have not prepared. Be ready. Otherwise you are lost. This is some heavy stuff! This is "things from God's point of view."

In Mark 8:35, Jesus quickly rattles off formulas for what our vocation is about. In two sections of that final paragraph He states the 'die is to live' phraseology a number of ways. I sense that between the lines the real message is still, "Love thy neighbor as thyself." And to achieve this you have to die to the hindrances and barriers preventing you from realizing this state of being and thus vocation—action. The last line is the money line: "If you are ashamed of me and my words…" Read on: the line can constitute our relationship to God. The opposite of ashamed is joyful, bold, and confident. The poetry is impactful. Try this –you can exemplify what being ready for eternity can look like right now. This last line is addressed to the apostles and disciples instructing them on their deportment as they stand in the marketplace.

The transfiguration follows these "massive attack" words from Jesus. It is correct that the next event be a mountaintop experience. On the mountain, the apostles have an incomparable experience. Jesus is phased so that the apostles see the lineage of holiness from Moses, Elijah, to Him, Jesus, at once. And so it is. Jesus is in line, a long line of saviors, yet more fully so at that moment. It started with Moses, pointed to Elijah, and is fulfilled in Jesus; first the Decalogue, then the Prophet, and doubtlessly in Jesus, the bringer of the kingdom of God to man. Each is crucial, each played a role, each fulfilled a vocation, and each pointed to the next one. And Jesus anchored the gospels, the good news, that life can be fully lived on behalf of others only after the kingdom is grasped, the secret seen and acted on humbly "the restitution of all things." This is pointing to the wholeness and fullness in the midst of the absolute infinite perfect One. The many are re-established and repose in the One. It is the garden again with God's voice, "listen to Him."

The Son of Man, or the Son of the Many, will die. He has to. In order to return to the source, the kingdom, people will have to renounce the message, the man, the real story. This is the most humiliating thing that Jesus could say; they will reject the good news. Me, I will be killed because it is so true and profound. Now it cannot be carried out otherwise. Oh, and they did this to Elijah, too! Not to worry.

What an indictment of the human condition. Deep matters to consider.

Revisiting Fruit of the Gospels (Mark 9:1–2)

This phrase has not been quoted often. In a way it is obscure and very enigmatic, but you'd guess it is the key phrase when it comes to this gospel. It is a complicated phrase of Jesus coming after the big question—*who are you?*—that is at the end of chapter 8, and the subsequent well-known lines about bearing our crosses that I worked on earlier. Again, this line is almost a tack-on to the beginning of chapter 9, yet with a deeper meaning than is noticed. It starts out with this line and flows to the transfiguration of Jesus, a grave event as well. But the line is, as many are, dense with meaning.

Who is the audience? The apostles, the crowd somewhere, the reader? Who?

It suggests the apostles, but I think not wholly. Fully, it is you and me, the readers, who get this passage in the heart. We have to break this into parts to liberate it.

Jesus starts with the word, assuredly, in the Revised King James Edition. The sentence following is in the imperative. I call it to mean "for sure," as in really, or "you can bet your bottom dollar," to use an idiom. It is also a verbal tic. It is very like the "indeed" that starts so many passages. It gets your attention: "Wake up, I am speaking to you!" I am "for sure knowing" that this is true—what I have to say is so. Jesus is sure.

This is followed with "I say to you." Another great attention grabber following the opening word, assuredly. This is coming from His heart, with very good emphasis. Heart is the location of the logos. Yes, not the mind, wherein you find the intellect. The heart has, throughout time, been the location of the "word." Jesus is speaking out of depth beyond the day's length, from the depth of his experience. And then evoking pointedly "to you," I say, you can feel His gaze on you. This is personal.

"That there are some standing here …." He is calling out, again personally, to those alive—here is "my point of view." If you are alive, listen up. Because there are "some standing here," well, what about the rest of us? There are only a few, some, not many, who are going to get this. *Some.* As in many are called, some are chosen, as in few. Fewer than you can guess. And this is a paradox of the seed, the market place, and the workers, specifically Matthew 20:1–16. "To them that much is given …." It is the deepest paradox. The gospel is for everybody, yet so few get it. Here it is again—*some.* Not *all*, but *some. Why?* And, Jesus knows this. Then the word, "here"— not much of a word. A sense of place, *here.* It is a four-letter word among other four-letter words. It anchors the line with a presence of now. Jesus seems to be talking about now, but hold that thought, because the next phrase moves you to another realm. It is *some*, I suspect, because only some look to the inner life. It is the choice of some to be active in the vineyard, the kingdom, or passive in the marketplace, remaining profane.

"Who will not taste death …." Ah, what are you saying? Everyone will die, Jesus as well. He is including Himself in this. We all end in death. But wait, it is such poetry: "taste death" is so simple, like a bit of pepper in your stew, a spice therein, merely a flavor, but not the finality, as in death, done, the end, *finita, la commedia*, lilies above your body—it is just a taste. Of course, Jesus means dead. Still, the phrase resonates. Look at it this way, "Who will not taste death?" Jesus says there are some of you who will not taste death, some of you will "be something else." There is a different outcome available, or "going to happen," something else that is to be achieved. This great, mortal fact that we all die does not make it impossible to achieve your calling. Jesus is God. God is eternal, the absolute perfect infinite, boundless One, and It is in Jesus. How can It die? Of course It cannot! Speaking to you humans, Jesus opens a path to eternity via the phrase and suggests a return to life.

"Till they see the kingdom of God present with power." Well, I suspect seeing is believing, just not seeing, in the sense of eyesight. Here is the produce of the gospel. In the life of consciousness, realizing the spirit, perceiving the deeps of existence, living the soulful life, all these point to an interior castle. Some call this mystical; herein lays the produce of the gospel. I am trying to suggest a view unheard of today. This brief, misplaced line, as I said, I think, is the culmination of the whole dying-to-live poetry that was at end of chapter 8. Jesus is giving us another vision of the power of the interior life. Not for the sake of itself but for serving God. *Then* and only then will your inclement spirit die. To see the kingdom of God present with power is the fruit of the labor (to die is to live), living in the vineyard of life as fully as humanly imaginable, tilling life for all to witness. The kingdom of God with power means seeing it completely, in all its glory, after you die in the marketplace. You have arrived, this is heaven now. This is timelessness, fully in the moment, not through a glass darkly, but full illumination. And, this is "the life" for some—their transformation.

Then again, maybe this is eschatology, pure and simple. A case can be made as well for this, and many have made it. But I think not.

Let us pray:

> Faith has blown away the market place. Jesus arrives in the silence of the night scattering Spirit in the world. There is shimmering in the trees and elation in the wind. Eternity utters a day. Amen

THE MOUNTAIN TOP (MARK 9:2–14)

To most, God is conjecture. A noted philosopher of the twentieth century wrote that there are five ultimate questions: who or what started it; are we going to make it; where are we going to put it; who will clean it up; and finally, is it serious?

Jesus's transfiguration is His pointing to God the Mystery via a trip to the mountaintop. This is Jesus's response to conjecture, and it is serious.

The transfiguration of Jesus comes late in Mark, almost two-thirds of the way through. Behind us are many miracles and ahead of us are some more miracles, the closing days of Jesus, his trials, death, and resurrection stories. Immediately before this section is the life-death poetry and metaphor and the line I call the "produce of the gospel." I wrote of this previously.

Let me look again at the transfiguration, since it is a key event to me. It develops more of Jesus's story and His impact on the apostles and us, the readers. It centers Jesus in the great paths of Hebraic tradition and grounds him in that string of leaders and prophets. Did Jesus do this, or was this an event in the hearts of the viewers?

This is a good question, to which I have no good answer. I feel and think, however, that the apostle's mountaintop experience as written and handed down to us by Mark was more confirmation to them at that moment of His immanence and grandeur. The confirmation of Jesus was complete. He was of God and man—Moses and Elijah. He was "of" in the sense that the apostles substantially saw him as God, historically in the lineage of Jewish greats, and powerfully as their Father. And God said so: "Listen to Him." What more do you need?

We needed more, I guess!

Let me start from the beginning of the section, as it is again full of "stuff" to unpack and weighty considerations. First, six days on the road, well, not to make light of it; yet six days. Did that result in the following paragraphs? Second, if not, then were those lost days? Where were you all? At the beach? Down by Galilee? Or taking a breather with the family before the big events to come? *What*? At no other time does Mark do this. Lost time. A holy gap, no doubt, as the transfiguration is a noteworthy event.

Six days is the same interval in which the Mystery created it all. (Yes, I know there were seven with the last as a day of rest.) The six can be reduced to three, the Trinity. A stretch, perhaps. Then there are the six angels of Zoroastrianism, the six systems of Hindu metaphysics, the six yogis of Tibetan Buddhism (Naropa), six retrogressions of Kung Fu Tzu, six virtue perfections of Mahayana Buddhism—overkill? No, look at them. They are all at the highest level of expression about the way life is from other points of view on the "religious" compass. Six days has some weight in the creative sense. It took six days to get amped up for this event to happen! The apostles were preparing for the last days too, though unconsciously.

And that brings me to Elijah. He was the prophet who expressed total belief in the one God—monotheism in the Old Testament. He was ascended to heaven in a whirlwind (no, not a UFO!). Elijah is tied to the end of times and the eleventh hour. According to some, He precedes the final hour and then comes the End of Times. So Elijah gathers the elect. Anyway, there he is with Jesus and Moses. The Alpha and the Omega of history, time all wrapped up in the experience of these three, a vision to behold, assuredly.

Jesus leads them up the mountain. Purposeful words. Jesus knows where he is going. If he knows what is going to happen, then it is a perfect echo of the baptism that started His journey, and it is the culmination for the apostles and the Jews, a veiled reference to the Messiah. But wait: this is a Messiah who is on the path toward death, not a terrestrial kingdom or power over the current lords there, the Romans. Jesus had to have sensed this. From the apostles' point of view, He is after this—the One. And it happens in awesome drama so that Peter wants to build a miniature temple all in white, totally transparent, to see the friendship among the triad of Elijah, Moses, and Jesus. Thus, witnessing to the Mystery's love of his servants, including the apostles, as they were privy there and then, to the glory of God, behold the Spirit. This is what a life-changing event is about. Jesus ends the section with end-of-times-speak, His sense or suspicion, not mistrust, of His final days, and His eleventh hour, death, and rise from the dead. Again, since this was written after the "event," well, the fulfillment is done. By then the apostles are witnesses to the power of the spirit. So, too, the scriptures.

On the mountain, Jesus is transparent to the way life is. He trusts them so much that He reveals His real being to them—the structure of being—God, the Son and the community of Man.

It is worth noting that the phrase Son of Man is first used just before this section and more frequently ever after. What is the "Son of Man"? My best thought here is that He is the one who has "pierced the veil" of the one-in-the-many metaphor. Jesus is at once the singularity of life in the midst of God's gift of life. He is all mankind in the One.

Jesus's Attitude and Prayer (Mark 9:14–30)

Something is going on in Jesus, if I may say that. Yes, He performs the miracle, but His attitude about the miracle business is very interesting. Just after the mountaintop experience there comes again a man begging Jesus to heal his epileptic son. It seems as though there are many who are stricken by this affliction in those times. Nevertheless, the man who beseeches Jesus does so in a manner that sets Jesus off. Jesus laments. He inclusively calls the man and "the people," his disciples, faithless. Jesus rues the effort it has taken Him to get this far, deplores the disciples as well for their weakness, taunts the man who asks for help (who thinks perhaps that Jesus is as weak as the apostles are) and then mockingly retorts, "If you can do anything …." Jesus is accused of being powerless. Amazingly sarcastic. Amazing.

Of course, the healing occurs as always it does. The boy's epilepsy is cured, but then the apostles ask, "Why were *we* unable to drive it out?" Indeed.

"Nothing can drive out this kind of thing except prayer." Since Jesus did this, he must know about praying. This is the first mention of this. What is prayer?

Before I share on that question, which has had many written interpretations over many centuries, I have four *a priori* thoughts on prayer.

1. God is an event, occurrence or experience, not a thought, conjecture, or invention.
2. God is a mystery.
3. Words matter.
4. Duality is a delusion.

With these as a position, I think I can talk about prayer a bit with you.

Have you prayed today? What were the words? When did you pray? About what did you pray? What were you doing when you prayed? Where do you pray? Do you pray in a group or alone? For whom do you pray? How often do you pray?

I pray in the mornings as I rise. I pray at night when I fall asleep. I generally do not pray during the day, though there are sometimes events that call for a prayer and then I pray. What I have found is that the words matter. The sentence formation is also crucial. I find that I rarely pray for myself, or things, or a solution per se. I recall an event after which I felt the urge to pray; it was an impelling experience. Subsequently, I reworked the *Our Father* over a long period in an attempt to make it relevant to me. Yes, that effort was prayer, a prayer before what I call the mystery of God, expressing my consciousness of life and my position in it and my relation to the mystery of God. Now the apostles are ineffective in their prayer, says Mark. Can there be a reason?

I suspect that they were praying as if there were trying to pull God down from heaven to aid them in their healing. God is in heaven, on earth, and in them. So what part of this do they not get? There is a duality—them and God. This was their delusion, as in false belief and mistaken notion. Jesus says as much, "Everything is possible for those that believe." God is not apart from the scene in which they are in. I guess they missed the mountaintop experience of the previous seventy-two hours. Furthermore, the apostles are trying too hard for a solution that they imaged. Perhaps their image of the epileptic boy is distorted. I have been trying to grasp what the significance of the epileptic is to them and to Mark, since he uses it repeatedly. I think it shows a deep distress to those who witness it, call it possession or the Devil, but this suggests an archetypal event or situation. It is not conventional. The apostles are still not able to go that deep; they have not prayed enough here in the sense of "seeing" what is going on. They feel outside of events, not in events. There is the event and there is them—a duality. It is hard to imagine what being inside of an event is; I suppose it tends to be an experience as being one. The apostles do not yet understand the phrase, "I and the Father are one." There is no separate "I." Jesus heals as God can heal. "Before Abraham was, I am."

Prayer keeps you in the space of God. Perhaps this is too abstract, and it sure seems that way writing it. Yet the mind prefers this empirical state over a lost ego to the kingdom of God. Jesus certainly is not unclear: "Except prayer." This is not a mental activity He's pointing to. Prayer is active. "[It] drives out this kind of thing."

Kneeling down to pray is not necessary, though this position offers a posture of humility. Sometimes prayer is whirling or prostrate (before the Godhead.) Even a walking meditation is prayer. This is not to say that everything we do is prayer, and yes, in the fullest sense of the term, it is. You arrive there after many preliminaries, which are the preparation. As they say, sometimes enlightenment is a flash, sometimes it is many cycles of lifetimes. It's your choice and creation, and your givenness, your character.

Jesus prayed. He had to have prayed. His life is a schema for what prayer looks like. There is nothing we cannot pray about, and very little that we can pray for. Prayer is an event in our interface with the Ground of Being. Results happen or do not, and the lack thereof or visibility should not deter us. Outcomes are terrestrial. And again, God is a verb to which we are mere adverbs.

I stated in an earlier presentation that the one is the many, the many is the one, the many is many, and the one is the one. We are in God. I pray to live these thoughts in action and still know that it is a total mystery, and to take myself lightly, being faithful despite life's bitterness. I have nothing to lose but the "I". Demise or rise.

Secret Teaching (Mark 9:30–32)

This section, though only two lines long, can become contemplation for us all for all our time and during the Easter season.

Who among you has not thought about your death? Been afraid of it, avoided it, forgotten about it, or denied it? Jesus, in two lines with a preface, goes to the heart of the matter.

We read that they are leaving a place and making for beyond Galilee. In this journey, Jesus seeks secrecy. Why?

Where has He ever done this? His life has been a crowded experience except where Jesus was off praying or with a handful of disciples, He is always in a group. But now, "Jesus kept his journey secret." Secret from whom, for what? "For he was teaching his disciples." He is keeping what He said restricted, on the QT, because what He has to say is paramount and has to be kept among only the believers, his apostles. There has always been a bit of conspiracy about the gospels, somewhat like passages in the Old Testament. Secret script, numerology, and so forth. A message that the initiate can hear exclusively.

Sadly, there isn't any such thing here, or not so sadly because we all know that death is part of life. Yet, we hear Jesus foretelling, as if warning, preparing the apostles about what is to come soon. Why is this so secret? Who among you has known the date, time, and circumstances of your death? *No one!* Oh yes, there is the offhanded stuff you hear or read about after the fact, but not prior!

Yes, there is an intuition about it all, that great event called death; that is why the biggest adventure is saved until the very last. Here, Jesus is like dead on. Okay, Mark wrote this after the event, so this could have been added like a testamentary story to the chronology. Give this to the skeptics out there. Or, on the other hand, to those who read this like a literal road map to Atlanta, Georgia. Rather, let me look at this like an extended contemplation on his imminent death and rebirth. Now what do we have here? What is the secret?

Jesus, like any shaker and mover, knows that His time is not long in the world. As the "Son of Man" (read Fully Realized Terrestrial Hero), Jesus is not self-referential enough to image himself as the Messiah. The phrase, "would be betrayed into the power of men," is the exact opposite of the Son of Man, very poetic. The Son of Man will be handed over to the power of man in betrayal, perhaps the echo in Jesus's soul that there is no perfect apostle, only a perfect fool, as in Judas. How could it be otherwise? The power men are out for his death. When there is such as Jesus, no one will allow Him to go on. They will kill. "And that three days after his death he would rise again." Father, Son, and Holy Ghost do away with the sentence of death and become life rising. There the sun will never set.

"But they were completely mystified by this saying and were afraid to question him about it."

Would you?

I mean really, the awesome fear and wonder of this tale must have been nearly crushing. To hear that your leader, your supreme love, is going to be killed by the powers that be and then rise after three days. To hear this so definitely told, with no hesitancy, equivocation, no "don't worry," etc., must have just been harrowing for the apostles. Yes, you call it mystifying; it is really flooring. You are on the deck. You have been hit with a low blow. And how can you say anything or ask for clarification after this secret? Jesus just shared his death, suffering, and rebirth, and you dare to say, "wait just a minute, what about us, me, them, this community? The movement of the Spirit, all of it, the feeding of the masses, and you are telling me this is *it*?" I suspect that they heard only the death part of the equation, not the resurrection or that to die is to live.

The secret is we all know the end. For lesser or poorer, greater or richer, our life's processes give us a glimpse of our ends. The secret is that rebirth through death is doable, practical, and essential. We will not die like Jesus most likely, but we see the image there in view before us. And if not in sight, then in secret before and with God. It is not so much in the details, though Jesus is down to earth in the facts. What is the secret He imparted to the disciples? The secret is that it can be done. He says so right to them. He has to talk only to them. Now it is here with us. It is our secret. Life can be fulfilled despite being betrayed to the power of men. Here and now.

Reference Point (Mark 9:33–42)

I think and observe as I move through the mid part of Mark's gospel that things are getting more intense, with more value to the reader and to my involvement. In other words, it seems that my life is intensifying along with the pace of the gospel.

I think and feel we are in times where there are fewer reference points, a time of seeming relativity, a time when there are hot emotions, feelings and zealotry, and little impelling analysis. We are in a time of relativity, seemingly a time absent of absolutes.

I have thought for a very long time that there is one question that matters: where are you on the question of God? I am not a churchgoing man. I do go to the synagogue with my wife occasionally and reflect on the meaning of life. Meaning I contemplate the question of God there. Of course, I do that just about anywhere, though not while I am driving or need to pay close attention to matters empirically at hand. At one time there were reference points. Such as what? Let's let the passage at hand guide us to answers.

The passage is approximately midway through Jesus's earthly journey. It is closer to his death than you'd suspect. And the apostles are more seasoned as well. By now there are certainly a few standouts and leaders among them, cliques perhaps, pairs of a few who are naturally attracted to each other, for good or ill. Though there is never a mention by name of who the leader is, nor even a name of who is there just then with Jesus, in a group of this size there would be a leader of the pack. This person is a source or a point person to whom you can turn to get some direction, clarity, or insight, an alpha male, as he's called today. This being a human group, it is natural for this to happen. No?

Well, maybe not.

Still, Jesus, smart man that He is, asks about it nicely. And the response is a bit of silent indiscretion as they argue about "who should be greatest." *Greatest*, meaning what? Well, recall that Jesus already told them about his death, which is to be soon. So who will lead this huge movement of the people? Incredible, no? Just the utter humanness portrayed herein is humbling to me. The apostles know He is on the road to His death, and yet they try to argue who the next "Jesus" will be! Who will take his place. Mortifying.

Jesus's response is the classic line, "If any man wants to be first, he must be the last and servant of all." Next, Jesus uses a child as a metaphor for his teaching.

(Off the wall question before I go on: Were the locations an artifice? Why does the location matter? Only the early reader would care.)

The first and last shows up in the Shabbat service, of course. The usual event in the synagogue during the service is an echo of this line, as when the whole congregation turns 180 degrees to the back door to welcome the Shabbat. Then the back rows are first to see it arrive, versus the front, who only see it when the Shabbat bride arrives to the front of the hall.

First and last—it makes sense. At the end of the line, in a way, you see the whole before you, so you can make a well-informed decision with better input. Now, the front has limitations. You only see ahead, not the group so well. Becoming a leader, first among equals, is a challenge.

First and last, this is the community over the individual. The last few words, though, make the line heavier, "the servant of all." This is the image of the suffering servant. As a servant you do that; as a leader there are other sufferings. It also puts into relief the idea of glory. There is no glory in leading from behind. To be last also suggests the possibility of an ignominious end. Again, an echo of Jesus's imminent death.

One more small point: the humility of being last has to be mentioned. To be the caboose of the train is not a spectacular position. And to carry that off with poise and bearing can only come from an interior life of strength. It suggests an inner being that is at home with God, and here, as Jesus said, is where the kingdom is. It also suggests nothing grand, no high, wide, and handsome. Or a total absence of ostentation or need to be noticed.

Using the little child is "the tell." In those days children were without status, just as the caboose is without status. Children were overlooked in that time and expected to serve the elders, or parents, and had no input into the circumstances that they were in. Children were seen. Children were not heard. As well as being small and weak, children learned by observing what happened around the home. Finally, children were not expected to offer anything of value. So to welcome a child as a source was truly a step, then, to humility, a humbling of the man, a lowering in their point of view. "One little child …," what a phrase! It drips with servitude. Jesus goes one more step and identifies himself with the child in that He parallels Himself to the child and witnesses to His servitude to God, the source of life. Finally, children have to be cared for from birth to about thirteen, when Jewish lads become men. This suggests the first part of the paragraph, the first and last phrases. In caring for a child, definitely, you have to put yourself last. So much to ponder.

This is a shock that shakes the apostles' foundations.

John retorts, almost defensively, and off topic, I'd add: "Master, we saw somebody driving out evil spirits in your name, and we stopped him, for he is not one who follows us." Not a member of the in crowd.

Jesus replies. "You must not stop him." Bang the gong! Not even a quarter to John's comment. Jesus states that if a person "exerts such power in my name, he would really not say anything against me." Absolute trust. Thus, if you or I, or anyone for that matter, were truly in the space of the gospel, in the kingdom of God, then that person is on God's and Jesus's side. This implies a Holy Spirit to me. Jesus drives it down a notch to something as simple as a drink of water, again echoing commensality, not often enjoyed in those days. If it is done in the spirit of recognition of the source of all life, God, that person will fully see the apostles as holy men on a mission from the Mystery, on an interior path, and "certainly they will be rewarded." *Not* with gold, silver, or coin, but with more fruits of love for the onward journey.

In closing, Jesus reverses the osmosis. If you ever get in the way of soul or spiritual growth or the path of righteousness, or squat on the gospel, woe unto you. So do not disturb the faith of one of the humblest (e.g., a child, or anyone just starting the path to God, being a child of faith, one who is just opening their sight concerning truth, life, and the light). Clearly, a person who is a little wobbly, like a child, about interior knowledge can be very aware and easily misguided. Oh, and lastly, like any child, this young one needs to be cared for. Here is where the "first" needs to spend time, talent, and energy.

The reference point here is apparent, the touchstone is hot. You are not the reference point, "not I, not I, but a fine wind that blows through me," (D. H. Lawrence) otherwise you are a faithless one. This section references the one who sends you. Wait. Not as one predestined, but one who journeys through the marketplace into the vineyard.

Otherwise, the millstone around your neck is very heavy.

What is Faith? (Mark 9:43 to End of Chapter)

What is faith?

This section carries on from the previous one about being the servant, being last if you want to be first.

It flows into an unusual section. It is almost a call and response if you read it out loud. We did this in the Catholic Church over Holy Week, and the stations of the cross, a litany.

It is nine lines, and they are a doozie. Philips terms it, "Entering the kingdom may mean painful sacrifice." There is something to this description. Let us listen and see. The context from the previous section is if you disturb the faith of another, even one of the humblest, one who is low on the ladder of spiritual development, you will get the millstone treatment, like cement feet. Maybe this is where it comes from! I do not know clearly what it means to "disturb the faith." I suspect that it means being arrogant, taking advantage of the spiritual hunger of the weaker one, or acting as a smart guy in your spiritual status to a younger one weaker in soul than you, taking advantage of the spiritual hunger, fear, and desperation of the young and weak of soul for your personal gain.

In contrast to the previous section, the context for this section is the personal faith of the reader. The gospel extends to "your faith," which begs this question: what is your faith?

Is there a good definition we can use to approach this section? A few synonyms—trust, confidence, loyalty, devotion—all cover the position of faith well. Of course, the question is about faith in God. The word *belief* is sometimes used interchangeably with faith. I think that it is okay for simple things that are lower on the totem pole of thought. Faith has the gravity of the other words in our vocabulary, like sin, grace, the Christ, and more. There are centuries of thinking on these words. In Jesus's time there was not a conjecture about God, it all started with God. God of the Old Testament was an experience, not a thought or a philosophy. It was action on you, in you, and around you, which is why "in the beginning was the word" is not a lump of logos, it is the activity of God in the world, and it could be identified to every man. God is a vibration that got into you, thus the "word." Second, as I referred to earlier, the Jews made a great discovery when they fell into faith about God. The posture they had and we have is faith in the one God of man. It is a faith for all time and for any condition that we are in.

Below are the "things" that get in the way of faith, and if they do, take drastic measures so that they do not suppress your faith. This surely cannot mean what is says. To maim, cut, or gouge out, these are not sober, rational steps to take when your faith is on trial or abandoned. Yet, the position of faith regarding the kingdom of God, the turning only toward the higher power, bowing before the way life is and not what you want or hope or wish it to be, kneeling before God, faith states have supremacy. The sacrifice, as Philips writes, is the sacrifice of the ego state, not the self, to the Godhead.

Fill in the blanks. If the ____ with your faith:

1. Hand interferes, cut it off.
2. Foot spoils, cut it off; throw it on the rubbish heap where decay never stops.
3. Eye spoils, pluck it out and be one-eyed.
4. "For every one will be salted with fire."

All this is very hard to fathom. (Please read this section now: Mark 9:43.) Each of these items is a clear, specific noun. All of us can see or touch or walk. The phrases each point to the first three in the list as potential spoilers of faith. Hm. At the end of each peroration there is a reference to the rubbish heap. The first three can get in the way of others, and thus your spiritual well-being, but how?

For example, if your hand gets in the way and spoils your faith, you must cut it off. Like that! Imprecatory sentence. And so forth for the foot and the eye. In the end there is a reference to salt and saltiness. The final line is, "You must have salt in yourselves and live in peace with each other." I have heard this line, but not the "live in peace" part.

A number of contemporary ideas come to mind. But, the thoughts in this section, two thousand years old, may have meant more or different things to the listeners at that time than to me now. I think this section is clearly alchemical in thought. That is the only way it makes any sense to me today, otherwise it is way too literal. Let me see if I can do this.

How can your hand spoil your faith and the faith of the humblest among us? Following on for the eye and the foot.

The "helping hand," the hand of God, the laying on of hands, and many more of these kinds of phrases identify with the self. The touch of the hand, a clenched fist—both portray different behavior and attitude. Jesus served with His hands, He was involved. Recall, too, that Peter was probing who was truly a follower of Jesus even if they were not among the twelve or the extended disciples. Jesus definitely shows in this line that if *figuratively* your hand hinders service to God then you had better cut off the hand rather than obstruct God. The hand is also essential in building. We have opposable thumbs so we can hold on to things and execute tasks. The task suggested here is the work of God, both external and internal in nature.

In Hebrew, the words for hand and power are synonymous. So it makes sense both then and today. Use the power entrusted to you for faith. Otherwise you are liable for the rubbish heap.

Next, the eye is a more easily understood representation for meditation than the hand. After all, "an eye for an eye" is a clear phrase. It was a common phrase and well-known, and acquitted with many years of thinking. After all, does it mean aggression, retribution, vengeance, and anger? Or is it a morality of its time, the Old Testament, and not apropos of the kingdom of God in the New Testament? How would the eye lead us astray, away from the faith?

The eye is also the seat of the soul and vision. It is crucial to see into the future, one's individuality, your outlook on life, the all-seeing eye of God, the evil eye, see eye-to-eye, are all phrases to capture the *augenblick*, the blink of an eye, the moment. The eye is the door of perception. Last but not least, the eye is a circle showing the little unity-totality that echoes the Unity-Totality that is God. Using all this, what can the significance of the eye in the question of faith be?

Again what "spoils your faith"? The well-known line, "those who have eyes, let them see." What? See what is, as it is, unvarnished, vulnerably, see the mystery that is God, see life as it is, not how we project it to be. Faith thus has to do with awareness of the deepest sort. This is called by the ancients the *Third Eye*, or eye of the heart, and can see into life and your life. The eyes can see the sun and the moon and the stars, the universal expanse. And it can see the evil in the world too, see the *summum bonum,* and the evil all at once.

The eye leads astray by being clouded or blind, thus all the healings of the blind in the gospel. This is healing to see, in this case not only to see Jesus, the Son of Man. Not just to see, to really and fully see the being, doing, and owning of all life; to see the sometimes pathos and suffering and comedy of being, as opposed to soulless blankness.

Next, yes, the bottom—the foot. Well, the lowly foot can carry us to the truth or away. It is more distant from the eye or hand, yet it is very important. The feet carry you in a direction, toward or away from the facts of life, your mission or vocation, not an often-used word today, and it is linked to purity of heart and integrity. The feet are your anchor and foundation. They can keep you stable or get you into the dance of life by following the music of the spheres. Your feet can follow or lead. Follow the footprints in the sand. Follow the yellow brick road. (Clichés, perhaps.)

Thus your grounding is in your feet. Faith seems to be mostly this, I think—where you stand in life. And if you are spoiling your faith by not journeying to the Godhead, well, you are headed for the dump. And the fires will burn your feet as fire from bottom to top and then to ashes, of course, from the fire. And now "everyone will be salted with fire." Whoa, a great juxtaposition, salt and fire. You know that salt extinguishes fire? Both are strong alchemical elements. We cannot live without salt. We cannot live without fire, as in body heat. So, can we live without faith? God? Biblically, salt is associated with Lot's wife. Recall the pillar of salt in the midst of destruction. She stopped in her tracks—feet—and looked back—eye. In alchemy there are three salts: elementary salt, salt of the earth, and central salt. They are associated with fermentation late in the process of inner vision. The point is that salt is common, yet profound in its effects. Perhaps it suggests an integrity or uprightness that is needed for the life as a "committed faithful." Salt is staunch.

The section ends thusly. Salt is a metaphor for faith: "Salt is a very good thing, but if it should lose its saltiness, what can you do to restore its flavor?" Well, how does it lose its saltiness, then? It gets dissolved, dispersed, and diluted, unused; each suggests its loss. When salt is added to a recipe it adds to the taste and strengthens the food's properties. Yet it has to be applied just the right way, with the right proportions, for it to work just right. This is a keen metaphor for faith.

Faith is the same. If you water down your faith, if you dissolve it, if you leave it in the box, they mean the same in effect—nothing. Have faith amongst each other, but "live in peace."

Now what could this mean?

"Keep the faith" was a funny saying in the past, yet it means a great deal. Internally, grow, yet never make that a source of pride, a source of division, a source of "who is better than the rest?" As Jesus stated in the earlier section, if you mean to be first you must serve and be vulnerable; if you are not, you are blanched, you cannot be touched, you are a pillar of salt to the Mystery and men and you are frozen dead, not alive to the good news, which is that to die is to live. You are all diluted ego.

Lurking in the background of this section is the issue of evil in the name of God. Can there be blind faith? Yes, and this leads to the worst sin, the sin against the Holy Spirit. This is the sin the devil adores. They are hypocrisy and layers of self-deception. It is a question of faith versus belief. Belief is in something. Faith is unconditional. Faith focuses on letting go and opening the mind to truth, whatever it might be, unreservedly.

MARRIAGE (MARK 10:1–12)

I am happily married and deeply in love. My arrival at this state and state of mind was a course of love action. Second, I have been married five times to the same woman. Third, what occurred was the will of God. Fourth, we are soul mates. Fifth, we are two different selves. Sixth, my wife is the wrath and face of God in my life.

Prelude

Tantric thought says that the action of the feminine created and greeted the terrestrial plane. (There is a cognate to this thought in Greek myth as well, represented by the birth of Athena via a blow to Zeus' head.) The feminine did this by reflecting to the Unmanifested itself, causing an experience, a desire. The feminine was the action, the reflection, and the impetus that produced the sacred desire for manifestation. Of course, there is more. And, the feminine is multifaceted; there are many stories. Despite the rich stories and folk tales, the feminine has been derogated by all the religions except Buddhism, and that is not a religion, per se. There have been female gods, spirits, and saints, as well as the role of Mary in the Catholic Church. However the female gods, et al., are all far too subtle in effect to override the deep-seated disdain for the feminine archetype by the masculine archetype. This position is also in denial of female biology and sociology. And this is not strictly a male put-down because men are disoriented regarding their own feminine. To make the matter more striking, the feminine is out of touch with its feminine archetype. So when we read about Eve "coming" from Adam's rib, or from God's hand, we see that the "female" creation is the second "thing" to occur. In Kabbalistic thought, the feminine is buried under the first Sephirot, virtually, in the dirt. Now these may or not be the male's intentional mind. Nevertheless, whether by the masculine or "allowed" by the feminine, this calls for a clearheaded and massive reimagination that has to be carried out for a purpose, which is the claiming of the anima by the masculine or the animus by the feminine.

There is another thought that Adam dreamed Eve forth from his unconscious—the anima. The feminine archetype is associated with the unconscious. The story is a point for meditation and reflection. The Genesis story, though there are two, has God separate Itself seven ways, always by division of two. I know that there were six days of creation. The other side of this holy action is supreme rest, and the feminine, via Mary Magdalene, who rested while Mary acted. (Earlier I said the greatest mystery is why did God become the many? Why did God decide to create all of us and the many things of this universe? Not "why am I here," important though this question is.) In this context Jesus is tested with a question about marriage.

Marriage—what a concept. It predates all other social institutions. It shows up here in Mark after three earlier profound chapters. It seems to be a sideways move rather than a deepening of the process we are in reading about Jesus. The chapter opens like all the earlier ones, and He was "teaching according to his custom." Again, it shows the Pharisees testing Jesus regarding a small item: divorce. (Why is this a test?) "Is it alright?" they ask. "Well, what does the "law" say? Moses?" Jesus asks. "Well, if you follow the rules, then you can divorce, they reply."

Jesus launches into a tirade, if you feel it, about this law, and his response centers on love. Love triumphs over the law, it overwhelms the law. Precisely, how "little you know of love." His response is flat-out incendiary. "In the beginning, (like from Genesis) from creation, God made them male and female." This must have set the Pharisees off. First, male and female are equal, He doesn't mention Adam and Eve. Second, beyond this, they leave mom and dad and join in a union—"become one flesh." To do that, again, they are equal in God's eyes. This was pretty confronting stuff then, I believe. "They are no longer two people, but one." This line is another amazing line in the gospels. They become a unit. They are unto themselves, they have integrity. This is the meaning of love. Two are one, and not individuals, but something that God has joined together. God is the "prototypical" unit. It is one. In marriage, the chance of this type of unity is possible, and in that possibility we mimic God, which is love. This is a primordial or ontological event. Recall that God made Adam and Eve, and, to go back to unity, Eden is the mission. It is unattainable, yet a vision. The joining by male and female parts in marriage is an act of divine providence. The dissolution of that is a tremendum, a shaking of foundations. In marriage, we can see the mystery of two unfolding in unity: the joy, happiness, and the contradiction, the human drama and comedy.

Finally, we can never separate what has been joined by God. Just as it is impossible to split the atom except with great force, so divorce is not such a light step. The choice of a partner to journey to God is an event like no other. To find, to discover, or to choose a mate, with all the weight of life, is an amazing experience. Then to stay in the context of the marriage at all times, you do need God's hand.

I avoid the last line. The question of adultery is like divorce, part of the marriage play. It feels out of place, almost like an addition, in a different voice.

I know I have left many thoughts, threads, and ideas hanging. Marriage is too big a topic to fully delve into via this book. Let me finish this unit with a reversion to the beginning of my thoughts. My wife and I are different. It is more than the idea that opposites attract, because positive and negative merely cancel each other out, so the adage that they attract is merely a conventional and superficial phrase showing a deeper state of life. Our marriage is an archetypal match: her jagged pieces fit my jagged pieces and form a picture. Both of us desired to form a picture from the pieces. The pieces are still jagged, yet there is unity. In my course of life, with many hiccups and feints to the left and the right and various attempts at existence, I have found three facts to be so. They serve as the asphalt of the road of life.

First, life is choice. Pretty simple, but everything on earth has a consequence. And some of those consequences are minor, major, or mortal.

Second, life is about finding out. It is a process of going deeper into the state, facts, and way of life. It never ends, never lets up, and produces all sorts of matters to digest, grow, build on, and recognize.

Third, life is about loving consciousness. If this is too hard to get, try this. Life is about absorbing one and two fully, deeply, madly, and still not succumbing or being tilled under. It is like Paul on the road to Damascus. He had an event that changed his life there and then. From that point on he loved that experience and made it his own every day. We all have events lesser or greater than this. It is our vocation to integrate what the essence of the experience is, and then to call it our own. To do this, I verily suspect, is the will of God. And, this *is* and can occur in the context of marriage, or, in any relationship when taken seriously.

Postlude

The state of marriage houses an implicit question about Christian morals. This section has posed a problem about divorce that I avoided and still will. I do wish to address a position about Christianity many have offered, supported, and espoused regarding what Christianity is. It is a morality, they say. Going around their positions immediately and not trying to describe them for fear that I will err concerning their propositions, I want to end by saying that though Christianity begets morals, it is not strictly morality.

First, Jesus says it explicitly: love your neighbor as yourself. This is the highest order of love. Second, Jesus says it explicitly: love God with your whole heart, soul, mind, and body. Third, these two lead to union with God. Fourth, God decided to become man; God incarnated on earth and this implies not a morality but rather a comfort with living, with life in general. Solely teaching morality to the exclusion of worship, interior life, and doctrine has brought the church to its state of difficulty. Though this is encompassing and overarching indictment, it speaks to the deep need for spiritual maturity across the Christian frontier.

WHY LITTLE CHILDREN? (MARK 10:13–16)

The little children visit with Jesus. The parents bring them to be touched. Pardon me, but it is a little like families bringing their children to be with Santa. It is good mana, and it is fun. It seems like magic, no? To have the powerful man touch your boy or girl. What do the parents have to lose? But is there more to it?

Well, this is a repeat of an earlier event in Mark's gospel, yet there is a bit of difference. The parable is more direct and definite, emphatic, if you will. Jesus is indignant because the apostles stop the children from visiting Him. Thus it appears that there is a point to this section, but what could it be? Children are children, after all, and often not well handled. And it isn't as if they had a jot to say about anything then, unlike today's precocious ones.

Two lines are all—and enough.

"You must let little children come to me; never stop them! For the kingdom of God belongs to such as these. Indeed, I assure you that the man who does not accept the kingdom of God like a little child will never enter it."

Some heavy words.

First, you have to get this in the gut. Experience the point and the weight of the delivery. Read it again.

Second, a few key words: must, little, come to me, never stop them, the kingdom of God belongs to such as these, accept the kingdom of God like a child will never enter.

Third, and then He blesses them. Here there are no demons to expel.

Fourth, He identified with the little children.

Fifth, the choice of words is courageous.

Well, what can be made of this short, three-line section after the middle of Mark's gospel narrative?

The life of children is very different from that of thirty-year-old men, Jesus for example. The children then were vulnerable, as today of course, but even more so then. Children live lives that are guileless, unpretentious, curious, and humble. They are open to be trained or taught about what is so. I have not used quotes to make a point, as that becomes scholastic or intellectual, versus the experience of Marks's gospel. This is a great insight adding to the thoughts I have. "Invulnerability means that one cannot be touched, and if one cannot be touched, one cannot psychologically be moved." (Charles Ponce, *Alchemy*)

Children are, by and large, completely vulnerable. They are not little adults. The balance between limits that foster a healthy ego can be hard. Not too conceited or self-centered, yet autonomous is perhaps an ideal. Nevertheless, children can equally be egoless, for that formation comes over time, paced by situations and the ability to absorb life at not-too-rapid a pace. What does this have to do with Jesus and the kingdom of God?

The being of a child is one of certain innocence, almost a type of foolishness. In literature, the child/fool is ripe with meaning because of its role in discovering the mystery or unraveling the "road to God." We recently had such an image in the book and movie series *The Lord of the Rings*. In this discovery process, the child pulled the entire situation into alignment. And it was not a simple task to save the kingdom; all manner of character had to be pulled into service, and still the road was narrow and sharp, with ruin always near.

Jesus, as the Holy Fool, took us to full realization about the mystery, depth, and greatness of life by his atonement to the Father. His posture or pattern as an innocent was the only way He saw to greet all of life's myriad possibilities, including death at the hands of the Romans. His oneness with all in the kingdom, known and unknown, seen and unseen, wanted and unwanted, was foolish, totally absurd beyond "surdity"! It was a must, a must because of the deepest level of choice imaginable, the holy choice regarding the Ground of Being. It was not a big choice with glory or with hubris, a "little" choice, a childlike choice, to enter God's kingdom and experience it fully. And Jesus was the child that is innocent in His moment, symbolizing total openness to the possibility of life.

There are five instincts: hunger, sex, activity, creativity, and reflection. Children are at the beginning of the instinctual development process.

They are innocent of the pretense of knowing more than they know. They are so in the moment that they can notice more than most adults. The kingdom is this witnessing, noticing, existing ensouled, surrounded by awe. What a wonder to be moved and touched on so many fronts. And here of all places we witness Jesus's personal warmth; it matters a great deal to the children. Amazing.

The Road to Salvation (Mark 10:17–31)

Who does not want to carry his or her load lightly?

Who does not want to sleep well at night?

Who does not want to fret less?

Who does not want to be happy?

Who does not want to be rich?

Who does not want to be loved?

Who does not want to have a meaningful existence?

If I missed one or two, add your own, because while these are important, the rich man's question is crucial. It has to do with the cross and eternity.

Leaving the little children behind, Jesus sets out on another mission trip. During the journey, a man comes to him for "help," but he actually wants a formula for spiritual wellbeing– in a word salvation. The 'rich man' hails Jesus, calling Him, "Good Master." This appellation is refuted: "No one is good –only God," making the point that all salvation derives from It, not from earthly code words for Messiah, savior, or someone who is above the fray of life and not grounded in reality. Maybe Jesus was being incongruous to throw the man off and get him to pay attention. Perhaps like a slap. Yet He sees into his soul and asks, "Are you keeping the Commandments?" This is step one in the journey to salvation. Can this really be so? Well, yes, the Ten are the "egos" steps on the razor's edge. They are the basics. As in, to get up on the tightrope of life like a razor's edge, at least use and keep the Ten and see where that gets you. Start out small and grow big in your soul with these Ten steps on the ladder.

Okay, I've got the Ten pretty well in hand, the man says. Oh? How so? Let's see. Jesus asks reading between the lines, the man a series of questions. Who is your God? What do you bow to; what are you in awe of; what are you truly afraid of; to what do you ascribe great, full, and total power; what has the ground of your being; what are you really serious about? Alright, well then, let's go to step two.

Let's make that which is really important to you relative, as in relative to the Almighty. Let's take your riches and push them lower on the totem pole of significance. Say, for example, money—make it immaterial. How about that? Now what? And the man was saddened, and left. Why? It says Jesus warmed to him, so He was not being confrontational.

Many would say that that the riches were the impediment.

Well, it says it right there in Mark: If you are rich you have a hard time getting into the kingdom. It is easier for a camel to get through the eye of a needle, children. Wow! That is some challenge. Imagine a large camel going ... well, it is impossible. I submit we do not know what the significance of rich is. Who is rich? Yeah, I know you have that pretty well in hand. Rich is the person just above your pay grade. Rich is a word you can really fill up with all kinds of definitions. As in, "boy, that is rich". Rich, in this context, means anyone whose spirit or soul fails to see the kingdom of God at hand. Anyone who fails to see Jesus representing the way life is. Rich here means blinded to:

1. the kingdom at hand
2. God as an experience
3. God, period
4. the next step in your spiritual journey
5. seeing that you are not synonymous with your riches or, for you dear reader, whatever you are synonymous with
6. the fact that we are all laborers in the vineyard and truly no better than the next in the labor

So who among you is richer than this man? Relinquishing riches equals accepting the call by Jesus to follow Him. What did Jesus do? He pointed to God with his knowing, doing, and being. And He healed the sick so that they could see the face of God too, which is love. Jesus showed this as real to all. The admonition to heal the sick, feed the poor, and clothe the naked cannot be carried out (in love) if you are worshiping an idol, riches, or another lesser god. For those who are cared for, what occurs is immediately seeing God in their lives and the possibility to receive the love of God through another. This is all about the first Commandment.

The section to this point is about sweeping the unimportant aside for the sake of the Kingdom. It is not easy, as we have read. "He went away in deep distress." The man's face fell. He was disappointed; he was un-enchanted. His hopes were dashed for a simple step to heaven. Sadly, there are no ways to cut the corners. Yes, you can be rich and be saved. There is no guarantee that if you are poor you are any better than the rich man. The road to salvation is detachment from all that is in the way of "accepting the Kingdom." (Mark 10:14)

The section closes with an enigmatic question posed by Peter. Well, if this is all true, and we are here following you, Jesus, what of us, and who can be saved?

Jesus says, "Humanly speaking it is impossible, but not with God. Everything is possible with God." Wow! So true, so true. With the Mystery of life it is all possible. What a meditation on this word; all is possible with God. More later on that; here we see in the closing paragraph what Jesus is getting at.

To paraphrase, leaving your community, leaving your riches and property, leaving your family, for the sake of God's word and Jesus, you will get back a hundredfold today and tomorrow what you have "sacrificed." And those of you who are blindly rich will truly be last, and those of you who are last will be rich in things and in God.

I suspect that this is momentous. It truly says that to die is to live. Give up the barriers to entry, give up the little experience and go for the gold of life which is: all that is, is good. Know that you are accepted, that your past is approved, and the future is open for your creation as a disciple of God.

Jesus's Apocalypse (Mark 10:32–34)

Mark brings us to the last parts of Jesus's life. The gospel is coming to the big finish, as the saying goes. We have the trip to Jerusalem, confrontations with the powers that be, Passover, betrayal. We come to the foothills of Golgotha and death scenes and the internment, and then resurrection. There are so many events told of that I am truly afraid of it all. What is apparent to me is the intensity of the narrative; Marks puts it down with great effect. In fact there is one more miracle, then no more other than the resurrection. Jesus has the demeanor of being at the Source of Life, with little or no room for playing nice.

The section after the "little children" experience is very short. Jesus tells his future to the apostles in three lines. In this section there are words applied to His followers that would be considered negative; they are dismayed and afraid. Jesus Himself clearly tells them what will happen to Him over the next month or so. He will be betrayed. He will be condemned. He will die. He will be given to the pagans. He will be jeered at. He will be spat on. He will rise from the dead. This is an outline or summary of things to come. It is apocalyptic. Even Jesus is alone with Himself. "Jesus walked on ahead." It seems as though He wanted to be alone.

I do not believe that it is a matter of prophesy here; it is a matter of knowing that this is what "pagans," the Romans, do to people like him. Not a big jump on Jesus's part to figure it out. Again it is not seeing the future or clairvoyance or something like that. Perhaps it is ultra-lucid, these three lines of prediction. Of course, in a phrase, every decision has its consequence. Jesus's acts are clear to Him, and He reflected, I am sure, on His behavior. It is clear that His decisions have consequences.

What about the rising word, as in "rise again."

Well, to Jews this word means at least two things: the rising of the group, as in an uprising, or a general rising of the body and thus of the "soul" as well.

I hesitate to think that Jesus knows that he is going to rise bodily. Yet, with God, everything is possible. It is available to the Source of All.

It seems that this section is apocalyptic in nature. After all, the community senses that the end is near, and putting these words in His mouth fits that cognizance.

Vocation and the Last Miracle (Mark 10:35–Mark 11)

From here forward the going gets rough, in a sense. Jesus has previously outlined the journey or pathway by which He will be going to His death and resurrection. Like it or not, the next six chapters are full—full of wisdom and tragedy, glory and sorrow, temptation and fulfillment.

This final section of the tenth chapter is a bit of a call to vocation for the apostles, who seem not to get it, just like the rich man previously! We, the reader, either get it or, like them, do not. Remember that though they have Jesus there to answer the dumbest question, this does not mean that the apostles are enlightened. They may be illuminated and have already experienced a baptism, but they are still a little thick. Notice the first part of this section.

Recall that Jesus has just, just, just told them that His end is at hand and death is nigh, and two apostles still, still, still ask, "Well, when you go, can we sit at your right and left hand in your kingdom?" You, Jesus, when you are dead and we apostles, when we will be dead too, can we be big shots like you and then we will be with you wherever you are going to go? What are they asking and who is doing this? Are they some newly appointed, recently anointed pair? No, they were the first to be called and the ones who responded at the lake back in the earliest days. And they have seen a lot of miracles, heard a lot of stories and secrets, experienced miracles, and even went out on their own to teach a ways back. Well, have they gotten the message? NO. They are still somewhere back there in the political phase of this organization. The question is purely a political question. Will we be powerful like you? Jesus's response to the question is, "What do you want me to do for you?" Like *holy smoke*! How stupid are you two?

"You don't know what you are asking," He says. Yes, they think they know what they are asking. And then He says, can you do what I said I will do and have what I said will happen to me? Oh yes, these two say, oh yeah. And Jesus says, well you will really get what I get fully, totally, undoubtedly, for sure. "But as for sitting on either side of me, that is not for me to give; such places belong to those for whom they are intended."

What a rebuke, but kind, in a way. *For those for whom the places are intended.* Let's think about what He's saying. Is this predestination? Does God, the Source of All, select us for such places?

Do you choose where you belong? Do you choose where you are going? What are the intentions you live by? Apparently, the intention selects the place you will end up. The meaning or purpose the apostles seek is earthly versus the soulful (eternal) that Jesus irradiates for all to see. The jump from earthly to eternal power is not possible; it is not an option Jesus can safeguard. The apostles figure that if they intend to conquer or rule earth by superior force, then they will surely because of this intention or vocation have the same result in eternity. Somewhat like a parallel universe. Intentional service, "to give life to set others free" will, in fact, earn them a seat on either side of Jesus. Nothing less.

The power to get there and the apostles' idea about power are not equal, not even close. In the next section of Mark He makes it clear how true intention takes place.

There is a deeper sense to the section. It is clear that Jesus has not a bit of control over who intends to gets to heaven. He will not get you or me to heaven; that is not Jesus's job description. God knows. And Jesus is God's Son and still He does not have the power to pull you or me to heaven. It is more or less up to you. It is your vocation, as it was for Jesus. As the sign says, "I promised you a safe landing, not a peril-free journey."

The apostles are thus totally duds. They are not fully illuminated to the facts of existence that life, each of their lives, is a creation and a calling—a decision, choice, and a loyalty. At one time this was called purity of heart or chastity. It takes intention.

Apostles, you want to sit by the *power*? Well, it is legwork (soul work?) and not guesswork. Jesus goes beyond the recent expression about his death, giving more details and outlines how the world works and how the interior world of soul works. It is the way of the servant that gets you to sit by the right and the left of the Source of Life; this is your vocation—to become the servant of all, to be the first you must be the last, to live you must die, to give your life for all. Well, what exactly is the meaning of the preceding formula for? We have seen these words before; they have heard these words before; the words are familiar to all believers, apostles, and disciples. Again, it is not actions that are necessary here, though the actions are eventually where the rubber meets the road. It is not social working. Again the working will be there. The key phrase "and give his life to set many others free." The freedom is not about libertine-ism. It is the freedom of loving the Mystery and

Source of Life with your whole heart and soul and your neighbor as yourself. This is to be subservient to God, the servant of God; this is so because you realize your union with the Transcendent that Jesus speaks of. This is not the way of the world, now or then. It is to be powerless in the sense of vulnerability, exposure, and fully before revelation—the way life is—and still serve, though it seems absurd. This is the calling that they faced, we all face, and will face forever. It takes intention.

Oh, and the last miracle.

Jesus is called by Bar Timaeus for a healing. He calls Jesus the Son of David two times. "What would you have me do?" Jesus asks. The blind man asks for pity! Jesus, can you spare a bit of power to heal me? Simply, Jesus says, "Go on your way then, your faith has healed you." It is in our power to heal ourselves; yes, it says so right here. The man knows he is ill; well, healing is facing that illness in the most thorough way you can. You can take it to Jesus, but the healing is in and on you. It takes intention.

By the way, above there was the request to sit on the right and the left of Jesus in the power and glory. Did anyone else see the cross and the two thieves hanging with Jesus on Golgotha? The places of honor at the cross went to two thieves and not to the expected apostles. The intention was in already for these two in a manner of speaking, if it was ever fore-ordained.

A second aside: is it not interesting that a blind man sees Jesus as the Son of David? Nowhere else is that title ascribed to Him in the gospel of Mark. Jesus was called the Son of Man and Son of God. Jesus had the nature of man, God, and David.

The Beginning of the End (Mark 11:1–33)

Mark now comes to the beginning of the "end process," the end of the line for Jesus. It is said that the candle burns the brightest at the end, and so here we observe Jesus in rare form. If before there was a hint of Jesus's attitudes and emotions, these hints now become reality. Whether by writer's design or Jesus's decision, personality traits become noticeable. In the previous section we saw this happening already, though slightly. Going forward, the evidence becomes overt. Could it be otherwise? Meaning, as we approach a significant point in our lives, the emotions are sharper—everything can become more deeply etched. Jesus definitely knows where this will end, but the details are less clear even if He is God.

Noticing and thinking about Mark's words, it is apparent that the oral tradition is wobbly to the point where certain words used in the section are peculiar, maybe out of place. There is a strange repetition, an echo of events or a revisiting, perhaps a retelling by or from another author, source, or point of view.

There are three distinct portions in this chapter as I see it: first, the palm march into Jerusalem; second, the scene the next morning concerning the fig tree and the temple; then another morning, the fig tree again in a different way, along with testy Pharisees. Using the days as markers, we have three events or tableaux. If you see it as a unity, there is really only one story, however, the story of Jesus acting as the leader of the movement and His actions in that context. Why the author portrays Jesus this way is harder to see. All through the gospel we read Jesus in a more remote role, almost diaphanous. With this chapter, the man is provoking and cosmic (not spacey, rather showing the order of the world and its structure). Recall the line by Paul, as though seen through a glass darkly; here there is no opacity, instead reality.

At the start of this chapter, Jesus instructs two disciples to steal a colt. Don't worry, He says, tell them if they ask that the Lord needs it. (Peculiar. It is strange to use the word *lord* here. It is generic. A Lord—terrestrial higher power? Or just any important personage? Or is it Jesus?) But He will send it back. So it's a loan. We see the entrance into Jerusalem, called triumphant, on the back of this colt. Quite a scene it is, with proclamations and huzzahs, great calls to greet the kingdom of David, our father. (Recall the recent words of the blind man Timaeus, who called Jesus the son of David.) This is some endorphin-producing event. There are calls from the crowd to save Jesus, "God save him from on high"—obviously a reference to the Romans and high priests. And this is all over the course of a day. This is one of the most political events in the Gospel of Mark. Here is Jesus fully taking in the adulation of the crowd and seemingly planning it. What are we to make of this? It seems to be fully orchestrated and planned; you have the feeling that the masses were in readiness and maybe wanted this to occur. From the inside, Jesus needs to give the powers that be a great and clear reason to put him to death. Is this His will to martyrdom? There is no confrontation with anyone this day. Jesus rides through the city and ends up at the temple, looks around, then leaves it and the city to go back to the suburbs. To where? A last thought: this event must have been very heartening to the followers, who are probably afraid of the Jewish leaders and the Romans too by now.

Next, Jesus comes back from the suburbs and is hungry for figs! But it is not the time for figs and He curses the tree for not bearing him any fruit. Wow. Pray tell. Surely He knows the season of the fig. He is victimized by the fig? Curious, or not. The fig tree–where else have we heard of it? In the Garden of Eden. Were not the private parts of Adam and Eve covered by fig leaves for modesty? And the tree is emblematic of woman and the male genitalia. It is also widely seen in the Middle East as a source of food. And, last but not least, Buddha achieved enlightenment under a fig tree. But in this context, it is nature, not nurturing. It is nature out of whack, so to speak, not fulfilling its "function." Jesus is not happy. The curse is downright sharp.

However, Jesus's action functions to end the curse of the garden, I feel, with His curse. Jesus, as the second Adam, is releasing humanity from having to go back seeking the unity of the garden. The ejection of man and woman from the nature of the garden with God's curse, caused by the first Adam and his downfall or sin, is herein reversed. Read: "May nobody ever eat fruit from you." Nobody means *nobody*. Ever means *never*. There had to be a fig tree in the garden, right? Otherwise, where did the leaves come from? In other words, don't seek the fruit in the garden back there, seek it in the kingdom of God now at hand.

This is perhaps a stretch, because there are many narratives and interpretations suggesting other *post hoc* ideas.

In the next section we read of Jesus arriving in Jerusalem and going to the temple. Here is the section that so many make a big deal of. He curses the temple businesses and acts out his anger by throwing out the dealers and sellers of goods and money exchangers, and stops the carrying of water through it. Well, what have we got here? A literal justification for much of the social gospel. Mammon out! Quoting the prophet Isaiah 56:7: "My house shall be called a house of prayer for all nations," Jesus continues, "But you have turned it into a thieves' kitchen." I think that again Jesus needed to provoke the powers that be to action, and this was a big provocation, since the activities were profitable to them. Now the important fact to me is that the Jewish leaders probably had to pay some of their profit to the Romans. Jesus thus is assaulting not only the Jews, but their keepers, the Romans. (Although perhaps this was the Sabbath and this was completely not okay. But this would've been mentioned. I do not know how secular they were at that time.) The provocation to the Romans could not be overlooked. The gospel says that the powers that be were afraid of him because he had "captured the imagination of the people. And every evening he left the city." Thus, Jesus did this many times. Repeatedly.

Then comes the last part of chapter 11. Jesus returns to the fig tree allusion. The apostles notice that the tree is withered away. In fact, it is more than that, it is shriveled up. Jesus replies in another fashion. It feels like an "our father" derivative. I am going to break it into pieces because of the import.

A. "Have faith in God." Well, what else can you have? Of course, there is a lot that can be deduced from the faith posture. But regarding the tree, it points back to that ban at Eden. What does a curse have to do with faith? With God, everything is possible—and confusing. Jesus first curses the tree, then suggests that we have power from the Source of All to attain what we pray for. Maybe Jesus is suggesting that a blasphemy, another word for curse, is the opposite of faith. Second, it may point to the first commandment.

B. Jesus continues: "If you say to a hill to get up and go over there, and you say it in purity of heart, chastely, coming from the source, God, the hill will jump to a new location." The between-the-lines here is that you cannot lie to yourself, doubt, or prevaricate. Otherwise it will not happen. Power—not the pornography of power—is the issue. You must not lord your power other people, for example, the powers that be. (Mark 10:37)

C. "Whatever you pray about and ask for, have faith that you have received it and it will be yours." Consider what this says or suggests. Don't diminish this process. Image it and it is done. What size of hill can you move?

D. "And as you stand praying, forgive anything that you are holding onto against anyone else, the result being that God will forgive you your sins." Wow. In the act of prayer you change the relationship you take to your actions. Prayer intends or directs love on the breach. So if you hurt someone or they hurt you, in the prayer about the event, you forgive the hurt; the event doesn't disappear, the sins go away. Existentially, the sin or separation is healed. Grace, maybe.

We could spend a lifetime here, no?

"So they came once more to the Temple." The powers that be ask Him an innocuous question. By what authority do you do what you do?

Where did a carpenter's son, now a rabbi, get permission to carry off this "revolt"? Well, this was my interpretation and reading between the lines, you know. And where did this son of a carpenter have the authority now equaling their power and project this power into the marketplace of Jerusalem with such ease? Then He presses them: since they put John the Baptist to death because of Herod's wife's wishes, he asks, "The baptism of John, now, did it come from heaven or was it purely human?" Clever! He boxed them in. Either way they answered, the powers that be were stuck. Checkmate.

Looking at this chapter as a whole, what is going here? Power is one piece of the chapter; there is provocation in the entry into Jerusalem at the powers that be, and anger in the temple. There is the allegory of the fig tree and meekness around prayer and there is a possible solution to the fig tree episode that also projects an attitude of dignity around His emotions.

Mark shows Jesus in this chapter in a manner that is not the stereotype most have of Him. And whether or not the oral tradition is close to the "history" we will not know. The message is the key. Drawing the meaning out into our lives and into the days of the week as it applies is Mark's point.

THE VINEYARD AND EDEN (MARK 12:1–12)

We come to a parable, more encounters with the powers that be, and apocalyptic imperatives in the next chapters. For indeed, we are (and Jesus is) hunkering down and focusing on the passion, crucifixion, death, and resurrection stories around the corner. But this parable is a mighty one. It relays a tone that is not usual because it seems so literal and superficial that we, the readers, give not a minute of thought about it before moving on to the next, more fun section about the coin face—Caesar and to whom render honor. So what of the vineyard?

It is a simple story, as I said already. A vineyard, an owner, hired hands, a murder, and various other mayhem. The vineyard image shows up prior to this story as a contrast between the marketplace and the vineyard, which I mentioned and discussed previously. This vineyard story is a bit different in that the workers have a different role. The other story had an oracular feel, where this one is more direct in some ways.

It starts out as a story to "them." They, we assume in this case, are the Pharisees, the apostles, and us. Everybody has just been hanging about since the last encounter concerning power and authority and where it originated. This parable sets an Edenesque line as the opening: "A man once planted a vineyard, fenced it round, and dug a hole for a winepress and set out a watchtower." In other words, the man set out a garden with all its lineaments. Okay it is a place for production of wine. All of the items are there in place for the wine. There are workers who will tend to the garden. But the man goes abroad. Why? An absentee landlord? A *deus ex machina*? The owner leaves, entrusting the vineyard in the hands of the workers; they will attend to matters in his absence. Strange. But consider that this vineyard is an echo of the garden story in Genesis. God makes an Eden, the garden in which man will live. He leaves matters pretty much to Adam. And while Adam does not murder anyone in the garden, he makes hash of life. Right? Tangentially, perhaps.

In this story, the workers are bad boys indeed. Ruffians, we'd call them if we were in pleasant company, but otherwise, devious, murdering, connivers—these words would describe them well. What was Adam? Well, not a murderer, I repeat. However, the rest may apply. Adam was a bit disengaged, it seems to me, a worker who left little to expectation. He connived with Eve, so to speak, he, who was God's first. Let's hold off on the deeper meaning of the garden and Eve and the Serpent. In this Mark story, the evil is carried out by the workers. You do not need a serpent to mislead these workers; they are on a bad road from the get-go to do what they do. So the question is, why was the owner such a bad judge of character? These workers rough up all the emissaries and kill the owner's son. Bad show. They are everyman. They're just unaware, unconscious, and conscienceless. In a sense, they are an undivided mass, so called, lumpen. Adam was this way before the apple. You might just call him soulless.

So the owner throws the workers out of the vineyard with no more retribution than that and "hands it over to others." The section ends with a quote from Psalm 118:22. This, to me, is odd. The Psalm points declaratively to Jesus. Is He the son who is killed by implication? Why are the men sent to the tenants? To collect the vintage that was the owner's portion. The owner wants what was his, what belongs to him, no more or less. Yet the tenants are ruthless to all of the owner's emissaries.

If we image the owner as God in this parable and the emissaries his extensions, prophets, maybe, then what is God trying to collect from the vineyard that matters to Him so? Were the prophets bringing in the sheaves, so to speak? Were not the prophets trying to bring people who had lapsed in faith to God? And the prophets were clear about God's destruction of the unfaithful, so here is the thought that the tenants will be replaced. The caretakers will be removed and others more conscientious will run the vineyard. This is an affront to the powers that be who are in the audience.

But back to the Garden for a minute, Jesus, the second Adam, though killed by the workers, rejected by them, achieves what the prophets could not. He becomes by incarnation the missing piece to point us back to the garden of God, to unite us with the architect of the garden, to be the cornerstone of the gate to God.

The "them" again show up as the powers that be, angry and wanting to get their hands on Him. Hm…like the parable, no?

But there is one more thing. This parable matters because the tenants' motive to kill the son is not out of mere manslaughter. It is premeditated. They said, "This fellow (son of the owner) is the future owner; come on, let us kill him, and the property will be ours." From this line comes more insight about the parable and what it may say to us. The tenants want to own and rule the production, to have the garden as their own, to have the power of the vineyard, the power of earth and to be godless (with all that that implies). This is what they seek. The earth as in the Garden of Eden is an emblem of the inner life. The owner only wants his share of the vintage, or his original intent or agreement about life, the fruit that was his, the fruit that is ours to share. We keep his gift, but he gets to have his too. The gift here is the life worth living as servants to God. Jesus already knows this. This makes Him the cornerstone to the structure of life or the spirit, the life of the earth, and its soul.

This is a family business, is it not? Owner, son, the owner's emissaries, and the workers all fit together as a picture. The tenants totally mismanage the vineyard. What is the mismanagement? They failed to bring the vineyard to its full fruit. Instead they wish it to be for themselves. They rejected the apparent opportunity, not participating in the process they were invited, hired, and chosen to carry out. The true intention here is fulfillment of a job; the workers do not perceive that their role is to follow the rule of the garden; they do not have the soul to do it. They live not for the calling. They lived for the appearance and not for the kingdom of God. How deep a sin is the rejection of a calling? It is a sin against the Holy Spirit.

Give to Caesar, Give to God (Mark 12:13–17)

"Wicked men obey from fear; good men from love." *Aristotle*

The section we have before us is ripe, to say the least. It is ripe today and for all time. In these four lines or so, Jesus states the gospel in miniature, in a short phrase. The matters are plain and clear. The powers that be, Pharisees and members of Herod's party, are trying to entrap Him with a question. Really, no one would fall for the ruse, certainly not Jesus. Here is the question, then, that they state and Jesus throws back at them, and I paraphrase:

"To whom do you bow? God? Caesar?"

Point blank. It seems very simple to me. Is it simple in the context of the tenants of the vineyard, who are everyman? To whom does everyman bow? What or Who is God? Is that not the question of the gospel? And is that not the only question?

"Then give to Caesar what is Caesar's and to God what is God's." Simplicity.

If I were to line up on a sheet of paper on the left, God, and in the middle, Caesar, what would we have? Let's find out what can be associated with each. What do we render to God? What do we render to Caesar? Perhaps a list of synonyms may help: submit, provide, give, or deliver. This helps.

God	Caesar
Awe	Respect
Prayer	Taxes
Obedience–following the law	Compliance–following rules and laws
Love	Deference
Our life	Authority
Full service	Just enough, what is due
Praise	Adulation
Blessings/sacrifice	The mob, inferior function
Soul/spirit	Indifference
Engagement	Protection

I suspect that we owe more silly business to Caesar and what's vital and crucial to God. Don't you? And this list is by no means exhaustive for either side.

Your list? Feel free to add to the above.

Paying tribute to Caesar is okay, Jesus says. And giving to God what belongs to God as well. It is with such ease that Jesus stated this, it is amazing. Many then and today would not be willing to carry this out. It must have struck the disciples as well, for they are a large group by now. If we assume that this was Jesus's teaching, knowing full well the import of the words, it must have had an impact and settled once and for all His position on terrestrial power. It is power. And it is God's realm of power as well. One is temporal and the other ontological, having to do with the structure of being. They are continuous and discontinuous to each other at once. They are not at all equal, yet touching. Implicitly, there is a question from the powers that be about the movement's intentions regarding the Romans. Will the movement attack and take over?

Again, the most important question is what belongs to God and what to Caesar?

Perhaps here I can state the oft-repeated phrase to illuminate this section, "Love your neighbor as yourself," and sense that the reader (or Mark) will hearken to the "love your neighbor" part as the law and skip the "as yourself" because to love yourself could be considered selfish or self-centered. Loving your neighbor is certainly the God part of giving to God what belongs to God. God would not need or want a selfish person, would It? But that "as thy self" part is vexing. How do you love your neighbor and how do you love yourself? At once? The gospel that comes to mind is to serve the poor, the sick, and those poor in spirit. It says little beyond that explicitly. If you flip the phrase to "love yourself as you love your neighbor" there comes to light a thought that "true" self-love and other love are commingled. The power of love is combined with the self and the other. More to the point, the why of this love is so that all can have the greatest good, God's love, God Itself. "To love another soul is to give him God." (Alan Watts) And as Jesus said before, "to set many others free." For that to happen, you must be free within the Kingdom of God.

Ideally, what belongs to God is true love of the other from the self, and what belongs to Caesar is true love of the ego. This is not intuitive, I suspect.

In the world, what we have, then and now, is the marketplace of Caesar, absent any real selves, merely slaves. This is a categorical way to reflect on an answer to the question I proposed. To whom do you bow and with whom do you dance? And the beat goes on.

A Knowledge of God (Mark 12:18–27)

After the last section can it get any more intense? You'd think and hope not. Yet it does. It starts with a challenge from the Sadducees who, according to Philips, do not believe in resurrection. They tempt Jesus with a paradox. By the way, they were another religious party of the time. It seems as though everybody is trying to find some way to trip Jesus up. They offer a seeming conundrum about a man who has a wife. He dies and sequentially each of his brothers marries her and then dies until the last, the seventh, leaves the woman a widow, who then also dies and goes to heaven. Who, they ask, is she married to in heaven?

This, the Sads thought, would get Jesus in trouble. Clever, these Sads. They hope that they can trap him in a mental or spiritual contradiction, just like the Pharisees tried to do previously regarding God and Caesar. Cutting to the quick, Jesus does not fall for the torturous logic and says God is for the living. It is all about life and not death or what goes on in heaven. Pow! Smack! Jesus gets the trick about resurrection that the Sads are trying to spring.

To not know the power of God: this raises the question of what it is to know or what is the knowledge of God? God is for the living, not for the dead. Whatever can this mean? These two questions are essential. I always thought that God was associated with death, and still do to some extent. Don't you? What you identify with makes a great deal of difference. If you say, as the Sads did, that they were concerned with this issue of who was the wife's husband in heaven, they identified with a hereafter, a heaven, a unknown place. Jesus's response hit this idea on the head. The Sads' intellectual conviction settles on this silly business and has no veracity. They present this silliness about marriage when the issue is that God happened to Moses, Jacob, Isaiah, and Isaac, to name but a few. These folks had an experience of God, not some mishmash of who was the husband to the wife at what place and time, so to speak. To have a God of the living implies an event! Thus, Moses et al. felt overcome by an experience of God. Jesus carries on by saying that the there is no marriage in heaven. Who cares! Care about the life what happens when you are touched by God. Now that is a resurrection, being raised from the dead!

To know God is to have an experience that produces an image, a story to be told to you, the community, and back to the Ground of Being. The burning bush of Moses; the God of Abraham; I am the living God of Jacob and Isaac; I am that I am. All these events "produced" shifts in the universe, so to speak, because they were encounters (experiences) with God. Moses goes to the mountain, sees the bush, and carries down the Ten Commandments. He is inspired, with God's Spirit, and shows the Ten Commandments. God lives. To know God is engaging with the experience, wrestling with it, and in this process, transforming your life. By changing yourself, you change history. This is "a living God."

The Sads were thus merely playing at life. I read in between these lines that there is a God out here living with us. By extension, the dead have no need for God. The effect of this thought is huge: live today and know it is favored as this time to live with God. Who better to show this than Jesus, God's Son, who realized this and ran with it? This is the "power of the living God."

What is More Important than the Externals? (Mark 12:28–35)

The Shema (and the Vehafta) and the Golden Rule are all that we need to know, do, and be! Oh?

That is it and I am done. "No other commandment is greater than these," says Jesus. They are the greatest commandments. The depth of the Shema along with the Vehafta and the Golden Rule in theory and practice are endless.

The Shema and the Vehafta are the greatest prayers and considered *the prayers* in Judaism. The Golden Rule is an elaboration of human relations attitudes. I have written of it previously, and Jesus talked about it in other parts of Mark's gospel. Interesting that first there were the Pharisees, then the Sadducees, now the scribes to step up to test Jesus—a neat array of talent.

Let me first spend a moment with the two since it is the most unfamiliar to many readers of the gospel, if you are Christian or merely secular human. (Let's suppose that there are a few who are totally atheist reading this as well.) The Shema is an awesome prayer even to a non-Jew, so Jesus's highlighting this is not a big deal. All Jews know what the Shema is. It is now, after the early centuries, a central part of Jewish services across all denominations, specifically the Shabbat ritual. I feel that a philosophical reverence for the Almighty, is a lost piece in Christian "thinking" and being. So much of Christianity is Christology unanchored to the Ground of Being. Not in every case, but predominantly.

I repeat if you get God, Jesus is easy.

Well, not a snap, just easier. The prayers together state how to love God: with all your heart, all your soul, your entire mind, and all your strength. This says that all your faculties are engaged, even the intangible, and the soul is stretching to ultimate reality. And this is the essence of the first commandment. What this suggests to me is not a limited response to life, but a full-out push at the five-yard line to get to the goal line.

Next, the love for the neighbor is based on the love of self and vice versa. Love yourself as you love your neighbor. Again, I have said this seems selfish or self-centered, but it is not. The pairing of these two commandments makes all the sense in the world. It is through the "other" that we have a chance to encounter the Mystery, to experience the presence of God. And the ability to have, be, and embrace this encounter and bear it is based on the health of the self. Merely running out and doing good is baseless, and may be the real selfishness with which we seek not to be tagged. Whole libraries are available to work this out. After all, only God is good, as Jesus said, in the sense that only God is the sinless One, Whole Being. To know God is to know your neighbor and yourself. The mystery, depth, and greatness are all there in the other and in us too. The union with God is a given. Prayer takes us there and celebrates and acknowledges this state.

Who do the Public and the Powers that Be Say I Am? (Mark 12:34–44)

The ancestry of Jesus is an issue that may never really get cleared up. As a supposed descendant of King David, certainly these few opening lines make sense. There are two points here. (The scribes continue to be in Jesus's crosshairs. And second, Jesus's lineage was first articulated by the blind man a mere two chapters back.) The Hebrews are hoping for a change, and a king's descendant would be the right person at the right time and place. Jesus, however, is not the one in every man's sense of Messiah. The opening lines are more of a play on words and Jesus poking fun at the powers that be. Thus, you have the crowd chuckling as they do. Wouldn't you? Mark called it "great delight" via Philips. Jesus just never accedes to being placed in the role of Messiah. He has better things to do, be, and have. Still, the question of his purpose is piercing, "Who do you think I am?" lingers in between the lines. The hearts and minds of the populace, the common folk, are as they are today, waiting for the daily grind to be smooth, peaceful, and homeostatic. Give us a chicken in every pot, a car in every garage, and a roof over every head, as the saying goes. Give us peace in our time.

And the shift in the next line to, "Be on guard against these scribes who love to …," comes as a stiff indictment of the powers that be, the scribes, and the leaders who are ostentatious, outwardly flamboyant, entitled, armored, thieves, and wolves in sheep's clothing; the high and mighty and their Roman friends and occupiers, their minions, and the many among men who are sanctimonious. All these traits are totally adverse to the kingdom of Heaven (God), the life of the soul. These Scribes are totally outward, exoteric in religiosity and in their poise. As in, "I am somebody special." They eat with the Romans. They live fat off the taxes of the poor and appear to be holy (outwardly), but we know who they really are, "They are only adding to their own punishment." Deep. They are snakes in the grass.

All this takes place before a vast crowd at the temple. Then Jesus placed himself before the poor box at the temple where the rich are dropping their tithes. Imagine this, please. Jesus is just sitting there, watching you as you drop your money into the box. Jesus is well known by now, a person no doubt who draws people wherever He goes—in this case, at the Temple of Jerusalem, no small building—and just looks at them as they drop their money in.

"Believe me," as in pay attention to what is happening here. See this poor woman, see her drop a nickel in the box? The ones who give because it is easy, well, that counts for little! They can easily afford it. No big deal, but the poor woman's gift of a nickel, this will get her into heaven. Well, He did not say that. What it means, though, is that the gift from her dearth is bigger in her life because the nickel really matters, yet she gives it from her heart and not from her head—not from the religiosity, not to be seen, not to grandstand. Instead, she gives it from her all. She is detached from the nickel; she is impelled from an inner set of principles, not from some external set of "shoulds." She is unconcerned about her life by dropping that nickel. Thus, she is giving up her life. Is there any greater sacrifice for her?

Many Prophesies and an Order (Mark 13-14)

This is the chapter in which Jesus proclaims what is to come in an apocalyptic sense. Because Jesus was not an oracle, I am sure you will agree, this chapter on prophecies echoes many topics that have been alluded to in previous chapters. What are all these prophecies that Jesus proclaims according to Mark? There are many. Depending on my count, there are about fifteen discrete ones. You might want to count them yourself just to see if I am correct. This section is troubling and it agitates me, not because the paragraph predicts dire events. I find them troubling because they are here, they exist, and it appears that Jesus says them. How do we deal with this set of predictions that Jesus utters before the apostles Peter, James, John, and Andrew as He faces the temple just after the affair there concerning the powers that be and the widow's mite? The apostles are quasi-straight men to Jesus declarations. Is Jesus feeling a bit testy or angry at the whole coefficients of adversity, so to speak? He is upset about the way the powers that be made matters really terrible. Is He expressing a deep-seated prophetic position about the way life feels for Him right now? Jesus is not an oracle, as I said before. Yet, He projected a whiff of the prophetic earlier. Jesus mimics the major prophets of the Old Testament in this portion of Mark. Was this Mark's effort to ground Jesus in the tradition? This seems a bit unnecessary. After all, Jesus is a rabbi, and rabbis teach and are often prophetic in tone.

The tone of this chapter is by far more intense than any Old Testament prophets because Jesus amalgamated them. Maybe not, in that there is repetition and genuine irritation. Jesus is expressing His humanness through His words about what is to come. He deplores the temple's pretentiousness, its ostentatiousness, the inattention of the people, the ease with which they are deceived, and their general unconsciousness. The entire paragraph is fire and brimstone. Jesus does not know that these events that He lists are going to happen. Rather, it suggests His fear, anger, and sorrow. He, in His humanness, though divine, cannot see the extent of what is to come. He is not a superman; He is not cunning in any way. He has the finite and precise character of a man who is speaking in tongues at the time.

I will not list each saying or prophecy for you. The phrasing is truly powerful and suggests force throughout the entire chapter. The small band asks, "When will the beautiful stonework be destroyed, as Jesus predicts? What sign will there be that all this will be accomplished? To whom is Jesus speaking or who is the audience?" Good questions that anyone would ask. Give us a sign for the end of times! Yes, this way we will be ready and connect the dots from now to then. Interestingly, the temple Jesus is talking about was newly built by Herod's party. It is opulent. This is a fact that no one can deny. Jesus's line is a condemnation, a proclamation, a conviction about likely events, and an augury not too far off considering that the temple is destroyed not much later.

First, be very careful that no one deceives you. Not just a little, be very careful. Calling attention to this repeatedly, Jesus seems to say that we can be affected and swayed as "the end" nears. Certainly we will experience trepidation and could easily fall out of line when matters get stressful. People around us will no doubt yell at the end, "but the end is not yet," Jesus says. Emotions will be high. Keep a cool head are the words between the lines. "Such things are bound to happen." This is reassuring. It almost normalizes the swirl around these circumstances.

Also, Jesus seems to say in the first line that there will be many who want to have his power over the masses, so they will come in his name. There is only one Jesus, so to speak. And these others will have power, but it will be pornography of power. From there He jumps, as if in a stream of thought to wars and rumors. Not to worry, your life is not in danger just yet. Why is this so important here? The band remaining after He dies is in fear, so their terror is magnified by their dire outlook. This emotion would easily occur and impel them to extremes. Again He says not to worry, "Keep your wits about you." You will have roughly the same done to you as was done to me, so to speak. And finally, let the Spirit speak. It will be awkward, but it will flow. Amazing, in that this is not a prophecy, it is common sense. It really happened to the apostles, Mark merely appends it here.

This next paragraph is not prophecy per se, but a prep course with warnings and instructions for the remnant based on previous happenings and Jesus's passion. Just follow all the "yous." What about "the pains" that are mentioned? I translate this as the apostles' coming passion and the pains from the birth of heartfelt knowledge. What is the connection between the pains and the apostles' passion? (Since they are set against each other.) The persecution of the followers suggests that the way the world is, its seeming chaos and disintegration is nothing to worry about because it is all in the course of worldly events. Even if they kill you, it is not anything of significance. Between the lines, "have courage" and "don't be alarmed." It seems to me that this whole first paragraph is like this. Followers, even if you see things that are destructive, this alone does not mean that there is no meaning to life. Remember the good news and the kingdom of God is in you. "For it is not really you who speak, but the Holy Spirit."

The following paragraph is more scary. Starting from the last line of this paragraph, "Yet, the man who holds out to the end will be saved," it seems to suggest that the struggle is both an inner struggle and the efforts of others, nonbelievers, to destroy the movement, to hurl the believers to their destruction. The sense of betrayal by those close to you because of your following Jesus is great. Internally, if you are a Christian, so to speak, people will not like you no matter who they are. And if they are family the anger will be very hard and harsh. Here again we interpret that the life of the soul is a favorable state. People will harm you physically, and they could be from your closest friends or family. Still, you will be saved. Meaning? Salvation will take the form of your nearness to and cooperating with the Ground of Being. Said another way, stay true to your faith; in today's vernacular, stay in character and be centered.

It gets a degree grimmer in that the sight of "the abomination of desolation" is the height of His warning. In the temple will stand a pagan god. This is not too far-fetched. Jesus correctly sensed that it was merely a matter of time until the Romans would destroy the temple. Since this is not only the external event but an internal collapse as well, He is pointing to the Jewish people's abdication of effort and their inability to stop this from occurring due to their somnolence. The radical actions point to the effects of the destruction on not only his followers but the whole of the Jewish population. I think this is a contemporaneous event and not a futuristic series of events. Still, the gravity of the temple's destruction is great. It deflated any chance of or for the culture to survive. Already, the factions made up of the Pharisees, Sadducees, and the numerous quislings are conspicuous of the breakup happening in their midst. And it's the same for internal life as well. The temple is the center of Jewish faith and culture. Its destruction scatters the seeds of Jewish life. In a sense yet to be pondered, Jesus moves the external temple to an internal temple of the Holy Ghost by his sacrifice via his passion and death on the cross. This death is totally in line with the sacrifices to Jehovah (God) carried out at the temple by all cultures at that time, including Jewish.

In the lines of chapter thirteen, there are repetitions and echoes of earlier presentations by Mark. If we take each paragraph of the chapter as a unit it seems to me that the oral tradition found repetition and elaboration as a way to communicate the gospel to the followers of the time. For instance, line 13.21 clearly echoes earlier lines in the Gospel of Mark. And the tone of paragraph three is like paragraph four but for the fig tree metaphor, which repeats the much earlier chapter about the fig tree. The overall style, tone, and character of this chapter is a jumble. The directive at the end of the chapter is to keep alert. Not a prophetic statement, but rather an order. And no one knows when all of this will happen but the Father. So again, the kingdom of God is at hand, at all epochs, places, events, and moments.

But what about the specific predictions regarding this generation? God's time, a time-lapsed photography, has no beginning and no end. I see these Jesus statements as part of the staying-alert admonition offered to the movement, which offered the chosen some solace about the pains at hand. The followers will suffer. And the suffering will feel like the end of time. The best you can do is pray for other signs of life and ultimately be a sign of life.

In closing, these statements attributed to Jesus by Mark are haunting. He must feel the weight of the mission on His being. The job at hand is heavy, as I said before. One, how do you prepare yourself for the crucifixion and death, and two, most likely, there will be apostles who will collapse under the strain of the task. His words are not enough; they do not carry the force necessary for the getting the followers through the complex process. The elements of prophecy herein only bolster the fact that Jesus is dealing with power beyond power. In this realm His union with the Ground of Being allows a certain grand dialogue to hail and foretell what He can about the change that the good news will bring to the world henceforth.

Finally, be ready for *it*. The event of the gospel's proclamation will cause the end of the past and an opening to the future where not even the angels will know what happened or what will. "The earth will pass away and the sky will pass away, but what I have told you will never pass away." This is the eternity of the mystery of life.

Anointing Jesus Before the Passover (Mark 14:1–10)

It is pre-Passover, a time of readiness. Passover is one of the most important ritual events in Judaism, the High Holy Days being the first. Jesus is with friends at their home for a visit, perhaps dinner.

How does this go, feel, in the midst of preholiday planning? I guess you are anticipating the event and all the solemnity. The women, no doubt, are prepping for it and the men are sitting talking about the weather, the Roman-Jewish politics, where they are in the process of impact from the movement's efforts, etc. Meanwhile, the powers that be, well, they are plotting the death of Jesus, and they don't want to do it "during the festival or there will be a riot." Clever, eh? I ask you, who was there to record this *tete-a-tete*, this parley? Would it not be in secret? Here it is in the gospel, as if Mark were a fly on the wall. Anyway, the "chief priests and scribes" are plotting away and make a move that we discover in the coming two paragraphs. The interesting word here in this paragraph is "consequently." What? Because of the feast of Passover, they are meeting before it to prepare for the murder of Jesus. What an inhumane juxtaposition. And they want to do it stealthily by a trick, so they can get Him into their power. The corruption is staggering. The venality of these people is immense. Pre-Passover planning for the festival for them is about death, not the celebration of freedom. No wonder God sent Jesus. Or no wonder Jesus emerged to take on this deficiency and despair. The powers that be are gravely mentally ill. They are totally "Caesar."

In contrast, we see the few apostles sitting at a friend's home, Simon the Leper. This is amazing as well. A leper's home, but this is the one He healed in body and mind earlier. Second stroke of surprise, there is a woman among them who broke and poured a bottle of expensive perfume on Jesus as in an anointing. Third, this is hearkening to the anointing of a king by a prophet, yet here turned on its head. A woman, not a man, did the act of blessing. Fourth, this woman must have been rich to be able to buy "expensive" perfume. Or is this allegorical? The apostles are aghast that she does this and does not donate the money to the poor. Fifth, this is the only significant exposure of a woman except Mary, Jesus's mother, who is only mentioned in passing. Sixth, this event, real or not, is the exposure of the feminine in clear action. Otherwise, Mark's gospel is truly a masculine story. I might add, the whole of Christian theology is masculine, but for the later Mary-ology and the many apparitions and miracles done through her. (This gets more important as time goes by; up to this day, though, less so. Women then were identified with darkness, earth, and hell.) Thus, to have this great a role for a woman is truly a big deal. The passage even gets at this because the apostles are "indignant" with the action of the woman. There was "a murmur of resentment against her." Putting it mildly!

Jesus calls them out with, "Let her alone … she has done a beautiful thing … the poor you will always have … she has anointed my body in preparation for burial … wherever the gospel is preached throughout the whole world, this deed of hers will also be recounted." It is a big accolade, I feel. Lastly, the act itself is an act of love. The anointing shows the gathered how to memorialize Jesus's life and being.

Overall, this paragraph communicates a definite fact. Jesus says He will be put to death, and whether it is a later addition or a foretelling around the corner, which is the betrayal by Judas in the next episode, the tightening of the noose around Jesus's neck is clear.

Betrayal (Mark 14:10–12)

This is a very short section. It is long on effect.

Who has not been betrayed? Slighted? This is a small betrayal or it may be larger than large. In two lines Mark sets the course of events. Of course, events and people were already moving in this direction from day one, chapter one, line one…from Genesis really. In God's mind as it developed, if I may say that, it was going to come to this. How can I ever say this? God knew the course of Jesus's life–that the Godhead had this course of events down in the groove way earlier.

Let's go once again for the first time to the thought or question of what is God?

Does God merely predestine, as Calvin offered? Free will anyone? Not a grain of sand!

And since Jesus shows up as God's incarnation in man flesh, was this hidden from Him? His blind spot?

In this I have no swift answer; the ease of earlier thoughts around Mark is absent around this topic. If God is the absolute, all-knowing, all-present, all-powerful, and all-encompassing, then this is all according to plan, right down to the smallest or largest person, place, or thing. At the other end from this is no God, atheism. And the third point, indifference. Right? So we have a trinity of thought: God, no God, and whatever.

Why am I talking about God and not Judas' betrayal of Jesus? Because, how can you betray Jesus? Can you betray someone who is already aware of the betrayal? Besides, Jesus had to have guessed that a, person at least one, would send him "up the river without a paddle." This realization is not a big leap for anyone. The movement, after all is enormous, so there has to be one person gunning for the leader. Regicide in a group is usual. After all, one individual's imperfect grasp of the kingdom of God is not a stretch! We hardly get it. I am still wandering in the desert of my mind, believe you me. There is Judas, supposedly the one who handled the purse. Power and money, you know, are notoriously close in unethical behavior. Okay, let's find cause and motive. Was there opportunity? Yes, as we will see.

For now there is the intent of betrayal; the giving over of Jesus to the Herodians and thus to the Romans is in process. Judas facilitates this process by his actions and words. Recall the previous paragraph, the powers that be were looking for the chance to get their mitts on Jesus, and lo and behold, Judas emerges from the troop to do the deed. If this is the meeting of the minds, what might be Judas' motivation? Notoriety? Money? Power? Revenge? Competing interest? Ingratiating himself with the authorities? All are possible.

Looking at the definition of betrayal, what is it? "A trade, to expose by treachery, to reveal a confidence and to be unfaithful in guarding" is the definition (Dictionary.com). Thus a light is turned on regarding the route that might have taken place. Assuming that Jesus's work was about the inner life, orienting the self toward the mystery of God, which is an esoteric understanding of existence, then Judas, in contrast and contradiction, is exoteric. Judas looks to the outside, the publicly externalized set of behaviors supported by the authorities. In this way the betrayal makes some sense. Judas is as every man in his desire to stop Jesus from uniting with power, totally opposite to Jesus uniting with the kingdom of God. The powers that be wished to end Jesus's activities, and they found the man to do it in Judas. And thus he is ready to carry out the wishes that are matching his. Every man is not interested in the "why of life," they are interested in the how, the means versus the end. Conversely, to ask "why" is to point outside, seek outside, but also to proceed eventually to the essence inside. Judas' act of betrayal is the loss of his faith in Jesus and the message of and about God's kingdom, the axial role of man in it, and our love of the mystery of God with our whole minds, hearts, souls, and being, and our neighbors as our selves. This is the essence of Jesus's gospel. Judas' existence is to sell out the apostles and Jesus to the Romans and Herodians for money. This step echoes the actions of the fallen angel before God to become Satan. Judas was inhuman in his actions regarding Jesus and hoped for a way to greatness.

Jesus healed the sick, the blind, lepers, and raised the dead, all those in need of their faculties because their faculties' absence severed them from the kingdom of God and their true aim as human beings. Jesus loved the human race, whereas Judas loved the idea of humanity.

The Upper Room (Mark 14:1–29)

The gathering for Passover, the feast to commemorate the flight from Egypt, usually occurs in a family setting today, though there are communal feasts at synagogues around the world where many families remember the Jews' episodic journey. In addition, there is a specific precept to invite anyone who has no family to join in the celebration. So, too, the twelve apostles were gathered with Jesus and each other to sing, talk, pray, eat, and solemnize this holiest of events. Again, not one man is named; we guess that they are all there. So too Judas, the betrayer. Why did the betrayal occur during the Passover phase of Jewish life? Also, the echoes of the triumphant entry into Jerusalem are here because of the instructions to two of them as with the donkey, to follow a person to a house and ask for the room therein for their supper.

Passover is a time of celebration today. Then as well, the passage out of Egyptian bondage was a great story of endurance and deepening of God's relationship with the Hebrew people. Here we have, smack in the middle of this fact, the handing over of the Man of Freedom to bondage. The falling into the hands of oppressors, Herodians, and Romans was in direct opposition to the message of Passover. Ironic or meant to be? From the God of Salvation to the God of Carnage! How come? It makes me think that Jesus was alone in this period. There is no call about the kingdom being at hand, no mention just now of God. It's all existential—in the moment.

The salvation of the Hebrews in Egypt was due to the lamb's blood on the doorstep so that the spirit "knew" not to claim the firstborn from that hearth. Where did the blood come from? Was it from the butcher or was it sacrificed by the household to accomplish the order of identification? Was it shared with others or did the blood amount to one lamb to one home? This is not known, but it strikes me. If you can, read Exodus 6:6-8 and look into the matter.

Jesus is identifies with the lamb, but also the shepherd of the flock, a striking combination. The lamb connects to the individual. The shepherd of the flock is parallel to the great self, as imaged by Carl Jung. Finally, the echo of the lamb's blood in the blood that will be soon sacrificed—Jesus's blood—which is likewise the co-relation of his blood and wine. It is all beyond my grasp. Nevertheless, the pieces are here so that we can fit them together.

Jesus instructed them to find a spot where they could memorialize Passover, much like He did for the joyous entrance to Jerusalem. And they do find it, just as He directed. I think the discovery of the room is exactly correct for them to be together for the last time. Whether because of prearrangement or intention, they find the accommodations. I do not want to make too much of this feat, as it is a bit irrelevant, though remarkable to witness.

Reading into this scene is not easy. There are no specifics except that the betrayal is there. The Passover event is transformed into a "love feast," so called. There is a magnificent amount of poetry to contemplate, and Jesus leads it all, as a rabbi of the time should. Looking at the facts, we have apparent elements of the Passover that still go on. There is the washing bowl, the unleavened bread, the wine, the apostles, a meal, and a leader. Of course, there are no apostles at Passover. The elemental choice however is still present. Those few who do celebrate this have self-selected.

Jesus's betrayer is called out and condemned. Judas will have a life of dis-ease after handing Jesus over to the powers that be. "It would be better to not have lived!" I paraphrase. Judas will be dead to the world and he will be recalled forever as the betrayer. This is his destiny. You can make of this what you want, that he enabled the end to come about, he was needed to for the process, etc. The fact remains that Judas is the agent in passing Jesus, the carpenter's son who is a troublemaker and the fomenter of a rebellion, to "them." All the sublime thinking wrinkles in the end—Judas is a treasonist.

Again, as I write I am fascinated; why was the betrayal and death of Jesus so tied into the Passover rite? Perhaps because the time is so solemn that any preventative action by the powers would be mitigated. The rite of Passover recalls the process of freedom from the Egyptians in all its trials and tribulations, facilitating the formation of a people and the eventual arrival in the Promised Land. In this night there is the process of the Holy Spirit, of freedom for the interior life, which is magnified because of the relationship to the God, a further elaboration of God's relation to man as incarnated in Jesus. To get to where they wanted to go, the "Hebrew people" had to die to their life and existence in the comfort of Egypt—this was a form of sacrifice. Jesus magnified and deepened that understanding with His death, and sacrificed Himself on behalf of his apostles and disciples. Here we have the sentient union of man and God.

In the midst of the Passover night, Jesus deepens the understanding of life and breaks our bondage and death's hold on us. There is no mention of heaven herein. There is the subliminal suggestion that deep roots bind us to the Mystery of Life, that eternity is the ribbon that runs through cells. Eternity is also in the most basic of items, bread and wine, in our blood moved seemingly forever by our hearts, in its rhythm, the beat in and the beat out. Eternity of liveliness—this cannot be denied. A new agreement, as Phillips calls it, is objectified in the final dinner among friends and an enemy in their midst. The dinner is the solidifying night of this group and movement, for it is a movement of the spirits of a small set of human beings who sense and will later apprehend the full meaning of it all. It occurred through a glass darkly then, among the community of believers.

Jesus transforms this night into the jumping-off point for centuries of struggle, glory, infamy, and transformation of flesh into soul called Christianity. He knew at the end of the meal that He was going to do the next days by himself, not with the aid of His followers. Good Hebrews that they are, they are not ready—yet. He is going down that big road by Himself. God is mentioned as a respite just before the dinner is broken, and they leave for the garden where the challenging ardor begins. Funny that the garden is perhaps an echo of Eden, full of olive trees, a sign of peace and victory.

BETRAYAL TO THE MARROW (MARK 14:29–36)

The last section ends with a quote from Zechariah 13:7: "I will smite the shepherd and the sheep will be scattered abroad." Smite, as in hit or kill, refers here to the unmitigated abandonment of Jesus by all who are his followers and Judas' hard act of betraying Jesus to the powers that be. Of course, in the heightened stress of the last days of Jesus, those around Him would scatter for the hills, leave Him bereft, forsake the leader of the pack, disavow all acquaintance-ship, leave the scene of the "crime," be a quisling and just plain run off abroad. Who would not, since the closing knot is there and the noose is tightening. Peter is not exactly a rock at the moment, although in other gospels he draws a sword (not bad for a fisherman). Bold action. But Mark remembers Him in another way.

In fact they all swear their steadfastness right then to Jesus. We do not read of it here. What is so interesting is the polarity of opposites in the section. Jesus, the Holy One, while the others are broken; Jesus praying while the rest sleep; Jesus, the Ascendant Blessed One, while Peter is bluffing; Jesus the non-victim of Judas the betrayer; and—the ultimate polarity—God allows the agony to play out. Is this true regarding betrayal and the agony of Jesus? Is this according to God's plan? These are profound, eternal questions.

This returns me to the question of what God is. It pushes me to raise the question of incarnation and why God did such a thing then. In order to answer the question, I suppose I would have to have the mind of Jesus or state God's intention. Neither of these is likely. The Christ event is now carried out to its conclusion; His betrayal, agony, crucifixion, and resurrection to the remaining apostles suggests in human terms God's timeless testament to His creation, mankind. It cannot be otherwise. Man has to be man and God has to be God. God shows up "where we are overcome, where we give out, that is the deity." (Carl Jung, *Memories, Dreams and Reflections*)

Sadly we see the scene in the garden of Gethsemane, where Jesus prostrates Himself before the Almighty, begging to be released. Knowing what is ahead, Jesus prays unto despair. Who has not known the silence on the other end of this type of supplication? And yet He prays. The innocent question is, "Why pray in a garden, this one specifically?" Why not a synagogue, or in the Passover feast room? I mentioned earlier that this is an echo of the Garden of Eden, and this is the end of the arc of Jesus's life, where the Genesis was the beginning. Interesting, too, that Jesus is interpreted as the second Adam.

There are points in the gospel where you intuit consciousness breaking into an awareness about the kingdom, but unlike an intellectual "mind thing." Such spirit points are rare. This *is* such a spot in the Gospel of Mark. Here the Trinity likely *is* present—God, Son, and the Holy Spirit, together in passion.

Of course, before this level of consciousness, everyman sleeps. The flesh is weak and the spirit is willing. A big Passover meal, it is late, and unconsciously they know what was at hand. "Look, here comes my betrayer." Betrayed, Jesus walks intentionally into the hands of evil men without abhorrence.

Dear Father (Mark 14:36–43)

"Dear Father," He says, "all things are possible to you. Please let me not have to drink this cup! Yet it is not what I want but what you want."

This is the prayer to God in Gethsemane; this is Jesus's vineyard. What to make of it? Supplication, entreaty, plea, petition, humility, meekness, vulnerability, exposure. The pain is transparent. Pain, in this context, is Jesus's awareness that His time is truly short.

This is the only overt prayer we know of that Mark attributes to Jesus. We know He prayed to God for those He healed. We know He prayed for the miracle of the loaves and fishes, and we know He prayed at the Passover meal. Jesus was constantly in prayer. In fact, no one knows whether Jesus prayed this at the time. Really, the garden of Gethsemane was not televised to an audience. This is Mark's holy intuition regarding what Jesus prayed and how He suffered.

"Dear Father," such an intonation. Calling the one who put you in this situation dear, well, that is something. We call people whom we are really close to dear, not an abstract It; that is not a "dear." It is a thou, It is God. Jesus had a relationship with God, a personal, up-close knowing, to call God dear. Jesus had an experience of God. This dear is both a decision and its obverse, a fact.

"All things are possible to you," in your wildest dreams. Yet all "things" are possible to you, God. Beyond time, space, and all dimension, and in this time, space, and its dimension, God moves and unfolds, disappears. We see it but through a glass darkly and then manifestly. In addition, we can be enlightened to God. To speak in this manner, Jesus suggests a kingly Father. Call it omnipotent, and yet there is no response but Jesus's knowledge of His imminent death. What is not possible to God? Really, what could or would God not do? Recall the beginning of the gospel: "this is my Son in whom I am well pleased." Okay, God is pleased now too, I assume, yes? And yet God is silent, or so it seems in the words on the page. We are both stuck with and struck by the question again, "What is God?"

"Please," The word of request. Here Jesus beseeches the Mystery to manifest Itself. The servant says please to the master, so to speak. Can I please get your attention? If only it were simple to ask and receive a reaction. This is what Jesus sought, a reaction to His life thus far. Perhaps like this, "You have seen what I have done; can I not die a gruesome death?" Oh, so real.

"Let me not have to drink this cup." We witnessed "the cup" at the Last Supper. Here is the symbol again. It holds something—wine, water, blood, life, and death. It is also the holy mixing bowl where life is sliced and diced. Can I say this: it is a symbol of the life force in that it holds Jesus's blood, so it is also the Holy Grail image. To drink of it is to drink to and drink of life; here it is imaged to be the drink of death. The phrase seems to center on the idea of God forcing Jesus to die. As if there were a command to the effect that this draught is God's will, and this brings the issue full circle to what is God's will here?

"Yet, it is not what I want but what you want." The force of this line is right up there among the many lines in the gospels which we must ponder. If there is choice, it comes to what God wants and we choose it. Very definite. What is God's choice? What does God want? There is not another option, so there is only this one step, to go to the cross through the ordeal and ignominious steps, ultimately to death, and from there to eternity with God. This phrase really implies a knowledge of God's mind; I am not too surprised.

Today, this section may seem a cop-out to many in this world of twerking. In this world of individual potential and faux self-realization, such docility is unheard of. Myself first, before any other Power. Today this Power of Being with which Jesus is entwined is one among many powers and principalities, a 'relative being' visualized and supplanted by George Burns and Morgan Freeman. Or, God is merely one with a throne, beard and hair. Jesus' God is not hip and definitely not cool. Very un-humorous. We are unaware, unconscious of the Godhead, and have no language to describe the experience, nothing like they did back then. After all, what is conjured when you read "Kingdom of God?" A long-lost something. Right?

"Are you still asleep and take your ease?" asks Jesus of the apostles. It may just as well be us.

Jesus, the Masked Bandit (Mark 14:43–53)

The opening lines read like a newspaper article, don't they?

The sharp shift from Jesus's desperation in the garden is in contrast to the calmness before the mob with swords and staves. It is almost like a shift in the universe, an electron shift in physics, or turning on a light in a dark room, as we see Jesus before the mob sent by the Pharisees and the other powers that be to gather Jesus before the Romans. There is a hint of sarcasm, a touch of resignation or let's-get-on-with-it mood in the passage.

Much of the early sentences of this section are odd to me. My sense is that Jesus is widely known. He is not a hidden figure, but ever in the public eye, visible to the powers that be and certainly a rebel whose face is recognized fairly easily. Though no "wanted" posters appear in the synagogues, still there is a stamp to his visage. Thus, the mob arrives armed for battle! Clubs, staves, swords, etc., are in plain description. "Let's get ready to rumble!" the loudspeaker is the absent voiceover. Again, the kiss must be metaphorical in that the mob is either composed of total boobs, mercenaries from elsewhere, or living under a rock, as if the kiss is needed to identify Him as the one to grab and hold, then hand to the Romans. The hoodwink, in as much as Judas' "kisses him affectionately" is double, with both the kissing and calling him Master.

Then two uncharacteristic things happen: the "somebody" cuts off the high priest's servant's ear and Jesus calls on His disciples to cool it, saying, "So you've come out with your swords and staves to capture me as if I were a bandit, have you?" This is satirical and mocking.

"Day after day, I was with you in the temple, teaching, and you never laid a finger on me." Why now? What caused His gig to be up? No worries: "The Scriptures must be fulfilled." As in, "This is really outside our hands here. You have to do what you have to do, and I will not prevent it!"

This scene is very intense. Judas, the purser, is the betrayer. He has already gone over to the dark side, and all of the apostles "deserted him as well and made their escape." Oh, my. Jesus is alone before His captors. And the desertion is total in that one of the followers is so scared that He runs away naked. Jesus is the only one with a shred of courage, character, or bravery. He, in contrast, is fully clothed and the personification of poise.

A few minor closing thoughts: Jesus did not castigate the disciple who cut off the high priest servant's ear. It is stated as a done deal, and there are no repercussions! The mob did not go after the attacker. Standing back from this section, I again wonder, why now? What brought matters to a head? Was it completely Judas's doing? Again, this is in the context of the Passover! This isn't just any old night of the week. The powers that be need an opening to capture Jesus, and this is it.

So They Marched Jesus Away (Mark 14:53–65)

Mark opens with the title phrase of this section.

Can you see it? Imagine the scene at night marching through Jerusalem. Is it night? It would have to be in the progression of the gospel. It would not be quiet. Could it be? Streets are empty, soldiers marching, a throng of people around Jesus, milling, motion, movement of a mob, His apostles, and "Peter followed at a safe distance." He is the only one mentioned explicitly, so perhaps Mark based this account on Peter's witness. Or is this section Holy Fiction? We will never know.

The high priest is not named. I wonder why? Certainly he is someone who is part of the powers that be who want Jesus dead. Along with the high priest there are lesser chiefs and elders gathered again clandestinely to find a way to stick it to Jesus. "But they failed completely." This scene is a kangaroo court, something out of a show trial from communism. False witnesses, perjurers, and so forth are marched in, all of whom point fingers at Him and then are ushered out and possibly paid off like Judas or any other quisling.

"But even so their evidence conflicted." Jesus remains silent through all of this. The high priest then accuses Jesus of blasphemy because Jesus confesses to the high priest's accusation that He is "Christ, the Son of the Blessed One." To this accusation He says, "I am. Yes, you will all see the Son of Man sitting at the right hand of power, coming in the clouds of heaven." What an elliptical phrase for which to crucify him. And, Jesus was merely quoting extant Scripture. Psalm 110 and especially Daniel 7 suggest that the line was a "midrash" on them. The phrasing is declarative in tone. The sentence seems to summon them to a higher plane.

What are these phrases, anyway? What could they suggest, because meaning is elusive and it may take a lifetime of essential reflection to unwrap them? First, here again there is absolutely no person who writes down the scene as it occurs, transcribing the words or actions among the participants. So what we have here is some oral history told to or by Peter, or another associate inside who eventually was converted to "Christianity."

Second, the high priest's question to Jesus was answered in two parts. The question in itself is curiously stated by the high priest, "Are you Christ, Son of the blessed one?" Could he even speak this way? I wonder. You see, if the high priest used this language, it came from his thoughts or they were put in his mouth by Mark. Or is this a translation issue? Nevertheless, Jesus answers the two-part question with a two-part answer, "I am," and states a theological truism, the Son of Man does sit on the right hand of the Almighty. This is not precedential; rather, this construct was indubitably there from the Old Testament.

Let me look at this more. The key to any good story is identifying the defining moment, it has been said. This is it. It's not the cross scene, it is not the rolling stone event. Why? Here Jesus existentially says what is! It is a statement of the highest order. This is Jesus on our behalf identifying humanity with God the Almighty, the Mystery of Life—I am that I am; I am God's servant on earth. And this is Christ. It is *the Christ.* Not an everyman Christ that will remove people from earthly struggles and daily chores of living, rather that Jesus is the universal salvation event of life. Jesus was doing this holy chore by choice alone, and he is the same one that prayed to have the cup removed. This causes him to wax poetical and say, "Yes, you will all see the Son of Man sitting at the right hand of power, coming in the clouds of heaven." This is the second part, as I said earlier, and is the natural amplification of Jewish thinking. Jesus, the first among equals, pioneered the way to salvation and points to the eternal, the source of life. The poetry suggests or describes to me the possible result of a life lived on behalf of everyman. And Jesus is comfortable with this commission.

A follow-up question comes: "Is the Christ also equal to the Son of Man who will sit on the right hand of power, coming in the clouds of heaven?" By tying the two together, Jesus suggests that Christ and the Son of Man are one. Let's say this is so as an ontological truth. The poetry is dense. Sorting it out suggests a union—God and man—which is majestic, powerful and the source of all that is. This intersection of God and man is the kingdom that all humanity can be within. More so, it implies an action or active force of divinity in the terrestrial plane, a revelation all will "notice here and now." But it is not the surmounting of this veil of tears by the Son of Man, but rather God's incarnation in Jesus to make the earth Its own. It claims this dirty, pear-shaped ball of sacred space: earth is God's stage.

This is, in fact, blasphemy! *It rocks* the consciousness of everyman. The public self of Jesus looks like a bandit, the persona of an ordinary, walking, scratching human being, when in fact, in Jesus, the kingdom of God is here and now.

Returning to the phrase that comes from Jesus's mouth in response to the high priest who indicts Him as the "Christ, Son of the Blessed One," He says, "I am." I note that He does not utter the word Christ reflexively. Then there is the phrase I wrote about above. Since He does not tie Himself to the "Messiah" title, but does unite the two thoughts, it is still not clear what Jesus is pointing to. Perhaps this is pointing to God's union with Jesus.

I do not believe in the assertion that there is another place beside this universe. To sit on the right of power is not a place, and heaven is not a space. I believe that the Son of Man's role is to be kindred with Absolute Being. As the ancients have said, "as it is as above, so below," all around us. Further, the "right hand of power" is a kingly picture, an image suggestive of a profound relationship with Absolute Being. It is regal, royal, and resplendent. It is man and God meeting as one, followed by the phrase, ethereal in its vision, "coming in the clouds of heaven." This is the unmitigated peace that passes all understanding. Jesus is in heaven at this moment, He is at peace when the phrase is uttered. The whole saying is numinous—Absolute Being in the cosmic realm. Cosmic here, imaging the structure of everything known, unknown, beyond time and space, and any dimension.

You know the phrase, "been there, done that"? Well, see His phrase as a Ground of Being condition. Jesus is expressing His experience of It. The only way He can say this is that He is with God, God is with him, and the utterance leaves the faithful in awe. As for everyman, they are in disbelief and remain unready and unconscious of their union with God.

It comes to this: you are either indifferent or live in faith at this point in the Gospel narrative or your life.

MEANWHILE, IN THE BACKYARD (MARK 14:66–END)

This is a short piece, but it is an important one for many. It deals with betrayal again. The best synonyms are perfidy, treason, and letdown. This is not so much giving over Jesus, the leader of the movement, like Judas did earlier. Peter is just plain scared; he is scared silly! Here he is in the backyard of the unnamed high priest in the midst of the enemy, being accused, called out, and pointed at as a member of the bandit group of Galileans. Admit it, you are with the Nazarene! When confronted, Peter gets defensive. You do not know what you are talking about; I do not know the man, and leave me out of this scene of terror. Peter is fingered. He cannot get away from this fact. Yet, Peter is gutsy enough to be there to witness to what is happening.

Likely, this scene was his to tell. And it took courage to reveal the weakness he showed. Finally, this betrayal "cracks his egg." The pain of the dishonesty drives Peter to greatness, I feel.

Each time he denies the accusations in a more emphatic manner, and the cock crows. Thus, the famous saying foretold by Jesus, "Before the cock crows twice, you will disown me three times!"

What am I to say? Jesus is a fortuneteller? An oracle? He has magic powers? What? There is little doubt that this event likely occurred. There are too many characters with specifics, though the high priest's name is missing. Still, it seems in character for Peter. The other people are real too, as Mark describes them. If Peter is hanging around while Jesus is interrogated, with some input from a few insiders who supported the apostles, the scenes from Judas's betrayal forward are likely in sequence. In the high priest's backyard we have Jesus behaving not as an oracle, but rather as omniscient. Jesus knew His man Peter well. Besides, the denials of Peter are typical human traits under duress. Any normal person would protect his hide when among the enemy—name, rank, and serial number. That's all, folks.

And Peter feels great sorrow, "He broke down and wept." This, too, is a magnificent statement of vulnerability, as I suggested above. It seems to me that the denial preceded the oracular statement of Jesus. Jesus's statement totally affirms the denial; it does not put it down, and is sympathetic. We put Peter down. We disparage him. We pour scorn on Peter for his weakness. Jesus does not. He knows the hearts of men. We are weak, we do prevaricate, we do become defensive, we do not listen, we are thin-skinned, we are full of ourselves, we fall asleep in the midst of Truth, we seek power in the slightest ways, we are Peters—every one of us. Look back over the events of Peter's life before this backyard scene. What a funny guy, this one. Jesus chose this one as "the rock" on which to build a future. Amazing.

What do you think Jesus had in mind by choosing Peter as the next in line? While Peter and Paul are the two who build a Community over the following decades, it is Peter who is the commander and Paul is the executive officer, if you will, of the movement of the Spirit. And in the end, it became more Paul's creation than Peter's; Peter was the Rock, the Atlas who did not shrug.

THE HANDOFF TO PILATE (MARK 15:1–21)

It is strange to me that the high priest and the council waited until dawn to deliver the bandit, Jesus. I guess Pilate slept in and was available only after daylight.

Pilate tries to free Jesus over the course of their meeting. However, like the high priest before who could not find squat to hang Jesus on, other than an ethereal charge of blasphemy, Pilate jumps in to ask the loaded question, "Are you the king of the Jews?" which was pretty much the same question as before the council, and the beat goes on and on and on.

Who recorded this scene or told it to Mark? Surely a follower, since except for the crowd who was gathered during the Passover, the high priest, scribes, guards, elders, et al. did not care a whit for what happened to Jesus. Pilate is cast as ambivalent about Jesus. He tries to set him loose. Why? Perhaps he thinks, "I cannot be bothered with this intrigue," or, "I am bored with this tripe; who cares, whatever; I really do not want to get involved with the nasty people who turned Jesus 'over to him through sheer malice.'" Being in authority, he could be noncommittal. And, I will play the role of civility, a good executioner, and offer the rabble the choice. Barabbas or Jesus, hmm, he thinks to himself. Barabbas may have been a fomenter, as the appellation "rioter" was hung on him by Mark. Could he have been a follower, or merely another crazy from Pilate's point of view? He judges him as Jesus's equal.

Now it gets surreal. Pilate turns to the rabble and asks them to decide Jesus's fate. As if! But then again, maybe it is this way, as Pilate may merely be playing along, even though this could not have happened just this way. The rabble cannot call for Jesus's crucifixion. The Romans rule the land. The rabble cannot succeed except that the Romans allow this proceeding to take place. Pilate is toying with them, "Well, what do *youuuu* want me to do?"

So it goes. As a matter of fact, the closing scene is an echo of the high priest's closing paragraph, where they mock and beat and torture Jesus. The guards dress Jesus up in purple and play with Him, humiliating Him over and over. In the end they put his street clothes on him, march him out, and begin the trudge to Calvary. It is at this point that Jesus assumes the cross and the cross is Jesus—servitude and acting the willing victim.

This is Jesus's death march. It is also probably the most factual. It is likely this process is what the Romans did with criminals—they gave them a cross and watched them struggle unto death. This is suffering beyond my ability to grasp. The cross was likely very heavy, as it had to hold the criminal up. And whether it was a "T" or what we image as the cross really doesn't matter. It had to hold up a man. We read that Jesus had the helping hand of Simon, whom the Romans conscripted on behalf of Jesus. Here again specifics are noted, in that he had a place of origin, Cyrene, Africa, and is the father of Alexander and Rufus. Thus

I would conclude that this is really an event. Who is he beyond this? What role does he play symbolically is a more interesting question.

The cross has been a symbol associated with Jesus, as in Jesus died for our sins by dying on the cross. The cross was the way to heal the breach between God and man. This begs the question of why—why was there a breach, a gap between God and man?

Second, what does death on the cross unite? And how does it do it?

Third, it is called the sacrifice on the cross. What did Jesus sacrifice?

Fourth, Jesus was hung on the cross as a criminal. The inscription "King of the Jews" reflected his crime. He dared to defy the Roman and Jewish powers that be!

Fifth, what is the "sin"?

But I am getting ahead of myself.

Simon is brought over to assist Jesus to get to His death. Why? Was this the usual process toward Calvary, wherever that is? Simon's role is as a quasi-brother-in-arms to Jesus. Was He so worn due to the torture that this help is called for? Simon carried the cross. I suspect Jesus did also. So, like the thieves later on, you have a kind of "Greek chorus," suggesting an interpretation of events. None of these people were interviewed after the event regarding their experience of what happened. Thus, they are placed there with a message. Simon is a counterpoint to the betrayer, Judas. He assists Jesus in the transition from life to His death. Jesus carries the cross, as I said, a symbol of life, through the streets to Skull Hill, Golgotha, Calvary, His crucifixion. He carries himself to the point of His death with willingness, choice, and purpose. This is heavy work. If all before was preparation for this event, then the transmittal of the cross is illuminating, and Jesus's death ended in a lightning storm, with illumination. Therefore, Simon is the service so that Jesus does not die *en route*.

The Cross is the combination of the Tree of Life and the Tree of Knowledge. Imagine that life is the horizontal axis and knowledge the vertical axis of the New Tree, the Tree of the Kingdom of God. Jesus fully realizes the role of the Son of Man in the Salvator, opening the way to man's centrality in the universe. Jesus opened the gates closed by a misstep, perhaps a fatal flaw, in the beginning—Eden—to both the Mystery of Life (the Transcendent) and man's life mission (incarnation). The cross shows the upward and downward direction at once, the intersection, man's position at the crossroads between transcendence and transience.

The cross and man stand as a choice. Jesus gives you an image about a life as spiritual journey in human garb. Jesus is not irritated one bit by His transit. He takes up His cross day one and successfully presents God's kingdom at Calvary, which, of course, is Jesus's outlook as well: a kingdom internal and beyond at once. God is aligned to Itself right there. The sacrifice is His life vessel and an ego with a body. And the sin? It is the separation that is life. It is the human condition that has fallen into abject disconnection from its mystery, depth, and greatness, an existence that forgets and ignores unity with God. It is mistaking disunity because of diversity.

Again, Jesus reopened the gates of Eden and unity not as an enclosed sphere, but rather as a center, a self-contained whole, which is unbounded by characterization.

Let us pray:

Called or not called, God is there.
Seen or not seen, God is there.
Felt or unfelt, God is there.
Touched or not touched, God is there.
Heard or not heard, God is there.
Experienced or not experienced, God is there.
Wanted or not wanted, God is there.
Known or not known, God is there.
Understood or not understood, God is there.
Spoken or not spoken, God is there.
Sword or no sword, God is there.
Possible or impossible, God is there.
Faithful or indifferent, God is there.
Life or death, God is there.
Faithful or indifferent, God is there.
Yesterday, today and tomorrow, God is there.
Now God is here.
Amen

SEE HOW JESUS DIES (MARK 15:22–42)

"They took him to a place called Golgotha, which means Skull Hill," a low-key beginning to a glorious end. This line jumped off the page when I read it. Mark, in his typical unexpressive manner, starts with "they," as in the powers that be, Romans or high priests? "They took him," how is this possible if Jesus is carrying the cross? Or is He? "Him" must be Jesus, so why not say it?

"They offered him some drugged wine but he would not take it." To ease the pain, this is standard operating procedure.

"Then, they crucified him."

Three steps.

The crucifixion is a symbol (literally "that which is thrown together or cast together" –Dictionary.com). It is an event that happens to Jesus. It is not His invention. Folks were executed in this fashion long before Jesus was put to death by crucifixion. Jesus's death filled the symbol with greater power than had been witnessed before. Because Jesus willed and embraced this event—not the reverse, where everyman sees himself as victimized—Jesus cast all together in the marketplace, the secular world (and what can be more commonplace than a hanging in those days), His aspirations for life.

Yes, He suffers. And the acidity of the vinegar offering shows it to be so, that this is the marketplace. Precisely here, on Golgotha, is daily bread and life everlasting. His aspirations, ostensibly, are the establishment of the kingdom of God, the community of the Passover, and the call to do unto others as you would to yourself. It has been said that Jesus died on our behalf. And He died for His reasons as well. He did this to Himself, and the world reacted. It stopped, the skies parted, and the earth shook. And people noticed. The first conversion occurred there at the foot of the cross by the centurion. The conversion was not to Christianity, but to grasping the fact that Jesus is a mensch in 100 percent sense of that word. He is the Son of Man. And that, yes, dying there is life in full despite the countenance of God's absence. "My God, my God, why have You forsaken me?" This is one of the most expressive lines in Mark's gospel, and Jesus utters this as God's Son. This thrusts us into the eternal mystery of the Trinity. It supports the idea that God has an aspect that God does not fully know or is conscious of. Yet, this mystery deepens the symbolism of the event.

In addition, the bandits who were crucified at the same time, "one on each side of him," emphasized the commonality of this scene. Witness the placard, "King of the Jews," among the common man, suffering fully. This triptych, a three again, pictures them utterly humanly. Recall the mountaintop experience of the apostles, the transfiguration, which seems to prefigure in hindsight, this profound scene of death (with profound life). This scene adds to the transfiguration's impact. And both are on mountains, spiritual heights, where life can be seen in full.

The spiritual mountain is tortuously climbed. It is done on Skull Hill, where everyman can look up and witness it. Here is the fact that they want to avoid. If you are looking for the Messiah to take you out of life into an ersatz heaven, then turn your head and eyes from this to Golgotha. There is glorious life at the transfiguration scene, and equally on Skull Hill.

This level of alteration of the physical reality there at the cross, the skies darkening for three hours during the day, occurred likewise during the baptism when the skies parted. God spoke to man (baptism), and Jesus (man) spoke to God (crucifixion). Jesus submerged His life in the beginning and at the cross as well. In fact, God does not forsake the Son of Man. At such points, worlds can stop and the Mystery will visibly respond. God's forceful response, however, made the disambiguation that much more profound. Time stands still at death and eternity takes over. A sudden transformation takes place, a shaking of the foundations; the props on the stage of life are realigned for the next feature. Truly, God ascended at the crucifixion, leaving behind the carcass of Jesus.

Finally, the scene at the cross ends with Mary of Magdalene and Mary, Jesus's mother, off in the distance. No Peter or other apostles, disciples, or followers mentioned, but the women. This is very interesting. They are named followers in the sense that they followed Jesus in His travels and even to the cross. Now why are they singled out? The gruesomeness of Jesus's death makes it more incumbent that the men should be there. Yet they are absent, unmentioned. And it is not clear whether this is Mary, Jesus's mother and if so, Jesus had four brothers, James, Joseph, Simon, and Judas (Matthew 13:55) and a sister. It is also told by Mark that there were many other women who came to Jerusalem. This feminine presence is noteworthy and plain.

From Baptism to Tomb to Resurrection (Mark 15 and 16)

I have chosen to consider the last two chapters of Mark together, though the last section from 16:9 to the end is an appendix of dubious provenance. Still, I can see them as one—a "whole cloth."

You may recall that Mark starts the gospel with Jesus's baptism. God speaks loudly and clearly about the satisfaction He has for His Son. Anyone would wish such an affirmation from his father. God also portends this end that Jesus reached. Reading between the lines, you know where His storied life is going, not because it already happened in work, word, and deed (God's mind), but to be pleased with someone implies a deeper knowledge than surface. Second, John the Baptist's baptism was a "mark of a complete change of heart and for the forgiveness of sins." This, ladies and gentlemen, is not an everyman hope for change or the coming of a Messiah, a current ruler of import, a person to "remove the struggles of everyman's life, give us comfort from this anxiety-filled day, night, year, and moment." This is everyman's prayer. Oh, and get the freaking Romans out as well! This change of heart suggests habitation of another sort within the kingdom of God.

The expiation on the cross and Jesus's cry of suffering and pain despairing God's presence is in contradiction to the grandeur of the Baptismal laying on of the hands, a sending out, so to speak. The cross is the abyss, the void into which we can fall. It is the "I do not know where I am going" cry of Jesus. This is equivalent to our instantaneous loss of sight. The cross, the World Axis, acts as the tower for the body and blood we heard at the Last Supper. Jesus sheds it unwaveringly. Everything that is holy is sacrificed right there on Skull Hill. Jesus dies and the new covenant is welded between the incomprehensible and *terra firma's* inhabitants. This had to happen just this way. Mark does not dress up this sequence of events at all.

Jesus's power grew continually from the baptism until He died, and this is carried on and described in this last section. But the baptism of Spirit, the baptism of Jesus, was a moment in time where the "heavens split open and the Spirit came down upon him." Secondly, Jesus did have a sword, as all kings do; his was a spiritual sword that dismembered Mary Magdalene's "seven evil spirits." What they were we do not know, we can only guess. Only a spiritual sword can dispel seven evil spirits and then eternally mend sins. Third, I am reminded of the ancients' song, "Without God, undertake nothing." On that cross Jesus visibly and completely united God and man forever, and this was initiated in love and pleasure at baptism. The breach was no more.

"The tomb wombed all this." Joseph of Arimathea speaks to Pilate for permission to take Jesus down from the cross and place Him in the grave. They prepare Him as anybody would be prepared at the time of death. Remember that this is Jesus, the rabbi as well, so the law has to be followed, I am sure. Into the tomb Jesus goes. The women of Jesus see where He is laid, a solid rock tomb with a big stone in front.

(Here the ancients knew the trip was to the underworld for three days, the metaphor for gathering the mana, spiritual energy, to rise from the dead.) The women are there to prep His body for this excursion wrapped in white; this is their job. And what a sorrow it must have been. Mother, friend, and relative, they weep. The grief is unfathomable. Such tears for a leader, a son, and a holy man, Son of Man, the one who opened the gates to the kingdom of God.

Rebirth. Resurrection. New Testament.

Let me repeat that the unification of the breach, the at-one-ment with the incomprehensible, the Mystery of Life, Higher Power, whatever you name it, occurred in the sacrifice of Jesus's life for everyman. The road through the forest of life was notched. The boat for the ocean of unknown was carved. The profundity of the event of Jesus two thousand years ago is a fact. The prior description of breaking unity into many, first heard of in the garden, and repeated earlier in the creation story, is enfolded by Jesus's rising and ascending to unity as Its representative, fully incarnated into the unity, God. Now we can, you and I, attest to the way it is done.

Perhaps all this begs the question of the resurrection as told in the final section of Mark. From the tomb—again there are the women of Jesus trekking to bring spices for Jesus's body, not the men. Perhaps this is what women did at that time. (Here, a why may be appropriate.) They are greeted by a young man in a white robe (purity, transformation, enlightenment, pallor of death) who informs them that Jesus is not here, and they must go see the (men), Peter, etc., and tell the men to go back to Galilee as Jesus told them to do. This is what is written.

The body is gone.

Well, where did it go? Was it there to begin with? So, it seems that the women accompanied and placed Him in the tomb and wrapped Jesus in a linen shroud. Could they have forgotten the location? No, yet there is not a body to be found.

Paul believed in the bodily resurrection as written in 1 Corinthians 15:52–55. "O Death, where is thy sting? O grave, where is thy victory?" And this is pretty much what all Christians believe. The resurrection is the faith statement or position concerning Christianity. And it is bodily, I repeat. It is a reconstitution, a complete restoring, or restitution, according to Paul. Let's say that Paul has this faith.

Can I?

I am drawing to the end of this process of contemplating Mark's gospel. Before I answer my own question, I have to draw back a little bit more and place my "cards" down on the table. I do not have faith in Paul's assertion about the resurrection. I thus fall outside of the Christian circle. I cannot say there is a bodily resurrection or else I would also have to have faith in *ignis fatuus* (apparitions). Yet even Jung mentions in his autobiography that for God, everything is possible. I do have faith in the Trinity, the Triune God, Father, Son, and Holy Spirit. And something happened here that is not exactly clear, as so many other items in the Gospel are not. This does not and should not lead me directly to a resurrection event, and thus faith. So again, what happened? No body—did it rise and go disappearing to Galilee?

This, 'the rising from the dead event', is not in the realm of fact. Some have suggested that it is a spiritual resurrection that happens in everyday life. Thus it completes the natural 'to die is to live' invention. It may also be expressed as a restoration or restitution in the hearts of the Jesus's followers It is an experience of God—in totality of body, spirit, soul and self.

There was a death on the cross no doubt; the powers that be wanted that to take place. Historically, this is as close as we will get in this and the other gospels. The historical debate about this is more or less open. There is no evidence for it or against it!

I conclude that the resurrection took place in the hearts, minds, and spirits of the then-and-always faithful. This is precisely our relationship to God—it is an experience. Science and religion use two different lexicons to talk about the same universe, the same kingdom of God or, if you will, the four-dimensional time-space coordinates. Resurrection is a concept in which the cross is a symbol. The cross is an emblem, whereas the resurrection is a statement of faith. Both have faith qualities, yet the cross is not something you have to have faith in except in connection with the fact that to die is to live. When the self dies (forget the ego's little deaths), when it dies to itself and its internal structures and its gods, the things that it bows to, and bows instead to the Ground of Being or the God beyond God, there is rising. Also, when Jesus said "I and the Father are one," there was no ego, self, or being separate from the Mystery of Life. There is no life and death, Both are vanquished, life becomes the eternal now and death becomes the eternal now.

More, in the crucifixion narrative, the night that falls at Jesus's death points to the end of not only His life, but also to end of day and the coming rebirth of light—here called resurrection. It is not a symbol, an internal event, nor clairvoyant, but His existence in the souls, hearts, and spirits of His disciples. Writing of the bodily rebirth, Paul alludes to this in I Corinthians 15:52–55. However, Paul does not have the "verbal technology" we do today. Perhaps I am pushing words into his mouth that are not there. Perhaps Jesus was so real for Paul that it bordered on physical, that there could be no other faith but full bodily resurrection, full restitution and restoration. If you read this, you will find Paul talking of the "end of times" with the trumpet phrases, and also a current, this-moment restitution as if it were an enlightenment event that cuts across the bodily corruption he sees at fault. This must relate to the Jewish position on the body as corrupted that was held at the time. Today it's a bit different. It is the dropping off of the body so that incorruption and immortality can occur, it is just that the putting-on part is so hard to get to. *How* do you put on immortality? Then, and only then, we read, "Death is swallowed up in victory." That's Paul for you! Here, Jesus may say, that is the kingdom of God.

Back to Mark's gospel: all that they knew, the two Marys and Salome, was that he was gone from the tomb and the disciples were to be met by Jesus in their home town.

Did they have a word then for *resurrection*? It is not in the gospel of Mark. Mark says according to the angel/man, "he is risen." Do they correspond, or am I splitting hairs? Rising is to go up. Jesus has expanded his "game plan." Resurrection denotes a different cup of tea. In fact, the word resurrection is from the thirteenth century old French, *resurgere*. God took Jesus to Itself. All souls go to the source. Yet, the intensity of this event at that time left a holy residue on the witnesses, moving them to grasp the possibility, nay the likelihood, that restitution or rebirth would happen. It had to occur in life, theirs palpably. He is risen with all the implications therefore in place. Please imagine the experience and the *future* of the apostles, Mary, and all the disciples. This, today, is called awesome.

A few minor points: I mentioned that possibly the first convert was the centurion who beheld Jesus's death. To use a phrase from this last section that applied to Joseph of Arimathaea, "who was himself prepared to accept the kingdom of God," this best describes the life of one who is a disciple or soon to be. For us it is like Paul's experience of being thrown off the horse. It is being struck with the experience of total wholeness and forgiveness of all your sins—the brokenness is healed, the gap is jumped, we experience acceptance by the Ground of Being, and we are in it faithfully.

Next, the daughter disciples go to Jesus's tomb in the morning as the sun is rising. Imagine it. At the tomb the "angel" says he is risen. Then, in the hearts of the believers is the risen Jesus, now the Christ. Surely you get it. And they "were trembling with excitement. They did not dare to breathe a word to anyone." Trembling with excitement—what an image from the daughter disciples. It is almost sensual. And this is the psyche talking here; it is their souls resonating in the experience, the prospect of Jesus's rising.

The ancient appendix is obviously not Mark's work, nor are the last three sentences. Okay, they were stitched into the gospel for good measure. By whom? Doesn't matter. The story rolls on into many meetings, sightings, and greetings by Jesus to His followers. It feels like an epitaph, the affirmation of what was already said. Certainly the last three lines are part of a creed for the faithful and the vocation of the apostles.

Mark's Gospel: Parting Thoughts

From the beginning I stated that Mark's gospel is an oral record, inspired and stimulating so that the listener has an experience like the one the teller had. Jesus inspired it, the disciples remembered it, they shared it, elaborated and embellished it, and eventually it was written down. To me, this gospel is clearly a record that stitches together a narrative that appears to be historical in nature. The gospel is not a reenactment. It is the breath felt today of the experience –being with Jesus.

Reading over the years as closely as I could, threading it and treading where not many have gone, I witness a Man of God, nay the Salvator (Savior), who is the Christ. Jesus had the nature of God. But Mark's gospel is gapped. The record is full of connectors and bridges and phraseology that evidences (experiences from which inferences can be drawn) the writer's own question, "What happened, next, then, and …." None of this diminishes the effect on the reader. Again, the writer affected us greatly. Written well here by Philippa Gregory, "What happened? What was said? It was a secret meeting, and no note of it has survived. 'Oh no,' said I the historian: We simply don't know what happened. 'Hurrah,' said I the novelist: This is where fiction comes in; I can make it up. Indeed I have to make it up." (WSJ 9/10/12, On Historical Fiction)

Is it irreverent to think and write this? I think not. Mark had to do what he had to do, assuming it is a he; we do not really know. This is not that important, really, as the daughter disciples played a big role throughout the life of Jesus and certainly were critical day in and day out in the generations after.

Second, I'm never sure who is speaking.

Is it Mark? Is it what has been told to Mark? Is it Mark's imagination? Is it inspired by the Holy Spirit? Is it Jesus, or interpretation, or a daisy chain of embellishment? All together now—it has become the gospel of Mark.

Certainly there were scribes later on in the movement. Were the apostles literate? Peter's epistles are of questionable provenance, as are some of Paul's. There they are for us, for our edification and inspiration.

I repeat, this in no way diminishes the impact or import of the Word. If this is the case, then why bring it up? This is crucial in that it forces the reader to grapple with the words and effect, not as literal, but as archetypal. If that Word is too loosey-goosey, try exemplary. The words in the Gospel and the Epistles have to be grounded in reality, the type we live in today, as the words have been passed to us from another reality, over two thousand years ago. People may not have been much different, but the times really were different compared to now. My thinking throughout has been archetypal theology, if I had to name it. Additionally, to say words and use them without knowing what they point to, such as sin, is to merely mouth three letters correctly. They have to be grounded in life as we know it today and be backed up by some experience. This brings the *sin* word to life and does not behave as a metaphysical cudgel.

So everything is true as written in the gospel of Mark? Yes, and to the point that as we carry the words into today they can become true for readers right this moment. Repeating for the nth time, the experiences of the apostles were likely miraculous. The experiences were theirs alone and also in their communities. They shared it among themselves, the events, emotions, and knowledge they had. But in time, even the most amazing, dazzling, highest mountaintop experiences were worn down and smoothed out. Our minds are like that. Jesus had an experience that everyone who encountered Him got. The written word can barely carry out and only in fragments what truly went on.

And some of the experiences were cryptic. Some of the passages are totally incomprehensible to me and most others. What of these? For example, going to the tomb and not finding a body. Recalling that Jesus said that He would rise in three days, what else could the disciple daughters do but tremble in awe? This was fear and trembling in greater magnitude than seeing a hummingbird light on your head. This was awe before divine providence.

Again, this gospel of Mark is what was remembered and canonized. What was not written down, forgotten, diminished, or gone under? Has it disappeared? Yes. This record is what was shared and inclined to be shared. There are other gospels that are halos to the four that are sanctioned. They teach differently and have their own impacts.

Overall, there are more holes here than in a round of Swiss cheese. Yet even the holes are worthy of reflection. Of course, in the beginning of the gospel, we read about Jesus fully grown. Why? Where was He earlier? Jesus shows up with John the Baptist as already matriculated, chosen, and ready to go, having a point of view with an end in mind, a heart, and a soul. Where does He really come from? In other gospels, Luke and Matthew, there is the embellishment of Mark's stories. Yet here too, much is 'out to hunch'. In the passages in the gospel where no one is there but Jesus (and since He did not have a tablet device to record His thoughts, experiences, and dialogue), these were obviously—what? These events were created by those who were close to Jesus and could project what happened. (Yes, I am saying that some was made up.) Even where there were groups of apostles or disciples, the dialogues are bare bones. There are the many miracles, some in a group setting and some among just a few apostles, that raise questions about the events as they were written. For example, two miracles seem to be the same in their wording. In both Mark 1:21 and 5:1, the "deranged" people's phrases and dialogue with Jesus are approximately the same. They are two different events. Perhaps this is idiomatic. What are we to make of this? There were many apostles present. Also, this could be the translation by Phillips.

I could go on, and you could find more instances of just this; see Mark 4:33–34. Here it is written, "So he taught them his message with many parables such as their minds could take in. He did not speak to them at all without using parables, although in private he explained everything to his disciples." Well, then there are secrets, inner sanctum knowledge and hidden truths. Again, what these are is anyone's guess.

Finally, a word about my method. Using a process of going from the narrative, we can drop into the psychological and emotional, followed by the theological, and ending in the essence –ontology, where we engage

God. Therefore we culminate in an experience of Ground of Being. I used what was once called the Art Form Method in order to unlock the meaning by being systematic. This was my approach and process over the many observations. Originally, it related to photography, as in photo-mosaic. It was applied and utilized by a radical group on the west side of Chicago in the sixties.

Wanted or Not Wanted, God is There. And So is Jesus, and Now the Holy Spirit

Over lunch a close friend and I spoke about God and Its action in our lives and of those around us. Worry not, I have atheists and secular humanists who are friends as well, and agnostics and lay-abouts. (Recognize that the opposite of faith is not atheism. The opposite of faith is indifference.) As it is written, it rains on the just and the unjust alike. We spoke about what God means to us. If anyone was listening in, they surely must have thought we were off our rocker. My darling wife says I pontificate; well, I have earned my stripes. In fact, according to surveys, a large number of people today do not identify with any mainstream Christian church. To talk of God openly is crazy talk and admitting any strong faith in the marketplace is calling down others' derision.

In any case my friend's support was deeply welcome, as my wife was very, very ill at the time, and we spoke of my life-trials. My wife has had a great many complications. It has been said that there is life, with its many events, and what we do in relationship to them. The confrontation between these two forces makes us who we are. So true.

Her illness delayed this book by a number of months. I poured my life into her, so I had little left to share in these pages.

In order to wrap up this book, I have to admit again that the most important question is "Do you or do you not believe in God?" To me there is no distinction between the God of the Bible or God in general. There was a God before the Bible. If that is too abstract, then try this: to whom do you bow or bend your knee? Start thinking here: Who or what is your god?

In an effort to formalize my faith, I have written a type of creed. As you know, I do not believe in a bodily resurrection. This places me outside of the Christian faith. I cannot say the Apostles' Creed, thus I am "around the bend" to the Catholics, a type of heathen, like Harvby called me in high school.

Here is the prayer that I want to use again as an opening to this ending discussion. This prayer is my creation over the years as reaction to what has been passing through my life. I wrote it earlier, so I repeat:

> God, Father/Mother, which is in heaven, on earth and in our hearts, everlasting love is Its integrity. We are awe-filled and acknowledge the Queen/Kingdom's majesty which is unfolding throughout time, space, and beyond any dimension. Thank you God for everything being as good as it is. God, do not forsake us when we are up against You; do not disappear and forget us when we quake, wish us well, and then drop us into the pit. Please champion us as we venture daily to incarnate into spirit Your mystery,

> depth, and greatness. In humility, responsibility, and joy, we unceasingly pray. Amen

One of the hardest "facts" to ponder in answering the question about God is Its remoteness. On most days you do not know that God is there but by faith. Mostly, there seems to be no God. For some, except the faithful, this is the answer to the fact that there is no God, "Why, if there was a God, well, I'd know." However, let me propose a question, "Does the rejection of something prove that the something does not exist?" Of course, there is the additional fact that because we cannot touch, feel, see, or hear, we have no sense of God. God is distant, and the poetry for that places God in heaven. When we get to heaven we will see God, except for Moses, who saw and felt *that* and had a burnt face due to the awe-full experience, and resulted in the Tenach to prove that something happened to him as he wandered down the mountain back to the Hebrews. Brothers and sisters, there is a God, Moses said, in so many words.

Then, too, there was Abraham and his near sacrifice of his son. Abraham got really close to God in that event. There are a few more people of the Bible who got experientially close to the Mystery, aside from Jesus. In the story of Job we first have a God who is very present. But after the experience of Job and God's experience with Job, It became remote. It disappeared from the Old Testament. God resided and continued on in the interpretation and the extension of the Old Testament, but God became remote. Jews know God, Jehovah, through the midrash. It did not walk among us in the New Testament, It was portrayed as Jesus. Again, we put the Godhead in heaven, which we created as Its residence.

God is remote. This is a hard pill to swallow. In a very early chapter I wrote about why people do not believe in God. I listed multiple reasons. These were strong and compelling. They were thought to be good reasons. These reasons can be summarized in the word *remote.* God is absent. Why, if God were God, how could it allow blah, blah, blah, blah? O blah! I am being derisive, aren't I? Wise people are perplexed and others just give up and make breakfast. Then there is science which attempts to replace God with science. The rational scientific mind will not *allow that* or *it* to be. It is silly to figure out how many angels dance on the head of a pin. Just silly. The rational scientific mind (RSM) thinks about experiments that it can replicate and get the same results, be predictable; of course, this gets a little difficult when we talk about the "action" of electrons and how they change from a particle to a wave depending how you measure or observe them, but that is just a silly electron. RSM is only about predictability, not all that squishy essential stuff. Religion, well, that is the opiate of the masses. (Marx)

The fact is that both religion and science are talking about the same world or universe with different words. It is the same universe in a different language. RSM is about the past and the future, while religion is about now and eternity. Eternity is not equal to the future, or heaven, or the other states we know–hell, limbo, purgatory, and so forth. Think of eternity as unchanging, or ageless. This should not imply rigid. Consider that if religion is about the now, then all there is, is the present. (By the way, you might want to look up the root meaning of the word *religion*. If not, here it is: *Religare*: to tie up, yoke, bind, unite, or connect. (Dictionary.com) Past and future are a rule or a principle. There is only the moment. And the desire to escape the moment often leads to that suffering we all know. We are intransigent against the preparing, procuring, and providing for existence, daily living, that daily bread we all need and hate to secure and struggle for. The "I" just wants to cut out. It begs God to get it away from the pain of living, "Please warrant a reason for all this suffering," we beg. In this, the "I" forgets God, rejects the offering of love from remoteness, and holds onto itself versus giving up the "I" adhering to the future or the past. Then there are the really smart ones. "I am just too bright for all this God stuff. I am way too smart. I am well read, I have seen the world," they mouth off.

God is very present. It is on the earth. It moves in mysterious ways. Sadly, it is not noticeable in Its actions. It's not a Dolce & Gabbana frock. It is mostly the fascinating mundane, or the really scary, and in Its synchronicity, this too is a way you can catch It. Or it might be the inspirational and enchanting; a flourish designated by the Holy Spirit. And it guides the Son of Man, the apostles, and other faithful, because in the kingdom there are many mansions. God is inconspicuously a place to come for shelter; God is an abode. It was Jesus's mission to guide the immediate faithful and today's followers to greater being, doing, and having. In Mark, Jesus repeatedly supported the apostles in their mission, and we read them able to sometimes heal, preach, and do as Jesus did. Again, can we see this today? Though there are disagreements as to whether the mission can be carried on, as in miracles, healings, and raising the dead, there is agreement that after His death, the Paraclete came. In the Roman Catholic belief, the saints do miracles and heal. So far, the dead are not raised. If we contemplate all this, however, the dead are coming back to life everywhere. Again, to die is to live, and lacking that, simply, there would be no tomorrow. We live in the epoch of the Spirit.

Faith has blown away the market place.
Jesus arrives in the silence of the night
scattering Spirit in the world.
There is shimmering joy in the trees and elation in the wind.
Eternity utters a day.

Amen

God Incarnated, Seen or Not Seen

The question you are all asking, consciously or unconsciously (as in publicly or privately), after the last chapter is, "Where is God or why can we not see It like those mentioned in the Old Testament or Jesus?" Has God exited stage left? Right? Is God really in our hearts? What are God's footprints *now*? These are some ripostes that I have heard and even thought myself.

"You have to admit that Jesus was born Jewish," my wife said. Jesus incarnated in a Jewish body, a Jewish culture, Jewish society, from Jewish parents, and became a rabbi. Now this is real; there it is in the story written down in the gospel of Mark. What the question here is why there and then, and why not Roman, Greek, Assyrian, or whatever of the time? God chose to incarnate among the Hebrews two thousand years ago. Jesus was hidden for about thirty years and then showed up, speaking now of Mark, not Matthew, Luke, or John. Jesus, as I wrote in one of the early chapters, had an event that I called the Christ event, wherein He was lit up by the Holy Spirit, and God said it was good. God became man, or the Son of Man became God. I'll go with either one. But where are the footprints today, many ask? Do you?

Jesus experienced God. Again, why or who cannot experience that today?

I have no answers, just some hunches. Let's assume that Jesus is real and is a historical man. The story that Mark lays out in his fashion suggests just that Jesus had the event of all events, a deeply internal, psychic, holy, and blessed event that moved Him to become a man among men so that God could redeem the fall, and redeem God's own severance from man. God had to incarnate to put Its stamp of approval onto us. This stamp makes us very special. But Adam was not enough, and merely initiated the process to get us to the point of possibility for Jesus. It is not the point that there was no Adam, sorry. Adam represents everyman living in sheer instinct, bland awareness, slightly conscious wakefulness, and with some sense for differentiation from the biological world. Adam was an acorn, as all acorns are potential oaks in essence. Adam exemplifies the first sketch.

Meanwhile, you see God doing Its doing, being Its being, and having a good time right up to the story of Job. Because of Job's ideal character, God got called on the carpet. Seeing Job get the shaft because Satan (one of God's own angels) was toying with God and Job, God had to make amends. Job stayed true in his faith to God in Its revelation despite all that transpired. And a lot occurred in that Job episode. So you have God in Its omnipotence being a little out of touch with Its omniscience. It did not know Its own mind.

Then came Jesus. It is the chicken or the egg argument really—what came first, God touching man or the Son of Man, Jesus, reaching and touching God? In this most holy sense, Jesus pioneered the possibility of reaching out and touching God for us. Jesus was ready to experience God, and God wanted to respond. Therefore, this state of readiness is the answer to the question of why we cannot see God, Its footprints in the sand, Its track across the pages of time.

But what if this whole story of Jesus and God is a mistake? More, that Jesus is a figment of imagination among four writers of the gospels. Many people believe this as a truth. Proceeding from this hypothesis that it is all bunk, a lie, gibberish, a dream, I ask, what of it? The impact of one life at the time on so many people cannot be refuted. The upending of human existence by Jesus's salvific behavior points to a Godhead bent on impact. Jesus, under the guidance of the Holy Spirit, wrought a new relationship to life. Jesus gave His life to man in love and faith. He pointed to the kingdom of God as eternal life on earth, which destroyed our spiritual pride as the creators of our own salvation. Therefore, the doubtful questions about Jesus are a bit irrelevant because it is much more important to get the meaning, the inner meaning, of the events of His life than to discuss whether He lived or not.

I repeat that God is an experience. Try harder. Go inside or go outside, either one. Love thy neighbor as yourself. But if you do not have a reputable relationship with yourself, you will never meet the neighbor, and you will never reach the self or the Ground of Being. This is not self-love in the parlance, idiomatic sense. Love is not a feeling, either. Love is a state of being so that we can act in the moment. And it is an elemental choice. Thus, love is healing the sick, giving eyesight to the blind, remedying innocent of suffering, and love enduring, whatever your inclination.

The experience, cultivation, and practice of praying, for example, places us in or moves us at once toward our hearts, minds, and psyches, where we can settle. Events can sometimes conspire to open an entrance to one or all three aforementioned, and there we may find the Mystery of Life. I suspect that Jesus had such an event with the added impetus of the Holy Spirit. Why? God knows.

If we notice, what do we see now? We see a mythic world, not a soulful world. We see fear of abandonment, subjugation, emotional deprivation, unlovability, mistrust, social exclusion, vulnerability, fear of failure, entitlement, and perfectionism. In the midst of this, the soul becomes and is still utterly in grief somewhere between sleep and death. It is cut off from the "gods." And the question becomes, if we dare to speak it, "Is it possible to love when there is nothing and no one more to love? Can the soul create love out of its own forces?" And here is where we encounter the Almighty. Perhaps.

Usually what happens is that we exist in this anxiety on-goingly. The anxieties intensify, their intensity leads to indifference, which prompts the search for comfort or surcease. Then we can slip into despair, depression or some loss of self. From there the long road back, so called, is hard, yet even here on the road between limbo and life, here is where we can or may encounter the Almighty. Perhaps.

Jesus's answer to the man lowered into his midst for healing as a paralytic was, if you recall, "Pick up your bed and walk." The impact of this image and offering is enormous. It was not an easy thing to do. Here too, is an encounter with the Almighty. Perhaps.

There is no rational or empirical answer to any of these interminable questions. In our world today that desires short and easy fifteen-second answers, these questions are glossed over. The experience is sifted out. The answers are overlooked. Where is God today? Everywhere we take in. Nowhere. It is not a grey area. There is no chance of a compromise between everywhere and nowhere in a merger or some type of politically correct phrase. Is this ultimate then? Yes, God is ultimate, absolute, and eternal. And, this too is merely belittling. Anyone who knows, knows not, and anyone who says, says not. I do suspect that there is a deep, panhuman, timeless desire for God. Look to Jesus's experience and see there the kingdom, a manifestation of the soul, with the confirmation of the Holy Spirit.

And just one more thing …

The Question of Evil in Mark's Gospel

It is right to leave this question to the end. Evil has been discussed, examined, considered, and explained forever by all of humankind. From evil spirits to Beelzebub, and to the revelations of John in the New Testament, the quest to define evil has been never-ending. Although the Old Testament has a restricted portrayal of Satan, it is between the lines. It can be called the "Stealer of the Soul." In more recent times, popular phrases such as "being jinxed" have the echo of the deeper issue concerning evil taking over the soul and self for its treacherous effects. We are called to protect ourselves from preternatural forces that prowl and troll for their sustenance off of our wellbeing.

In all the writing of Mark, we read and image Jesus as above evil. He healed the blind and sick, raised the dead, fed the masses, uncovered the falsehood in the Pharisees and their minions, taught and parabalized, speaking in riddles and blessing those who beseeched His power. Throughout His life, Jesus pointed to eternity, and even though He died, He showed the way to God's kingdom.

Not a word about evil specifically. There is only one event wherein Jesus faced Satan down prior to His desert experience and right after the baptism and God's laying on of hands. It seems to me that Jesus is above evil. I know that evil exists and did and will. The whole tussle with the powers that be is a remarkable struggle with evil and its cousin, malevolence. Again, Jesus is above it all. To operate at the level that He did is magnificent. The evil still existed. Jesus did not vanquish it. The powers that be killed God in the form of one Jesus Christ. The powers that be did not pay attention to the reality before them, to their detriment. They damaged themselves totally, fully, and completely. They were, in the totality of their actions, evil—evil in their being and in their minds. The powers that be were conscience-less? Is this even possible? This would imply that they were not aware of their actions as evil. They were merely following Roman orders or they saw Jesus as another rebel leader equivalent to Barabbas or a blasphemer. Thus taken together, I offer their knowing, doing and being as defining and equaling evil. Or were they just afraid and threatened, perhaps? And do these emotions justify to them the crucifixion of a purported messianic leader?

Before going further, let me admit that this is a bit of a fool's errand. This topic of evil is much too large to tackle in a few hundred words. Nevertheless, the issue is pressing more now than in the past. Why? Because of the potentiating of evil today due to our 'higher' awareness. The power of an uncontrollable event can strike at any moment, laying low many more people. The effect of an evil act two thousand years ago did not have that potential. Putting aside the question of evil and the end of times, there are four questions to put on the table:

1. What is the origin of evil?
2. Is the unconscious evil?

3. What is the relation of good to evil, or God to evil? An overarching question.
4. How should we deal with evil? Or again, how did Jesus deal with it in Mark?

Prior to diving into these questions and answers, I have to suggest that even pondering these questions leaves or pushes evil to bay. It will not recede, but will halt its advance. First, the objectification or naming something evil surely focuses the awareness. The word evokes a sense of space, a distance of observation followed by a yes, no, or maybe. Enough for a sacred pause. If that is too highfalutin', then count to ten and see again. Second, there are three structures that I offer as identifications in order to halt evil's advance to some extent. First, the person is unaware and indifferent to its existence; second, evil exits and it has no valence to the person; third, the person sees it, knows it, and recognizes evil in themselves and thus, they notice it terrestrially and empirically. With this introduction, the four questions have to be answered.

Beginning with question number four: "how should we deal with evil?"

Jesus, as I said, really did not call it out or name it, though there is a case of the "madman" in the graveyard with many afflictions who, through the lenses of his disturbance, named Jesus as the Son of Man. This talent, faculty, or ability suggests that evil sees the *summum bonum* (the Highest Good) and vice versa. Jesus did not let on to being the Highest Good and repeatedly requested that the one healed go quietly aside and be well, as in, soak up the full meaning of the healing. Jesus often asked that the one healed keep quiet about the healing, though each one promulgated their experience.

At many points in the gospel, Jesus faced accusations, falsehoods, malevolence, and total ill will from the offices of the powers that be. He did not name the name, calling it evil. Of course, Mark did not witness all the events. Perhaps someone was there, who then passed the story to him. Nevertheless, his depiction of the scene paints the picture well. Mark portrayed the evil. Jesus did not struggle with the powers that be at all. Jesus, more or less mutely, filled with the Holy Ghost, took the hits. Not in any part of this or earlier at Judas' betrayal did He call God down or curse the participants. His character was strong. At the heart of reality, the powers that be are what they are. It was theirs to do or not do what they chose, and God again appeared distant from this event as well. Yet, to name God as absent offers no surcease to the disbeliever because Jesus was able to carry out the divine mission supremely. Jesus looked for life everywhere. Evil is a human judgment. God, in Its wholeness, is immaculate and illimitable. Evil's locus is man. It is our calling to rumble with it, call it out, name and objectify it, and thus bridle it.

Some have asked "Can we deal with evil by loving it?" While this may have an answer, its scope and depth is beyond this limited discussion. I will offer a slight theorization. Going back to the question of God, absent an affirmative answer or even a limited begrudging assent, the individual is outside the chance for accepting the union with It. The potential union can undercut the hubris that is the groundwork for the evil's rooting in the conscience.

Question number three: What is the relation of good to evil, of God to evil?

The origins of evil can be tied to question four. Evil is often related to the unconscious, and by extension, a shadowy part of the personality. Or evil emerges as a deficiency of good. Perhaps as it is for some, it is just a bad point of view. In any event, evil is real, it is a problem, it is more than an adjective, and it is certainly a matter of active awareness. Using Mark's gospel, Jesus sensed the evil at hand in His prophetic behavior. Also, in His curious formulations about the murder of the landowner's son by his servants, Jesus told the story of murder. Evil? I think so. I do not want to reduce the scheming of the servants as merely evil in Jesus's parable. They were distinctly motivated by inhuman ingredients that, taken together, were totally wicked, thus evil. So human beings created evil. God allows evil to exist. So God is a participant and at fault for the earthly events like this. *No.*

What then? Is the unconscious evil? Some would posit that the fall from grace in the garden of Eden was the root of evil facilitated by the snake's cleverness. Here we have to reach outside the practiced, usual, and easy views for a formulation that holds the complexity. You can name the murder of Abel by Cain as evil quashing judgment and contrition. Conscience is the capacity resting in the human beings' interior. It seems to be 'embryonically' panhuman. And to a greater or lesser extent, it has endured in this way. The shattering of conscience (to behave within constraints) by acts, heinous thoughts, or monstrous traits can certainly be identified as evil. This fragmentation or disintegration on a great scale leads to the human evil we undertake to surmount.

Jesus's divine vocation was never in danger, and it was at a level that the powers that be were unable to diminish. *This* was the Holy Spirit's infusion throughout Jesus's life, taken ultimately to His death and life in God's realm. Evil could not lay a glove on Him because Jesus saw not the God in the other person, as some say, but rather, Jesus humbly modeled His interpretation of God's present kingdom to the one He healed. If the kingdom were in the powers that be, they would not have acted to kill possibility in their midst. Jesus enabled not the highest good, but rather signified the Way, the Truth, and the Light in the midst of destructive evil. Evil did not go away, it did not disappear, it did not wane, it was contained. It has been written that the opposite of war is not peace, it is poetry—it is creation at the ready. Jesus was God's poem in loving action.

There is finally the first question regarding evil's origin. If the unconscious is not the sole place of evil's genesis, then where did it come from? Is it merely a human epiphenomenon, something bubbling up from somewhere unknown? A product of free will, a result of genius? Going back to the Eden description, the garden of Unity within consciousness, where man and itself and God were one, the break with wholeness would produce Original Sin, the experience of everlasting separation from the Source, and be passed forward to all souls. This is not only high poetry, it makes sense, precisely for God's other son—Satan. We see his "behind the scenes" interplay, which I alluded to earlier, in Job. Satan ran amok with Job as God sat idly by, allowing its way. The fact is that Job neither cursed God nor was he victimized by Satan. Did Job see Satan? He did talk to God or heard from Him. Satan was only on God's level and not visible to Job. But what happened to Job was what I would call malevolent; Job did not name it evil. The evil, and coincidentally the ills that fell on Job, did not originate from God. Perhaps tacitly, the cause was Satan.

Thus I have more questions. At least twice Satan had a caustic effect on man; first in the garden of Eden and second in Job's travail. How is this possible? Also, was Satan God's other son, on par with Jesus? And is this the hidden fourth in the Trinity as Jung hypothesized? Is the starting place of evil a divine imbalance? Notice what Jesus did to Satan in His encounter with it right after His baptism. Jesus threw it down, and subverted it. But still, evil remains. At His baptism, Jesus experienced an act of becoming, putting Him face to face with its opposite, the unseemly, the disunity.

Evil is like the air we breathe. It's both a thing and invisible. We can smell it and not see it except in certain states of analysis. Not enough air and we die; too much pollution and we suffocate. This may be the best analogy I have for the state of evil. Paul gets after it in attempting to describe his and our state of being. It is not the goodness we are, but the weakness we act out. Sometimes evil wins, forcing its way forward. It is ascendant. Then comes the good to expose the evil and make it descend back to its place to sit quietly like an unprincipled, good dog. In ways, evil has to be trained. And as its master, we have to behave well with it. The master knows its place, as does the evil; both have wills and different motivations. With a master's hand on the leash, guiding both evil and man home from wandering around the four quarters to face reality in the Godhead. In the full sense of the first commandment, we cannot invalidate, nor elevate, nor raise up anything before ultimate reality. This would be evil.

Evil, though not in the gospel of Mark, is there stealthily. The Godhead added a degree of consciousness by becoming temporal—human—to fully personalize evil into an entity, Satan. Many fine books have tried to get to the heart of darkness, to interpret the Prince of Fools, which may be a better phrase. It is, I suspect, a development in time and a bit obfuscating to objectively drop evil fully into an earthly form. Nevertheless, the secular political evil of the French Revolution, Stalinist-Communism, Nazism, Maoist China, and North Korea each do well as examples of evil incarnate in our time. The Prince of Fools had a *sub rosa* role in each, I bet. And, it is still not at an end.

And in the End ...

I started writing in 2008, having very little idea where I would end up. Now, after over ninety chapters of reflections and extended ruminations, that statement is very true. Prior to the beginning, I was psychically moved to explore my Christian background. It started one day while I was driving my car back from an appointment and I suddenly felt the need to pray. This was about two years before this book was started.

I was raised Catholic by my mother and the Benedictine Sisters in the Midwest. My father was, at best, an agnostic Hungarian Unitarian. The distinction is that he was born into the church in Hungary and was not a Universalist. I never really knew what his faith was. In this ecology I was baptized into the Catholic Church via my mother's decision. Dad went along because he loved my mother; I had no choice just then. My mother was a devoted Catholic, not stereotypical, however. I thought of her as a bit superstitious at the time. My voyage over the rough waters of life got me to today, after all. Born into the culture of the 1960s–70s, surviving to this age is a real awe-producing experience for me. It is a bit awkward to look around and not feel out of place writing about these things when most of my cohort is worried about more mundane things. Some pretend not to be worried about this at all, this being the gospel of Mark, the good news.

I said somewhere in the beginning that the only unadulterated question is, "Do you believe in God?" Or alternatively, "Is there a God?" Up until the last fifteen years I prayed the agnostic's prayer, somewhat like my father. "Dear God, if there is a god …." I felt cool about that, as in hip or at one with the cynical, secular, humanist state of the world. Events, internal and external, fused and moved me to engage in this process that I call "let's take another look" and follow it where it might lead me. I repeat, life is about finding out. And, here I am.

Coincident with these events was the power of the gospel itself, precisely Jesus's message, which is not easy to abbreviate. If I can, it would be that love of neighbor is a function of your own relationship to yourself. He says it elegantly: "Love thy neighbor as thy self." This is rock bottom, because therein you will also meet the Ground of Being, community of man, and the Universal Sainthood, and what you were looking for at the beginning, your *self.*

Mark's gospel is amazing in its simplicity. The phrasing, pace, and prose are not eloquent. It is like tensile steel. Whoever wrote it was not a Pulitzer Prize winner, yet the person portrayed the life of Jesus perfectly. The bearing of the reader, what you bring to it, is the important factor in convening with it. I mean, who do you identify with in the narrative? Who is the farthest from you? Where did you go out to lunch, fall asleep? What is hardest to get? What is furthest from your mind? What offends you? And what is admirable? There are more questions to contemplate. These question-experiences were at the heart of my encounter with Mark's gospel.

There were moments of ease as I produced this work, first as a blog. The writing often went like a hot knife through butter. At the other end were the passages that I, along with others, found unexplainable. These left me asking what resonance they had then, two thousand years ago, and what we are missing now. I could not bring any of me to them.

The gospel often called me to work on it. I came to it at times fatigued or obligated to write about the next section. Then there were times when I was inspired and experienced satisfaction with the effort, and so, too, disquieted with the results. There was also the enjoyment, hoping against hope that I was making some sense to myself as well as to the reader. My wife was a key reader. If she got it, well, then, most would. She often called it subjective, or stream of consciousness, and it is a stream of words organized well enough to get the message of the gospel out in another way. Hear the word of the Mystery as a friendly whisper. Or not. I do suspect that there will be a lot of upset too.

These are the ending thoughts, neither final nor the end of a comedy, feeling good about the last laugh. Sometimes life is serious and at times a joke, tragic, miraculous, dull, dumb, and even these experiences are not *it*. I have faith in God, the Mystery of Life. My weak attempts at revitalizing God have now reached an end in this book. And yes, just like many facets of life, we must revitalize our relationship with God. I have come from moral relativism to an absolute. If you get God, you will get Jesus—with the help of the Holy Spirit. We live in the time of the Holy Spirit. The Jews lived with Yahweh—God. The next step was Jesus, the Savior, and then Holy Spirit leading us to the Ground of Being. And the final word about life: All that is, is good, the past is approved, the future is open, and I am accepted. Knowledge of this matured me late in life. I could not marginalize or sidetrack powerful experiences. God breathed on me and brought me to life. It was an experience in the middle of an intense episode over the past years. Trust me, it was not fabricated, it was visceral.

None of this makes me special in any way. God is an experience—sometimes it happens and sometime the experience does not. Yet God is. Nor does the experience preclude constant sin. I am broken just like the next one on the bus. "We are all bozos on this bus," as the Firesign Theater stated years ago. But the difficulty of life is admitting this and still getting God. No joke. The biggest step in life is admitting how much there is to learn about it—and thus God. To paraphrase, there is God and there is us, and the interaction of these two "facts" forever creates who we are.

I am headed up the road to everlasting possibility, choice and demand.

Coda

During the review and editing I realized that I left out a very important factor. It is too late to add it to this body of work. It will be incorporated in a future book already in development. If Mark is the beginning of the Gospel journey, then St. John is a kind of terminus. It will be here that many more journal entries will find a place and uncover more perspectives. St. John has a distinctly different understanding of Jesus, the Son of God.

Thank you,
George Andrew

BIBLIOGRAPHY/FURTHER READING/REFERENCES

Over the course of forty years, a great many books, texts, articles, and workshops have suffused this book. Here are a few key items for your edification:

The New Testament in Modern English, by J. B. Phillips. Macmillan (1972)

Hero with a Thousand Faces, by Joseph Campbell. Pantheon Books (1949) There are too many of his books that are worthwhile. The second one that is included here is *The Inner Reaches of Outer Space.* Alfred Van Der Marck Editions (1986)

The Saviors of God, by Nikos Kazantzakis. Simon and Schuster (1960) The second one is *The Last Temptation of Christ.* Touchstone Book. Simon and Schuster (1960) Though it is not referenced, it is a keen observation regarding Jesus as the Christ.

Answer to Job. Princeton University Press (2010) and *Jung's Seminar on Nietzsche's Zarathustra*, by Carl Jung. Princeton University Press (1997)

The Wisdom of Insecurity and *Behold the Spirit*, by Alan Watts. Pantheon (1961) and Vintage Books (1971) respectively

My Search of Absolutes, by Paul Tillich. Simon and Schuster (1967)

Love's Body, by Norman O. Brown. Random House (1966)

Three Faces of God, by David L. Miller. Fortress Press (1986)

Alchemy, by Charles Ponce. North Atlantic Books (1983)

Jung on Evil, by Murray Stein. Princeton University Press (1996)

The Myth of the Eternal Return: Or, Cosmos and History, by Mircea Eliade. Princeton University Press (2005)

The Gnostic Gospels, by Elaine Pagels. Vintage Books (1989)

Prayers of the Cosmos, by Neil Douglas-Klotz. Harper One (2009)

The Gnostic Jung and *Jung and the Lost Gospels*, by Stephan A. Hoeller. Quest Books (1982) and (1989) respectively

Spirituality by the Numbers, by Georg Feuerstein. Tarcher (1994)

The Eleventh Hour, by Martin Ling. Archetype (2010)

The Soul's Religion: Cultivating a Profoundly Spiritual Way of Life (cassette tape), by Thomas Moore (1990)

The Art of Worldly Wisdom, by Baltasar Gracian. Shambala Classics, 2000.

In addition, *The 2000 Year Old Man* comedy routines on CD were perfect for writer's block. Carl Reiner and Mel Brooks are the antidote to this irritation that all writers face in the process of creation.